RESISTING EXCLUSION. GLOBAL
THEOLOGICAL RESPONSES TO POPULISM

LWF Studies 2019/01

THE
LUTHERAN
WORLD
FEDERATION

Resisting Exclusion. Global Theological Responses to Populism

Edited by
Simone Sinn and Eva Harasta

LWF Studies 2019/01

EVANGELISCHE VERLAGSANSTALT
Leipzig

Bibliographic information published by the German National Library

The Deutsche Nationalbibliothek lists this publication in the Deutsche Nationalbibliografie; detailed bibliographic data are available on the internet at http://dnd.dnd.de

This book was printed on FSC-certified paper

Cover: LWF/Sean Hawkey
Editorial assistance: Department for Theology and Public Witness
Layout: Department for Theology and Public Witness
Design: LWF-Office for Communication Services

Printing and Binding: druckhaus köthen GmbH & Co. KG

ISBN 978-3-374-06174-7

Published by Evangelische Verlangsanstalt GmbH, Leipzig, Germany, under the auspices of The Lutheran World Federation
150, rte de Ferney, PO Box 2100
CH-1211 Geneva 2, Switzerland

Parallel edition in German

Contents

APPENDICES

PREFACE

Martin Junge

Dignity and justice, respect for diversity, as well as inclusion and participation are core values of The Lutheran World Federation (LWF).[1] The global Lutheran communion, together with ecumenical, interreligious and civil society partners, actively engages in reflection and action to overcome manifold forms of injustice and exclusion.

In view of this long-standing commitment, the LWF is deeply concerned by recent developments in public discourse, on national as well as international levels. Public discourse has become significantly more aggressive and divisive, as ethno-nationalist populist movements have gained traction. Political agitation and hate speech have led to hate crimes, especially against vulnerable groups like refugees and migrants. There is a tangible negative impact on the cohesion of societies and the infringement on the rights and freedoms of diverse groups of people.

Exclusionary populism unfolds a negative dynamic, which undermines the very fabric and existence of public and civil society space. It perverts basic norms and values of how we want to live together as society and as international community. Therefore, it is vital to jointly address these challenges by scrutinizing its ideological foundations and denouncing its harmful assumptions. Furthermore, the LWF sees the need to articulate with renewed clarity our vision for just and participatory living together, and live out this calling as churches. [2] We need to give an account of the

---

[1] The Lutheran World Federation, *With Passion for the Church and for the World. LWF Strategy 2019 - 2024* (Geneva: LWF 2018), 8f.
[2] The Lutheran World Federation, *The Church in the Public Space. A Study Document of the Lutheran World Federation* (Geneva: LWF 2016).

theological perspectives that emerge from the gospel message, which points to God's compassionate and liberating presence in this world.

The international conference "Churches as Agents for Justice and against Populism" held in Berlin (Germany) in May 2018 brought together sixty-five people from twenty-five countries in order to deliberate together on the topical issue of exclusionary populism and provide stimulating theological conversations. It is of vital importance that such reflection is done in a collaborative way, by people coming from different contexts, with diverse backgrounds. We thank all who prepared papers and engaged in discussions. The insights emerging from such intercultural theological conversation are indeed much needed today. We are very grateful to "Bread for the World", Evangelische Akademie zu Berlin and the Church of Sweden for their collaboration with the LWF desk for public theology and interreligious relations in preparing this event. The steering committee members Almut Bretschneider-Felzmann, Eva Harasta, Chad Rimmer, Simone Sinn, and Dietrich Werner have jointly conceptualized and implemented this conference.

With this publication of many of the papers from the conference, the LWF wants to stimulate further theological conversation, encourage joint reflection on what it means for churches to resist exclusion today, to dismantle its ideological foundations, and to engage in creative and effective action to foster respect for diversity and inclusion of all. With this publication of many of the papers from the conference the LWF wants to stimulate further theological conversation, encourage joint reflection on what it means for churches to resist exclusion today, to dismantle its ideological foundations, and to engage in creative and effective action to foster respect for diversity and inclusion of all.

INTRODUCTION

Eva Harasta and Simone Sinn

In a wide variety of global contexts, populist political movements pose serious challenges to churches and theology. Churches are called to reflect more deeply on their public role in view of populist exclusionary policies. In a situation where populist movements misappropriate Christian rhetoric to justify their aspirations, churches cannot remain silent, but need to resist exclusionary strategies. The contributions gathered in this volume offer analyses and theological orientations, and invite readers to compare their experiences to thoughts and action in different contexts.

Changeable and fast-moving, populism takes on diverse forms. Further-more, populist movements often obscure their stances and aims (including their non-democratic agenda), thus making it even more difficult to grasp. This volume aims to clarify the problems inherent to certain forms of "populism", and highlights the current wave of right-wing, anti-establishment, anti-elitist and exclusionary movements. The second chapter—"Analyzing the politics of populism"—further discusses the understanding of populism. This volume views "populism" as one of the causes for a crisis of democracy that can be observed in different parts of the world, be it in emerging democracies or in states with a long democratic tradition or in countries that have recently moved towards establishing democracy.

Churches and civil society at large in different global contexts experience these developments first hand. Their effect can be described metaphorically as a "shrinking" of public space. Obstacles to critical social and political discourse are put into place, and exclusionary tactics hinder meaningful participation of all. Ethno-nationalist populist movements work on depriving parts of the population of their access to public discourses, or even on depriving them of their right to participate. Social and political exclusion undermines core values—dignity, equality, freedom, justice, and transparent decision-making processes. Yet these values are a core part of the Christian world-view. Thus it is not for the purposes of a political system that the churches are called to public witness, but rather for the sake of their mission as churches itself. The third chapter—"Public theology in context—resisting exclusion"—offers insights into responses to this challenge in different local contexts, while the first chapter—"The churches as agents for justice"—offers approaches from the perspective of church leadership, i.e. responses to this challenge on a regional or even federal/national level.

In spite of their contextual and theological diversity, the contributions of these chapters agree in one important regard: The churches need to be self-aware and self-critical when engaging in public witness. Exclusion, discrimination and even unjust power structures are present in the churches as well. Theology and the churches take part in societal dynamics, and can be influenced by exclusionary politics without realizing it. The fourth chapter—"Responding to Sexism"—focuses on one aspect that has proven especially hard to grapple with both for academic theology and for the churches. The contributions aim to encourage self-critique by showing how faith flourishes in communities that cherish equality and dignity of all.

Democracy needs to be rejuvenated and renegotiated in each generation. The fifth and final chapter—"Populism and truth"—discusses how such renegotiation may look in this current generation. Exclusionary political movements feed on fear and aggression in the face of complexity, ambiguity, and diversity. They offer fictional narratives of uniform cultural, religious, racial or national identity, arguing for the exclusion of "others". The contributions of the last chapter offer theological responses to different aspects of coming to terms with diversity and ambiguity, and work with an understanding of truth that follows the Johannine principle that truth is not a proposition, but a living person, and a promise of liberation.

THE CHURCHES AS AGENTS FOR JUSTICE

In the first section of the book, several church leaders offer perspectives for constructively engaging with challenges in society today. In order to analyze the situation, they describe contemporary developments and dialogue with philosophers and political theorists to more profoundly understand what is at stake. Each in their own way speaks from a place of personal commitment to resisting exclusion.

Antje Jackelén addresses the need to reclaim democracy in the face of polarization, populism, protectionism and post-truth. She reflects on the ambivalent impact of digitalization, especially the emergence of digital swarms, and passionately pleads for nurturing democracy through education. In her view, the church should engage in public space by keeping the quest for truth alive and fostering a sense of direction. From her experience in Sweden, she points out that the church may face fierce opposition and blatant hatred. In view of this, the church is called to form viable partnerships with diverse stakeholders to strengthen hope, justice and peace.

Reflecting on the role of the churches in Germany as agents for justice and against populism, *Heinrich Bedford-Strohm* proposes focusing on the grand narratives that shape the self-understanding of society. The rise of the right-wing populist party "Alternative für Deutschland" (AfD) needs to be addressed on this deeper level as well as on the level of individual political issues. The churches in Germany must speak up decisively against all attempts to make nationalistic ideas acceptable again—yet they should do so without framing this discourse as a *status confessionis*. Instead of discussing whether certain people are Christian or not, the topics at hand need to be discussed soberly and clearly, first and foremost among them immigration and social justice. The churches need to propose their grand narrative of hope against populist narratives of fear, and they need to mediate this high-minded narrative with everyday political discourse and its constant search for compromise.

In approaching contemporary populism in Hungary, *Tamás Fabiny* draws on insights of Hungarian political theorist István Bibó. In 1946, Bibó analysed the destabilized situation of Hungary and other small Central European states after the two World Wars. He argued that these societies were traumatized to the point where they might not be able to build their own identity for the foreseeable future. According to Fabiny, the challenges that Bibó describes continue to haunt Hungary even seven decades later, after forty years of an illiberal communist state and thirty years of post-communist democracy and neoliberal capitalism. Hungarian populism offers easy answers to the deep questions of identity that have been left unresolved by the ideological upheavals of the 20th century. It envisions a homogeneous Hungarian "nation" and strengthens cohesion by openly discriminating against minorities. The Lutheran church positions itself against these political dynamics by advocating for inclusion, diversity and democratic participation.

A sharp analysis of the intersection of populism and racism in the US today is offered by *Linda E. Thomas*. Doing public theology from a womanist perspective, she underlines the importance of looking at the historical depth of these issues. She introduces the cultural knowledges that emerge from black and womanist experience, and shows how these connect with experiences of others e.g. First Nations People. Remembering the past, the abuse suffered, is indispensable. Equally important is unveiling the persistent dynamics of power and privilege. Thomas views racism as structured, systematic and institutionalized prejudice. In order to counter this, Thomas argues for shared analysis, i.e. those who are in one way or another in a position of power or privilege join the efforts to disrupt racist structures. Another concrete way in which churches can help transform oppressive systems is to accept leadership from historically subordinated people.

In his account of populist politics in India, *Roger Gaikwad* points to three interrelated challenges: religious fundamentalism, communalism and nationalism. Gaikwad speaks of *Hindutva* populism and shows how it creates an intolerant and coercive climate in society. Such climate gives rise to attacks against women, dalits, adivasis, religious minorities and working people. Gaikwad briefly introduces the historical emergence of the ideology of Hindutva in the late nineteenth century. He argues that the politicization of Hindu religious sentiments entails fascist elements. The churches in India have responded critically to these developments in various ways, in public statements as well as by forming civil society coalitions. Such coalitions help to raise awareness in society and activate all available legal mechanisms to protect minorities.

Pascal Bataringaya writes about the Rwandan churches' efforts to contribute to the healing process after the Genocide against the Tutsi in 1994, when more than one million people were killed in a period of 100 days. The Genocide traumatized the people of Rwanda on the individual level, but it also traumatized society as a whole. Bataringaya stresses that justice is a necessary precondition of reconciliation. This concerns the role of the churches as well. The churches had to come to terms with their complicity in the circumstances that contributed to the Genocide. After so much violence and suffering, justice and reconciliation can seem impossible. For Bataringaya, the heart of the churches' witness for reconciliation consists of the trust that justice as well as reconciliation are graceful gifts from God.

ANALYZING THE POLITICS OF POPULISM

Populism is a contextual phenomenon, it responds to challenges within a particular society. Yet populist movements have become influential in numerous different global contexts, a fact that points to inter-contextual dynamics and parallels. This chapter offers analyses from Hungary and Croatia, from South Africa, from Brazil and the US, concluding with a statement from the perspective of a German development agency. Populism emerges as a form of politics that uses social resentments in order to gain power, and that, once in power, contributes to a crisis of democracy across different global contexts.

In their article "Radical Right-wing Populism and Nationalized Religion in Hungary", *András Bozóki* and *Zoltán Ádám* offer a definition of populism from the point of view of political science and analyze populism in Hungary and its relation to Christianity. They describe populism as an anti-elitist approach to politics that primarily seeks mass-mobilization and that positions the person of a charismatic leader in the place of political principles. Populism's rise in Hungary originates in recent history. During the three decades after the collapse of communism, countries in Eastern Central Europe have transitioned into democratic structures quickly, but have also faced economic and social challenges. Many citizens have become disillusioned with "the West" and with neoliberal capitalism.

Nico Koopman approaches populism from the perspective of a South African academic public theologian. He focuses on populism as a logic and idea, not as an ideology or a political movement. Thus populism appears as an anti-intellectual flight from complexity. In response, Koopman calls for a theological ethic of intellectuality and catholicity. Embracing intellectuality takes its cue from the conviction that faith includes loving God with one's entire mind, which leads to affirming complexity and ambiguity in society as well as in theory. Embracing catholicity implies that the churches pay attention to God's work outside of the church, both regionally and globally.

Rudolf von Sinner and Marcia Pally both look for the societal hermeneutics of populism. *Rudolf von Sinner* calls for a deeper understanding of the centrality of the people. He writes from within the contemporary Brazilian context and begins with an analysis of former president Lula's popularity in order to decipher the meaning of populism in Latin America. Here, populism is also understood in positive ways. This has been theoretically elaborated by the Argentinian political philosopher Ernesto Laclau. He does not regard populism as manipulation of the masses, but as articulation of the subjectivities of the people. Against false harmony there needs to be legitimate space for political conflict, so that the voices of marginalized be heard. In his own theological approach, von Sinner underlines the need to look more closely as to who and where the people are.

Marcia Pally investigates why neo-nationalist movements are so persuasive to many citizens in the US from the perspective of cultural studies. She defines "populism" as a program of solutions to economic and sense-of-place duress and uses the word as a synonym for "neo-nationalism". Drawing on political and theological interpretations of the covenant by Johannes Althusius, John Winthrop, and Alexis de Tocqueville, Pally delineates models of political participation, liberty and belonging that contribute to the persuasiveness of exclusionary political stances in the US.

Dion A. Forster and Branko Sekulić look into the relation between the church and populist politics and into the use of Christian ideas and rhetoric by populist movements. *Dion A. Forster* offers a theological response to contemporary populism in South Africa, which takes its strength from a disappointment in the slow pace of transformation, from the re-emergence of identity politics, and from growing concerns of state corruption. Christian rhetoric plays a significant part in current South African populism. Forster points out that there is a blurring of the lines between the political and the religious discourse, and that the churches are in danger of becoming embedded in the actions and intentions of the state. In order to work against this tendency, Forster points to the South African Kairos Document (1985), which calls the church to prophetic witness, and reminds theology and the church of their spiritual responsibility for distance from the state, and their public responsibility for justice.

Branko Sekulić analyses how churches in ex-Yugoslavia are entangled in the promotion of an ethnonational mythology. He underlines that mythology is not to be understood as a distant concept, but as a mindset that has practical consequences and shapes reality. When a church institution supports are certain ethnonational mythology, it is entangled in political struggles which thus acquire a certain sacred characteristic. Furthermore in such mythology, the people are given a special status as chosen people. The historical narration is fixed in such a way to support the mythology. The idea of hostility toward other ethnic, national, confessional or religious groups becomes and intrinsic part of the mythology. This can develop into a precursor to ethnic cleansing and genocide.

At the end of the chapter, *Dietrich Werner* introduces an inter-contextual perspective on populism. He writes as a representative of Bread for the World, the development agency of Protestant churches in Germany. In the past few years, strengthening civil society actors has been one of the primary objectives of Bread for the World as it responds to a disturbing development that can even be addressed as a global crisis in democracy. Nationalist populism contributes to this crisis in many global contexts. Werner stresses that the churches need to remain strong in their witness and service to those in need beyond all cultural, national and ethnic boundaries. Inter-contextual ecumenical exchange is an important tool in this situation.

PUBLIC THEOLOGY IN CONTEXT—RESISTING EXCLUSION

Wherever Christians live in difficult or oppressive situations they have to find ways to stand their ground. There is a wide range of strategies from confrontation to cooperation by which churches try to live out who they are called to be in this world. Out of such struggles public theologies in context emerge that defy exclusion and work toward recognition of a plural public space.

Sung Kim argues that the current development of public theology in Hong Kong needs to be understood in relation to the religious-political reality in the People's Republic of China (PRC). While freedom of religion or belief is guaranteed in the basic law in Hong Kong, Christians in Hong Kong fear looming changes in view of Bejing's increasing influence on the "Self Administrative Region". Some theologians in Hong Kong favour the concept of "localism" to allow for some grade of independence. The debate on the impact of "foreign influence" continues, however with different nuances in Hong Kong and in the PRC. Kim points out that in the midst of these political questions, public theology should not loose sight of the growing socio-economic challenges that produce glaring marginalization.

The introduction to the quest for independence and democracy in Myanmar by *Samuel Ngun Ling* provides insights into the different histori- cal stages. He then points out that there are currently two approaches to peace and reconciliation in the country, one through inclusive political dialogue, the other one aims at ending internal conflicts by military force. Neither approach has yet achieved peaceful coexistence. Furthermore, a particular challenge is the fact that government authorities have tried to promote Buddhist religion and culture to form national identity. In view of this hegemonic dynamic the minority ethnic Christians struggle through non-violent means for recognition of diversity, justice, dignity, rights and freedoms. For churches in Myanmar, Jesus showed the way to resistant evil powers and systems and to stand for the disenfranchised.

Jeevaraj Anthony describes how the United Evangelical Lutheran Churches in India as a minority church responds to the challenges of the Hindutva movement both in theology and advocacy work. Minority communities in India, with Christians among them, currently experience a context of fear and suffering. Anthony calls for a public theology "from below", i.e. a public theology that involves the everyday lives of marginal and minority people. Furthermore, he calls for a dialogical public theology as it is practiced at the Ecumenical Dialogue Centre India (EDCI), because dialogue is the most effective method in responding to exclusionary ideas and practices.

Daniel C. Beros analyzes the term "populism" and focuses on phenomena that are usually attributed to "populism": xenophobia and racism. These phenomena are on the rise in Latin American contexts, where neoliberal authoritarian regimes currently gain ground, often with the help of media monopolies. In his theological response to this situation, Beros draws on the category of idolatry. This concept can help to analyze the use of images in the media and it can help to recognize "false gods", i.e. deceitful claims of justice and peace. However, it needs to be employed self-critically, as it has been a means of oppression historically.

The use of religion by right wing Israeli and Christian Zionist groups is scrutinised by *Munther Isaac.* He describes how biblical and religious language is used in these two movements to legitimise a certain political agenda. He calls this "imperial theology" and criticizes such theology as resulting in prejudice and fear and leading to dehumanizing Palestinians. Isaac argues for a theology of shared land as the only meaningful way forward.

Almut Bretschneider-Felzmann writes from the perspective of the Church of Sweden's international department, which cooperates with partners in sixteen countries. For more than a decade, the issue of democratic spaces in society and civil society has been of central importance in these global relations. "Democratic space" designates room for civil society discourse between different actors. In many cases, certain groups are denied access to such democratic space. Yet excluded voices need to be heard in the public space so that decision making processes can be truly participatory and beneficial to everyone involved. Living out the public witness of the church needs continual reflection and care. For Act Church of Sweden, the development organization in Church of Sweden, sexual and reproductive health and rights have been focus areas for many years as well as gender justice.

RESPONDING TO SEXISM

This chapter focuses on exclusion based on gender, i.e. sexism, as a populist strategy in five different contexts: the US, Zambia, the UK, Sweden, and Brazil. Theologians face a dilemma in this respect, as the tradition they are part of has been strongly influenced by patriarchy. Thus, responding to sexism in the public space presupposes a self-critical investigation into the exclusionary structures within theology and the churches.

Constructive theological resources that help to re-evaluate tradition and critique misogyny and sexism are brought forward by *Kirsi Stjerna*. Her aim is to strengthen persistence in the face of multiple expressions of injustice. She remembers women during the Reformation period who have become models of persistence by their theological engagement with the questions of the time. Looking at contemporary challenges she underlines that making the world a safe place for women as exemplified in the #MeToo movement is not only a secular matter, but a Reformation concern. She highlights key insights from the recent statement "Faith, Sexism and Justice. A Lutheran Call to Justice" of the Evangelical Lutheran Church in America. Stjerna is convinced that the way theologians speak about God is of vital importance, and that a fundamental theological reform is needed. In her view, it is worth revisiting Luther' Genesis commentary and use it a resource to include women's experiences.

Mutale M. Kaunda and *Chammah J. Kaunda* focus on the public challenge of sexism, though never losing sight of the interconnection of sexism and Christianity. They analyze how Zambian Pentecostal women politicians, though successful in gaining political influence, have failed to resist patriarchal structures. This dynamic is particularly apparent when these politicians use the religious discourse of wifely submission in order to exercise power in a male-dominated political context. Patriarchal models of gender relations that claim to be Christian are a part of populist rhetoric in Zambia. Zambia mirrors other global contexts in this respect as well as in the underlying power structure: Women achieve positions of power, but then fail to challenge patriarchal attitudes, instead conforming or even actively strengthening them as long as it helps them to stay in power as individuals.

Esther McIntosh's paper investigates sexism in current public theology, and shows how male-dominated hermeneutics prevent theology from responding effectively to public challenges that are posed by populist sexism. Male-dominated public theology interprets the public sphere based on Jürgen Habermas, David Tracy and other white male theorists, ignoring feminist critiques of the distinction between the public and the private, and remaining deaf to theological witness on public issues by marginalized groups. McIntosh stresses that public theology needs to overcome this bias and needs to start engaging with public theologies of many different backgrounds, e.g. with Elisabeth Schüssler-Fiorenza, Rosemary Radford Ruether, Jacquelyn Grant, Delores Williams, Mercy Oduyoye, Musa Dube, and Kwok Pui-Lan. This is especially important in a situation of rising misogyny in the public sphere, as sexism proves to be a salient part of populist politics in many different contexts.

Gunilla Hallonsten discusses the role of sexism in nationalist populism in Sweden. Hallonsten points out that sexism—together with racism—is an integral part of nationalist populism in Sweden. Women are seen primarily as mothers, reproduction being seen as woman's first duty for the nation. Nationalist populism stresses the nuclear family as the only legitimate family model and discriminates against the lesbian, gay, bisexual, trans- and queer people (LGBTQ) community. Hallonsten then draws on the feminist post-colonial thought of Paula de los Reyes and Diana Mulinari, whose criteria for intersectional thinking are useful for critiquing gendered theological spaces, and for developing public spaces that are in accordance with gender justice.

Looking at the pervasive presence of violence against women in Brazil, *Marcia Blasi* argues that such reality is nurtured by a destructive political discourse that is not simply populist, but actually fascist. Blasi describes how in such public discourse there is a binary typology of women, being either "beautiful, modest, and housewife" or angry and dangerous. This discourse could be heard in the fierce debates in relation to Dilma Roussef's presidency. Blasi denounces the involvement of religious leaders in the misogynous public discourse. She pleads with churches to hear and believe women's stories, and to provide safe and just spaces for women.

POPULISM AND TRUTH

As populist discourse began to either control or demonize certain media outlets and started to attack journalists, questions of fake news and post-truth became a matter of public concern. Communication in public and private spaces seems polarized and distorted. These developments call for a renewed reflection on what truth is, which implies asking what is meant by factual evidence, as well as looking into philosophical and theological perspectives on truth. Furthermore, it urges us to reflect on rationality and the plurality of truth claims.

The scene that surrounds Pilate's question in John 18, "What is truth?" is the starting point for *Chad Rimmer's* reflection on truth. By analysing the socio-political context of the situation, Rimmer shows that the prosecution of Jesus as narrated in this biblical passage can be interpreted as a case study for unveiling populist dynamics. The populist tactic of blurring deliberation is questioned, and truth is invoked to work toward justice. Rimmer argues that Jesus embodies political agency, not least from the cross, where the disintegration and exclusion is exposed. Furthermore, when the church gathers a community of faith of diverse people in the face of exclusionary populism, this is a political act.

Olga Navrátilová discusses the chances and limits of a multi-religious society. She underlines that guaranteeing freedom of conscience of an individual person is a key component in plural societies today as it enables the persons to live according to what they hold as truthful and binding. She demonstrates that the claim to universality of reason as put forward by Enlightenment thinking needs to be critically discussed. She takes up John Rawls' idea of overlapping consensus to make the case for the need of different world views to interact with one another and to create shared space. She argues that the experience of truth shows that truth often comes as question; this, for her, is a strong argument to see that reflection on truth opens space for plurality.

From within the Swedish context, *Michael Nausner* identifies a polarization between secularism and religion on the one hand, and a polarization between religions on the other as problematic developments in public discourse that need to be critically analyzed. He pleads for reconnecting the Abrahamic faiths, and refers to reflections of Rabbi Jonathan Sacks and of perspectives from the Muslim writer Navid Kermani for working toward mutual understanding. Theologically, the Noah covenant plays a key role in overcoming diverse polarizations.

According to *Joona Toivanen*, it is important to trace the historical legacy of atheist discourse In order to understand public discourse on religion in Estonia today. He calls this a post-Soviet eclipse of religious consciousness. He diagnoses a vacuum in which people are looking for saviours and solutions, as a sense of purpose and the experience of belonging and being loves is eroding. He sees that people cling to fragments of faith and Christian morals, and questions whether this is based on an authentic relationship to God.

Florian Höhne approaches social media communication from a theological perspective, asking whether social media algorithms may be a factor that fosters populism by confirming biases and fears. After all, Google, Facebook, Yahoo and You Tube filter and personalize the information they offer each user based on previous preferences, thus strengthening those preferences. Populist politicians and movements use digital social media actively and effectively, but by way of the "filter bubble" mechanism, these media further populism implicitly, or latently, simply by doing their job, i.e. accurately diagnosing preferences in order to ascribe advertisements most effectively. Finally, Höhne draws on two of George A. Lindbeck's four types of theories of religion in order to find ways to overcome the filter bubble mechanism.

In view of the negative impact of diverse forms of fundamentalism and radicalism in society, especially for disenfranchised groups, *Elisabetta Ribet* calls on theology to provide critique and analysis of current developments in society. Theology needs to shed light on the relationship between truth and reality, between belief and knowledge in order to empower people to discern complex situations. Based on insights from Jacques Ellul she discusses the power of propaganda in a technological society. Ribet makes the case for Christians to more deeply understand what it means to be a witness. The calling to give witness is starkly different from propaganda. Christians are called to ask questions about meaning in life and about what is sacred in life. This critical reflection can help counter paternalistic populist dynamics, and give space to the truth that will set people free.

These papers were presented at the conference "The Churches as Agents for Justice and against Populism" in May 2018 in Berlin (Germany). The insights emerging from the plenary discussions are captured in the "Summary Findings" of the conference included at the end of this volume.

THE CHURCHES AS AGENTS FOR JUSTICE

Responsible Church Leadership in the Face of Polarization, Populism, Protectionism and Post-truth

Antje Jackelén

Church Leaders between Tradition and Transformation

In dealing with the socio-political challenges of today, responsible church leaders find themselves in the midst of a familiar conflict between tradition and transformation. This conflict affects not just the church sphere, but every area where there is a call for responsible leadership. There is, however, often a difference between the emphasis placed on the two components, at least when viewed from the outside. If, for example, in the field of economics the *cantus firmus* is one of constant transformation, then in the church the focus is more on tradition. That comes, indeed, as no surprise in a movement whose "business concept" is not exactly a start-up one but has been tried and tested in a unique fashion for over 2,000 years. Why should we change at any price something that has survived the storms of the centuries? That would be unwise.

From that point of view, it is understandable that for the church tradition often becomes a hallmark of truth. The closer it is to tradition the purer and truer (and so much more "classical") the theology is. Therefore, it is understandable that, particularly in times of uncertainty and challenge, the early church is idealized and romanticized as a time that cultivated good traditions. Certain periods of church history may be idealized in order to "prove" that the church of today and its leaders to a greater or lesser extent have fallen short. Or perhaps another part of the worldwide church is elevated as a place which remains particularly faithful to tradition and to orthodox faith, again with the aim of exposing the current church and its leaders as deficient. This tension concerning tradition is nothing new, and there is nothing to suggest that it will ever stop.

Yet, as we know, tradition has not made its way through the centuries unscathed. Without phases of particularly loud critiques of tradition and without the constant quiet tweaking of traditions, we would not be where we are now. Yes, in a sense, tradition, as the passing on of what needs to be handed down, is already a form of transformation. For this process requires communication and communication always comprises the possibility and the reality of transformation.

Moreover, Christian tradition is congenial with the call to transformation. If life in baptism is a life of constant conversion, if the Spirit of Pentecost is a Spirit of renewal, then it follows that the church, the people of God, is also in need of constant transformation. This is not a case of change for its own sake, but of ongoing renewal or reformation. *Semper reformanda*, even. Incidentally, I love the gerundive in this expression—if this is a matter of renewal, then it is a clear corrective to any zealous activity to which we may be inclined. "*Semper reformanda*" does not actually mean "always reforming", as it is often rendered in English, but "always in need of being reformed".

In the years following the 500th anniversary of the Reformation, it may not be out of place to remember that renewal and transformation will perhaps be particularly successful when we engage in encounters with others. The second imperative in the Lutheran-Catholic document *From Conflict to Communion*, calls on us to "let ourselves continuously be transformed by the encounter with the other and by the mutual witness of faith".[1] The 800-year-old Pentecost prayer, *Veni Sancte Spiritus*, which is attributed to the Archbishop of Canterbury, Stephen Langton, expresses an appropriate way of dealing with tradition: *flecte quod est rigidum, fove quod est frigidum* (bend that which is inflexible, warm that which is chilled). This healthy tension between tradition and transformation is a proper context to all with responsibility for leadership, including those in the church.

Polarization, Populism, Protectionism and Post-truth

What makes this conflict between tradition and transformation appear special in our own time? Polarization, populism, protectionism and post-

---

[1] *From Conflict to Communion. Lutheran – Catholic Common Commemoration of the Reformation in 2017* (Leipzig: Evangelische Verlagsanstalt, 2013), 88.

truth are the four Ps that hang together and strengthen one another. Taken together, they form a seductive but poisonous cocktail, which is eagerly swallowed in many places today. And, of course, the church is in no way left untouched by this. First, the Ps operate within the church; second, the church in the world is caught up in this poisonous area of conflict; and third, the church is exploited repeatedly in this area of conflict, so often that it is hardly able to recognize itself in the mirror of criticism that is held up to it.

However, the increasing consciousness of the dynamic that the four Ps bring to today's world, including the church, offers us a sign of hope. In a time of populism, we can respond by remaining open-minded and steadfast. We can be open to the world, critical and self-critical in our eagerness to learn, and yet, at the same time, steadfast, firmly anchored in the gospel and thereby also in the Universal Declaration of Human Rights (UDHR), which was in parts inspired by Christian tradition.

Polarization is a result of the ever widening gap between people who have plenty of wealth, education, health and power at their disposal, and those who do not. The fact that the combined wealth of eight men is greater than that of 3.6 billion people, half the world's population, says something about the polarizing potential of our world. We can also see this from a less global perspective: the things that belong together in a functioning society are being more and more pulled apart, or even ripped up. Consequently, we have created a society where there is little comprehension of the living conditions of those who are different, which leads to open hostility. Those feeling they belong to society's disadvantaged are drawn to protectionism, which often reveals itself in nationalism. Brexit, Britain's move to leave the European Union, has clearly demonstrated how polarization between town and countryside, young and old, those of higher or lower levels of education, influences people's views of reality and strengthens their desire for protectionism. As we know, that does not in any way mean that populism is only to be found among angry young men who feel themselves to be disadvantaged and of limited education.

As is generally well known, Brexit was also a classic example of the influence of post-truth. The old saying "Lies have short legs, [... you are soon caught by the truth]" seems to have been replaced with its very opposite by certain politicians and opinion formers who set the tone for the Brexit debate. But that is not the worst of it. The fact that lies suddenly have long legs and that public liars, when caught out, instead of showing any shame, strut about shamelessly, is to all intents and purposes an attack on the network of human relationships. Human relationships, which sustain our societies, presuppose a relatively high degree of trust. If post-truth is successful in dismantling both this trust and our fundamental sense of the truth, then the argument about the extent to which relativism inevitably follows on from post-modernism becomes nothing more than trivial banter. For without a fundamental sense of the truth, democracy cannot function over the long term.

As a result, it may well be entirely right for us now, after the cleansing bath of post-modernism, to argue once again for, and enter, an enlightened universalism. If post-modernistic over-eagerness leads to seeing nothing more than a deconstructable claim to power behind every claim to truth, then universalism completely falls by the wayside. Concern for the general good, whether in the form of common interest, or in the form of common values, succumbs to tribal interests. Universalism is replaced by tribalism.[2] Perhaps for that reason it has latterly become more difficult to get acceptance for the idea that at least Judaism, Christianity and Islam speak of the same God, since, from a logical point of view, it would be difficult to have several different creators of the universe. For those who, above all, feel a need to exclude Islam, using the slogan "Our God is the opposite of Allah", it does not seem to matter at all that in so doing they are reducing God, the creator of heaven and earth, to a tribal god.

But let us return to post-truth. Where the network of relationships and the sense of truth are broken, the formation of opinion in society suffers. In accordance with the philosopher Byung-Chul Han, we could say: collective expressions of opinion in civil society get hidden beneath digital swarms, which materialize on a grand scale and then quickly disappear; the responsibility of voters is confused with clicking a "smiley"—or the "like" button; citizens are reduced to consumers.[3] Such danger lurks wherever democracy and the church are subdued by an entertainment culture. Even if church activity has its own entertaining qualities, the purpose of the church goes far beyond entertainment; it always comes with a taste of provocation.

Han's digital prospects certainly deserve more theological reflection. The "digital swarm" for him is something quite different from people demonstrating. The swarm has neither soul nor spirit, no sense of "we", no voice. It is noise. That is something different from the dialectic of a proclamation of the word as *viva vox evangelii* and of God's presence in stillness, to which we are theologically accustomed. Digital culture leads to self-exploitation, according to Han. We provide a constant flow of data, with hardly any idea of how it will be used. We do not know what monitoring systems and manipulation op-

---

[2] See Susan Neiman, Widerstand der Vernunft: Ein Manifest in postfaktischen Zeiten (Salzburg: Ecowin 2017), 57ff.

[3] Byung-Chul Han, *Im Schwarm. Ansichten des Digitalen* (Berlin: Matthes & Seitz, 2013), 87-90; English translation: Byung-Chul Han, *In the swarm: digital prospects*, translated by Erik Butler (Cambridge, Ma: MIT Press, 2017), 61ff.

portunities we are feeding into. The Cambridge Analytica affair, in which the firm has been accused of possibly altering the result of the United Kingdom referendum on Brexit, has at least justified Han in this. Transparency and a constant presence are the core of this.[4] Both history and the future appear empty, which is difficult to reconcile with significant theological categories such as history of salvation and (divine) promise. A rather aimless culture of acceleration has replaced the processes of growth and maturity.

The smartphone has become an icon for the individualized digital culture. Concrete reality is in retreat in favor of the imaginary. The smartphone opens a narcissistic space for self-absorption.[5] As is well-known, *digitus* means finger. A finger that is mainly used for counting. Han maintains: "Digital culture is based on the counting finger. In contrast, history means *recounting*. It is not a matter of *counting*. (...)* More than anything, friends on Facebook are *counted*. Yet real friendship is an account, a narrative."[6] That applies, of course, also for the friendship of God. Recounting! Narrative! Can theology ever manage to get along, even in the digital age, without narration?

So what does this excursion into the digital realm have to do with the four Ps? I believe that the four Ps and digitalization can influence and also strengthen each other. Han asserts: "(...) the phenomenology of the digital knows nothing of the dialectical pain of thinking. It might be called the Phenomenology of 'Like'."[7] That sounds like a fairly ideal philosophical basis for a four P world.

From what has been said above, it is self-evident that critical scrutiny and the critical verification of sources are more important than ever before. It is as important as it has ever been for this to be taught in schools, universities and further education, perhaps even more important than ever. But when mistrust exceeds a critical level and when manipulation corrupts confidence, then even criticism of sources is of only limited use.

There are signs of danger which deserve attention. These include the loss of honesty, accountability, respect of others, readiness to compromise and social cohesion. On the other hand, there can be acceptance of hate speech and fake news, the propagation of outright lies or half-truths, the identification and pursuit of scapegoats, the demonization of groups, shrinking space for civil society, and subtle changes in the meanings of words.

In Sweden, there are a number of examples of slippage in the use of the language, especially when talking about immigration and Islam. There is also an increase in ethno-nationalism—a phenomenon that is not

---

[4] Ibid. (English translation), 21.
[5] Ibid., 26
[6] Ibid., 35f.
[7] Ibid., 49.

confined to Europe and North America, as is illustrated by the Hindutva ideology in India.

Populism is a beneficiary of the crisis in journalism in a changed media environment—at least in Sweden. There are too few journalists who have the necessary security of employment and the resources they need in order to carry out systematic and rigorous investigations. Too many of them are forced to get their information from social media. This contributes to the proliferation of the black-and-white scenarios that are so common in social media, thus adding to polarization. In this way, a culture arises in which fringe phenomena become blown up, while the broad middle ground is downsized and the majority seems to be turned into a minority. The marginal is marginalizing the mainstream!

POPULIST PROPAGANDA AND THE CHURCH

Since the church is part of the world, these dynamics can, of course, also be found in the churches. There is polarization here as well, and fake news is also produced here. Not-so-holy alliances are being formed and it is relatively easy to use the populist recipe book to sow distrust of the church leadership: as having lost contact with people; as an elite who flirt with minorities instead of caring for the unity of the church. Interreligious dialogue (especially if involving Islam), engagement in public affairs or the pursuit of inclusion and equality appear in populist rhetoric as liberal, left-wing, feminist betrayals of the church. Populist propaganda against the church has invented the aphorism: in the past, people left the church because they did not believe in God, now people leave because they do believe in God. Even though sociological research pursued with meticulously scientific rigor proves that this is simply not true, it is still repeated over and over again until it does have the appearance of being at least somewhat true. And it then doesn't take very long before the first journalist from the mainstream media asks the question: What is your comment on the fact that devout Christians are leaving the church because it has become too political? And *voilà*, a new pseudo truth has received a nice rubber stamp of legitimacy.

The demand made of the Swedish church is to become more Swedish, i.e. nationalistic, and to be more like a church, i.e. to put up a front, above all, against Islam. The allegation that the church is being political instead of Christian, if it expresses itself on public issues, often comes from people who have themselves adopted a resolute political position. The so-called politicization of the church is often more a projection "from outside" than a strategy "from within". But it is a thoroughly effective projection. It puts the speaking and actions of the church in the public arena under the cloak of suspicion, which can lead to discouragement, self-censorship, and eventually, to silence.

In 2017, a reporter from a regional daily newspaper revealed how he, following the methods of the undercover journalist Günther Walraff had gained access to a so-called "troll factory".[8] After being recruited the first task he was given was to damage the church. The Swedish church has close to six million members, making it the largest civil society organization in the country. Destabilizing it seems attractive. Up to now, this destabilization has taken the form of constant intimidation rather than large-scale attacks. We do not find ourselves facing water cannons but are rather under a leaking faucet. At first, the constant dripping is hardly noticeable, then it becomes irritating, and finally the only thing that matters will be how to escape from the torture. The first question is, then, no longer a matter of what we wish or ought to say or preach, but what negative reactions will be stirred up, once again, by what we want to say, in which case perhaps we would rather not say it, or at least not just now. Thus, discourses are changed; confusion emerges. Alarmism can blur our sight and lead to a resigned shrug of the shoulders, where it would be better to have a critical and self-critical analysis and resolute energy.

In this situation significant risks arise: an erosion of civil society, political parties acting in a short-sighted and reactive manner, a lack of vision, and weakened democracy.

WHAT THE CHURCH CAN DO

The church must not allow itself to be brought to the point of only taking care of its own interests. It must not allow itself to be content with less than what has, for example, been expressed in the Vision of The Lutheran World Federation (LWF): *Liberated by God's grace, a communion in Christ living and working together for a just, peaceful, and reconciled world.* This is to be achieved, as it always has been throughout the history of Christianity, through prayer and work. *Ora et labora*—pray and work.

What might that look like? Seven points:

1. I think that it is once again important to pay great attention to the worldwide community of the church. Church provincialism is not a

---

[8] https://www.ekuriren.se/tjanster/granskning-sa-styrs-den-svenska-trollfabriken-som-sprider-hat-pa-natet/ In English: https://www.ekuriren.se/sormland/the-secret-swedish-troll-factory/ by Mathias Ståhle, published on 16 February 2017 in Swedish, on 23 February 2017 in English.

virtue. The Gospel of Jesus Christ was and is transnational, crossing borders. "There is no longer Jew or Greek, there is no longer slave or free, there is no longer male and female, for you are all one in Christ Jesus" (Gal 3:28). The ambitions that we in LWF have expressed for the Reformation anniversary can be formulated just as well for the following years: we will worship, think and act publicly in ways that are ecumenically responsible, globally aware and with confidence in the future. This is perhaps less about arguing for radically new ideas, and more about standing up for a renewal of thinking. And for good alliances, which will reinforce hope, justice and peace.

2. It is also important to think through the role of the church in the public space boldly and consistently. It is self-evident that faith is not just a private matter. It is also person-to-person and leads to consequences in the public space—both for us as individuals and for the church as a community and an organization. This is not about party politics, but rather about trying to make the work of politicians easier by providing background and giving a sense of direction. I have found the LWF study document "The Church in the Public Space" helpful in this. It gives five guiding principles for action in the public arena: a) assessing public issues in participatory ways; b) building relationships of trust; c) challenging injustice; d) discovering signs of hope; e) empowering people in need.

3. We must also recognize that in every generation it is necessary to reclaim democracy. In Sweden, we celebrated one hundred years of democracy in 2018. Equal and universal suffrage was introduced in 1918 by decision of the parliament. Up to only a few years ago, it felt as if democracy was as stable as a centuries-old stone wall—indestructible and essentially maintenance-free despite wind and weather. But now we need to compare it rather with a wooden house, which is constantly in need of maintenance work, if it is to brave the rain and storms and offer its inhabitants and visitors, not just protection, but also a good place to live together. This co-existence is indispensable, as we not only have to confront populism, but we also need the strength to tackle climate change and the so-called fourth industrial revolution. Democracy needs democrats. They don't just fall from heaven, but they are nurtured through education.

4. If democracy is to survive, it must be constantly fed a diet of values. For this, it needs not just democrats to feed it, but also healthy food— the values that arise from constantly fresh encounters with the great

traditions of human ideas. Some of these values will always have their roots in religion. Modernity and scientific development have not led to the disappearance of religion. On the contrary, the insights of cognitive science point to the human being as a *homo religiosus.* Seen collectively, this means that, despite criticism of the Böckenförde paradox, there is something in it: The liberal secular state is based on prerequisites or values that it cannot guarantee itself. Or, according to Habermas, reason, being serious about self-criticism and its own limitations, cannot help but encounter what goes beyond reason. This is not the same as a drift into the irrational; it is not something less than reason; but it is an openness to that which is more than mere reason. Reason that recognizes its boundaries can, therefore, hardly withdraw from having a theological interest. In this sense, it is also in the interests of democracy to deal wisely with the sources of cultural values. And this indispensably includes, once again, the great faith traditions and the organizations that represent them in a particular way, such as the churches. That naturally involves criticism and self-criticism of the traditions and institutions, but also naturally excludes any blanket condemnation or banning of these institutions from the public space.

5. Populist movements challenge the churches in positive as well as negative, risky and painful ways. On the positive side, I include a closer alliance with the sciences. Although it has long been convenient to represent faith and (natural) science as enemies, it has become much clearer, in the light of populism, how much both are bound up in the service of the truth. That means a constructive partnership rather than opposition; that means practice-oriented dialogue instead of an apparently lost power struggle on the side of theology. This dialogue can also help us to expose populist accusations that the church is promoting politics rather than Christianity as a diversionary tactic. For what is criticized as improper political interference is often only the fruit of good interpretation. It is clear that, in the public space, it is not possible to engage in argument directly by using biblical passages without further ado. For example, if we want to advocate in public the importance of the child's perspective, then we hardly do that by quoting Jesus blessing the children, or by using his words about who is greatest in the Kingdom of Heaven. We do it by pointing to the UN Convention on the Rights of the Child (UNCRC). If we do that with the same concern for interpretation that we naturally apply today when speaking of God's activity in creation, by using the terminology of evolution, then we can be sure that the public voice of the church is in accordance with the gospel and the love of God towards the world.

6. In the confrontation with the four Ps, a new narrative of hope and participation is called for. In this case, hope, as distinguished from optimism, is a theological category. Optimism is essentially no more than the extrapolation of facts, such as they are perceived. Its basis is not necessarily reliable. The philosopher Susan Neiman says: "Optimism is a misjudgement of facts, hope is aimed at changing facts. Understanding hope as an ideal means not just taking it as given, but that it must be achieved."[9] As a theologian, I would add that it also can be achieved. I say can, because hope is oriented towards the promise of God, with which God comes to meet us from the future, as it were. This hope is different from optimism because it bases itself, not on the shaky ground of our more or less successful compilation and interpretation of facts, but on God's act of salvation. For that reason, we do not counteract the pessimism of our time with optimism. And for that reason, too, we do not answer the dystopia of our time with the mirror image of Utopia. Instead, we proclaim and portray hope as the salt of the earth, in the shape of a public theology as well as the priesthood of all believers, as advocates for a public space, that allows full participation and involvement for all; as people who, by the power of their hope, are able to not only endure ambiguity and complexity, but also to demonstrate their fruitfulness.[10]

7. In times of populism, we will have to show resistance, and in doing so have a sense of our own wounds and also the wounds of others. "Peace be with you! As my Father has sent me, so I send you" (John 20: 21). That is what Jesus said to his friends when they saw him again after his resurrection. It was not just the victory over death that they saw, they also saw the wounds, the marks of the nails, which had been driven through his hands and his feet by the fear of the people. The sceptical Thomas was even invited to reach out and feel the wounds. "Peace be with you! As my father has sent me, so I send you." Yes, I would like to have this peace, but when I look at the wounds, do I really want this mission? Do I want to accept the task given by the wounded, helpless-looking God? Only because I am certain that it is the risen, living one who bears these wounds. Therefore, be open-minded and steadfast! And then—as the children's song says: '*Mut tut gut!*' It's good to be brave. Very good!

---

[9] Neiman, op. cit. (note 2), 75.
[10] E.g. by not playing off universalism and particularism against each other. This should be obvious in the Lutheran mindset that is used to thinking dialectically!

Messengers of Hope. The Churches in Germany as an Agent for Justice and against Populism

Heinrich Bedford-Strohm

New Right-Wing Populism in Germany

The right-wing populist party "Alternative für Deutschland" (AfD) is currently represented in the European Parliament, the German Bundestag and in all of the 16 German state parliaments. When it was elected as the second strongest political party in the state parliament of Saxony-Anhalt in 2016, the Protestant Bishop in Saxony-Anhalt Ilse Junkermann very clearly set the standard she would apply to the AfD in the new Magdeburg parliament: "Working soberly and competently for realistic solutions, instead of polarizing with simple slogans and increasing fears—that is the standard by which members of the AfD in the state parliament have to be measured."

I would like to add two more aspects to this clear assessment by Bishop Junkermann. First, understandable fears of citizens need to be recognized in the public debates of our country. 900,000 people came to Germany in just one year to seek protection against war, terror and misery in their countries of origin: This of course requires a great effort, even for a rich country like Germany. Nobody ever said that this would not be a challenge. The high number of immigrants in 2015 was an exceptional and singular occurrence. A courageous and pragmatic political response—sober, competent, and solution-oriented—is all the more important when coming to terms with such a big challenge. Any solution, however, needs to rest firmly on the basis of our humanitarian traditions. It is on this basis that we need to engage with anxieties and fears especially. The authorities have made significant progress in exactly this sense, registering refugees, and supporting civil society initiatives for refugee aid as much as possible. Billions of Euros have been made available for immediate assistance and integration measures.

The second aspect that I want to emphasize concerns the public voice of the church in the face of right-wing populism. We must speak up decisively and clearly against all attempts to make nationalist ideas and right-wing extremist martial rhetoric acceptable again in Germany. Right-wing populism is accompanied by a collapse of values in online communication, especially in social media. The waves of hate that we currently see in comment columns of some websites testify to online disinhibition, which certainly has to do with the fact that people on the internet remain anonymous and do not have to give account for their words. Yet more and more people deposit what they say hatefully with their real name. Obviously, the internet is seen as a space where everything is allowed. It seems that it is not conversation or discussion with others that is sought, but a militant reinforcement of one's own prejudices and one's own hatred. Such online discourse does not promote real communication, but brings communication to a standstill. This is not about restricting freedom of speech. Rather, it is about stopping hate propaganda. Those who hate others under the guise of freedom of expression must be stopped. Those who criticize "political correctness", but in reality only want free rein for the spread of misanthropy, must be clearly countered. Those who stir up hatred of people who are among the most vulnerable are in clear contradiction with the basic orientations that our state and our society stand for. In any case, such voices cannot invoke Christianity as their basis. Yet, this is not about a *status confessionis*. We do not need to discuss whether certain people are still Christian or not. Rather, we need a clear and courageous discussion about the topics at hand—without being led astray by the rhetoric of propaganda. Where the name of Jesus Christ is invoked, the gospel needs to be present, too. Jesus gave us the double commandment to love as the central commandment and basis of all inter-personal relations.

Three groups of AfD supporters need to be distinguished: protest voters, right-wing conservatives disappointed by chancellor Merkel's policies, and finally, right-wing extremists. This varied basis of the AfD makes engaging with it difficult. On the one hand, democratic protest and fears need to be taken seriously, and the decisive question in engaging with them needs to be: what can be real solutions? On the other hand, however, we need to stand firm against extremist racism, and avoid giving any legitimacy to it. Staying in dialogue with protest voters and with right-wing conservatives needs to be balanced with a clear distancing from right-wing extremist positions. In this situation, my suggestion is to go beyond immediate questions of policy and seek the heart of the matter: what is the narrative we want our society to be shaped by?

The Christian tradition is a rich resource for societal narratives, and the churches have played an important role in shaping the self-understanding of societies in the past. They have something to bring to the table of civil society discourse even today, in the context of religious diversity and secularism. Speaking from a Lutheran perspective, when thinking of a "grand narrative", Luther's distinction between the *theologia gloriae* and the *theologia crucis* comes to mind. This can be re-interpreted in the sense of a narrative of self-elevation versus a narrative of humility and responsibility. In terms of interpersonal relations, one may distinguish between a narrative of distrust or even hate and a narrative of trust and neighborly love. In eschatological terms, one may think of a narrative of fear versus a narrative of empowerment and hope. All of these dialectical models can be applied as hermeneutical keys to the situation of facing right-wing populism, and they yield a variety of interpretations as well as resources for dialogue.

How such deep background narratives shape perceptions of public issues has recently come to the fore in the debates about the Bavarian state order to hang up crosses in all public institutions, issued by the Minister President of Bavaria Markus Soeder. The political viewpoint here suggested that the cross could serve as a symbol of civil religion, a symbol of "the West". However, in a situation where right-wing populists in Europe use the notion of the "Christian occident" to further their nationalist agenda, we need to focus on the religious message of the cross, and the churches need to bring attention to the meaning of the cross. The cross is the most powerful message against right wing populism and xenophobia which one can ever imagine. However, the churches need to speak up publicly against any use of the cross as an exclusionary symbol, as a gate-keeping symbol, so to speak, that is meant to discourage diversity and inclusion.

THE NARRATIVE OF FEAR AND THE NARRATIVE OF HOPE

The narrative of fear is a constant presence in civil society discourses and in the media—be they traditional media or social media. Fear pays attention; and attention is the most valuable currency of our time. The backbone of the narrative of fear is xenophobia, closely connected with a fear of losing one's wealth and privileges. Elements of this narrative are the model of the "clash of cultures", and a paradigm of shame and honor that structures the nationalist perception of international relations and internal politics. Populist politics both stir up fear and alleviate it. They offer grandiose fictions of nationalist pride that speak to the emotions, and make us forget the struggle for real-life solutions. Examples come to mind easily: "America first" and "Make America great again"; or in Europe Hungarian and Austrian references to the "defense against the Turks" since the 16th and 17th century.

The narrative of hope is the basis of the Christian self-understanding, and it is rooted deeply in the traditions of Israel. It can take its initiative from the Exodus tradition:

> My father was a wandering Aramean, and he went down into Egypt with a few people and lived there and became a great nation, powerful and numerous. But the Egyptians mistreated us and made us suffer, subjecting us to harsh labor. Then we cried out to the LORD, the God of our ancestors, and the LORD heard our voice and saw our misery, toil and oppression. So the LORD brought us out of Egypt with a mighty hand and an outstretched arm, with great terror and with signs and wonders. He brought us to this place and gave us this land, a land flowing with milk and honey. (Deuteronomy 26:5-9).

God's eternal covenant of peace, illustrated by the rainbow, which will be kept by God despite all human sins and weaknesses, is the consequence of this narrative.

And the Christian conviction that God became human in Jesus Christ who died on the cross and was resurrected after three days is the most powerful confirmation of this narrative which one could ever imagine. This narrative of hope is inclusive, as the gospel of John stresses: "For God so loved the world that God gave God's one and only Son, that whoever believes in him shall not perish but have eternal life" (John 3:16). The whole world is reconciled with God through Christ (2 Cor 5). It is decisive to understand whom we see when we look at the cross, we see Christ's radical love. And the cross becomes a symbol of hope for all through the resurrection of Christ. On the cross, we see a human being who dies with a cry of desperation as a victim of torture. We see a man who preached a universal love which reaches out even to our enemies. We see someone who did not respond to violence with violence but with meekness. We see someone who identifies with the hungry, the prisoners and with the strangers. In the resurrection, we see the new beginning, we see hope triumphing over despair, we see solidarity with the oppressed and liberation from suffering and inequality. In the resurrection, we see graceful justice, and just grace. Therefore, the cross of the resurrected Christ is a symbol for inclusion, not for exclusion. (And I say concerning Bavaria, one can only be glad if the cross is visible in public with exactly this message of justice and inclusion, delegitimizing all political strategies oriented towards exclusion!)

Re-generating the narrative of hope instead of the narrative of fear: Churches as agents of remembrance and reconciliation

The grand narrative needs to be made accountable for everyday issues as well. It needs to prove its relevance for giving direction to active engagement in societal issues, and for finding solutions for contemporary challenges. However, grand narratives have to be mediated well, and they need to be shaped and re-shaped by their interpreters. The people that identify with a grand narrative shape their society as well as the grand narrative itself. And the churches are important mediating institutions in this regard, it is the very nature of the church, one could say, to manage and distribute the grand narrative in the different contexts of communal live. So at the end of my contribution, I want to take a moment to consider the mediation between the high-minded principal "grand narrative" and the level of everyday political discourse with its constant search for compromise. I focus on the churches' way of mediating in the German context.

In describing the churches as mediating agents in the political public sphere, I take inspiration from Max Weber. I think that dividing up an ethics of conviction (a direct ethics of the grand narrative) and an ethics of responsibility (a "realistic" compromise between grand claims and everyday limitations) between church and politics does not do justice to the complexity of the motives on both sides. Rather, conviction and responsibility need to go hand in hand on both sides, that is, in the church and in politics—the question is how they relate to each other in the political sphere and in the religious sphere respectively. When Max Weber introduced the distinction between responsibility ethics and conviction ethics in his lecture "Politics as a Vocation" (*Politik als Beruf*) almost one hundred years ago[1], he started with distinguishing the two from each other, first stating that people who act on the basis of an ethics of conviction do not take into account the results of their conduct or are not ready to take responsibility for the results. People who act on the basis of an ethics of responsibility, on the other hand, consider the possible results and then decide upon their actions accordingly. However, they do take convictions into account, and need to come to terms with how to balance their convictions with their responsible flexibility. If the conviction is a Christian one then responsible conduct will mean looking at the consequences the decision will have for the weakest individuals in the situation when seeking a solution. This agrees with liberation theology's preferential option for the oppressed.

---

[1] Max Weber, *Weber's Rationalism and Modern Society*, transl. and ed. by Tony Waters and Dagmar Waters (New York: Palgrave Macmillan, 2015).

We have got to stop pitting humanitarianism and realism against each other. It does not aid the public discussion to have one political position claim to have an approach of "realism" while suspecting all other diverging opinions as being naive or saintly. Truly being realistic, from a Christian point of view, cannot be understood without viewing Christ as being the reality that grounds our reality. Dietrich Bonhoeffer illustrates this position impressively in his ethics by emphasizing God's reconciliation of the whole world in Christ.[2] Realism cannot ignore what Bonhoeffer calls the "view from below". With respect to refugees, this means that realism always has be able to give a satisfying answer to the question: What does the realistic option mean for those weakest individuals in the situation? Or once again in the words of Max Weber: each ethics of responsibility is based on a certain conviction. For that reason, ethics of conviction and ethics of responsibility can never simply be placed opposite of each other but have to be placed in relation to each other.

At the conclusion of my remarks, I want to name important instances when the churches have mediated their conviction in the narrative of hope in the public sphere. In Germany, remembrance politics are a special concern in this regard, given the recognition for Germany's historical responsibility in the crimes of National-Socialism, and the constant work towards renewal, justice and peace. In this regard, the narrative of hope turns into a paradigm of humility and self-reflection. We need to stress that our political freedom, and the democratic order of Germany, are granted rather than achieved, and this must lead towards humility, thankfulness and the readiness to share one's wealth.

I want to give a few examples for how the church in Germany tries live out the paradigm of humility and self-reflection:

- The common European remembrance of the First World War was an important moment in the public witness of the church in 2014, when we distanced ourselves strongly from any triumphant nationalist celebration of the "Christian Occident". We discovered how different the narratives of the First World War in the different countries still are. However, in the Community of Protestant Churches in Europe, through dialogue, we managed to agree on a common narrative which found its expression in a joint statement on the First World War. The Protestant Churches in Germany (EKD) took it as the basis for their own statement.

---

[2] Dietrich Bonhoeffer, *Ethics* (*Dietrich Bonhoeffer Works*, volume 6), ed. by Clifford J. Green, transl. Reinhard Krauss, Charles C. West, and Douglas W. Stott (Minneapolis: Augsburg Fortress, 2005), 55.

- In 2015, after long preparations, a worship service in remembrance of the Armenian Genocide took place in the Berlin Cathedral, and President Gauck finally called the mass killings of Armenians in the Ottoman Empire, which were aided by German troops and started on 24 April 1915, a "Genocide".

- On March 6, 2017, I took the opportunity in the Paulskirche in Frankfurt to express—on behalf of the Protestant Churches in Germany (EKD)—our shame and deep regret to Jewish Leaders for Luther's hate speeches against Jews. In my view this had to be a clear consequence of Luther's own emphasis on the need for continuous repentance in the first of his 95 theses. In order to actively strengthen the work of countering anti-Jewish hate speech, the EKD decided to fund an endowment for a chair of theology with a focus on Christian-Jewish relations.

- In 2017, the EKD offered a declaration on the Genocide of Hereros during the German colonial regime in present-day Namibia. Colonialism and its long term consequences of robbery and injustice remain a challenge for remembrance politics in the coming years.

- In November 2018, I have celebrated a common service with the Archbishop of Canterbury in London to remember the end of the First World War.

The Churches have a lot to contribute to the shaping of a societal narrative which is inclusive, and they need to embrace this public theology responsibly in the future just as strongly as in the past. The challenge of populism for the churches' public witness remains, what does an open, inclusive identity for society look like, and on what can it be grounded? In the above, I have offered my insights on how to work towards strengthening the narrative of hope.

Churches as Agents for Justice and against Division in Hungary

Tamás Fabiny

Introduction

Over recent years, populism has become an increasingly prevalent issue in both the United States and Europe. We experience how more and more groups in society are prone to give simplistic, emotive answers to old and new questions, often not respecting the integrity of others. These often very crucial questions tend to be related to past burdens in each given society, the responsibility for the lack of solutions rests on many shoulders. However, while it is of course relevant to raise a question, this is no justification for giving the wrong answer.

Public theology is closely related to context and it is my task in this paper to present the situation in Hungary and the churches serving there. Comparisons can be made with other Central Eastern European countries given that there are many similarities. There are historical and cultural reasons for this, and our countries have also had similar routes of development and faced similar challenges.

Let me turn at this point to an excellent political thinker of the 20th century, István Bibó who already in 1946 gave a very clear analysis about the situation of the countries in our region. Bibó was a Democrat at heart and a committed Protestant. His most fruitful period was the so-called coalition time between 1945 and 1948. In 1945, under Soviet occupation and controlled by the allied powers, a multiparty democracy was born which lasted until 1948 when the Communists gained power in Hungary. During this period, Bibó still hoped that it would be possible to use rational arguments and good analysis to convince politicians and ordinary people.

In 1946 Bibó wrote an essay with the title "The Miseries of East European Small States. The Deformation of Political Culture in Central-East Europe"[1]. The pessimistic title refers to the fact that the nations in Central Eastern Europe had been subordinated to the interests of greater powers for most of their history. Shortly after World War II, Bibó was looking for an answer to the question whether those small states would be able to gain strength without turning against each other, and at the same time build their own identity while maintaining their contacts with the West, to which they had always claimed they belonged. Bibó mentioned several obstacles to this process and those are alas still relevant seven decades later.

In relation to populism, we can refer to the incoherent political philosophies and lies mentioned by Bibó. He defined political hysteria as "a characteristic feature of the unbalanced Central-East European political mentality"[2] and related it to an existential anxiety in the community. In harder times, national consciousness brought with it the appearance of authoritarian leadership. Bibó described this type of politician as follows: "besides their undoubted talents, [they] had cunning and a bent for aggression that made them perfectly suited for running and epitomizing anti-democratic governments and aggressive political pseudo-constructs in the midst of democratic trappings".[3]

According to Bibó, in Central European nations not only the social structure but also the political culture and mentality have been deformed. Balance between possible and desirable things has been shaken. From a socio-psychological point of view, this has been accompanied by "self-documentation", oversized national vanity, the constant underlining of achievements and moral irresponsibility. Or as Bibó put it:

> All manifestations of national life were subjected to the most furious national teleology; all their genuine or imaginary achievements, from Nobel prizes to Olympic records, lost their spontaneous purpose in themselves and were put in the service of national self-documentation. From forgery to assassination, everything was sacrosanct and inviolable if done in the 'name' or 'interest' of the nation.[4]

Bibó sees political journalism working with false categories as the main tool for disseminating this attitude. (Political journalism today is also an

---

[1] Citations from István Bibó, *The Art of Peacemaking. Political Essays by István Bibó*, transl. and ed. by Péter Pásztor (New Haven/London: Yale University Press, 2015), 130-180.
[2] Ibid., 149.
[3] Ibid., 152.
[4] Ibid., 155.

efficient tool for populism.) Distortions then influence the scientific sector of each country and immerse it in corruption. This type of political thinking is unable to hear criticism coming from outside, as Bibó put it:

> If they were called to account for their internal disorders, dictatorship and oppression, they would point out the wounds they had suffered from [...] the Turks in defending European liberty and democracy. If they were reproached for their thoughtless and vain foreign policy, they would invoke the centuries-old, moreover metaphysical, 'meaning' of their history, which fatefully defined this or that policy of theirs.[5]

I assume I do not have to underline how relevant the logic sketched out by Bibó is even after seventy years. In addition to experts in social sciences, politics and media, representatives of the church also have to define their attitude in the light of this analysis and the questions of our time. Churches have a huge responsibility in how they react to certain phenomena in their societies and how they orient public opinion.

I have served 12 years as the Bishop of the Northern Diocese of the Evangelical Lutheran Church in Hungary. I serve in a region where lots of people have lost focus after the change of the regime. In my experience they are the most keen to react positively to any populistic ideologies.

It is a well-known fact that for forty years (between 1948 and 1989) Hungary was not a free state. The change of the regime in 1989 brought big changes and not everybody was able to cope with the sudden freedom. Living standards rose slower than was expected and dreamt of, and many people were disappointed. This situation provided a firm foundation for populism. The once "happiest barrack" became the saddest supermarket. In what follows I do not claim to give a systematic overview but rather some personal reflections.

THE SITUATION OF ROMA COMMUNITIES

Although a Roma community of a considerable size has lived in Hungary for centuries—and there are also quite positive examples of cooperation—an anti-Roma attitude repeatedly emerges from time to time. Especially in times of economic or political hardship, this national group tends to be chosen as a scapegoat.

In past centuries, statutes were passed on the forced settling of the Roma and there have been examples of internment and repeated raids. This led to the establishment of Roma ghettos and Roma labor service. During the Second World War, many Roma died in concentrations camps.

---

[5] Ibid., 156.

The Roma community met prejudice also in the Communist times. In the fifties, so-called errant Romas received a special black identity card and in the 1960s and even in the 1980s there were examples of forced washing of Roma people in the segregated Roma settlements.

There were also official attempts to integrate them—often against their own will. It often meant that Roma people from the countryside were brought to Budapest and allocated to blockhouses not matching their own culture. The state sought to integrate them in the labor market, many Roma people became trained workers who lost their jobs in the first wave after the change of the regime in 1989.

Public opinion turned against the Roma especially related to certain well-publicized crimes. They became a target for extreme right-wing youth—unfortunately also in a literal way. In 2008 and 2009, infamous attacks happened against unguarded Roma families. In several locations in the country, Molotov cocktails were thrown at houses on the edge of Roma settlements and people who ran out of the houses, including children, were assassinated. The authorities were unable to solve the case until they found evidence of the deeds of paramilitary groups. Extreme right-wing forces were behind these brutal actions. At that time, our church spoke very clearly against the brutality and we organized a remembrance service in the biggest Lutheran church in Budapest. The motto was from Romans 12:21, "Do not be overcome by evil, but overcome evil with good".

Education and awareness programs are important tools for fighting discrimination in congregations and church schools. We also strive to accept more Roma children in our kindergartens and schools, and we run a Christian Roma College in Nyíregyháza which is part of an integration network of the Hungarian state.

In addition to schooling, we are also present in the field of *diaconia*. To only mention a few examples, we are present in Roma communities with social agriculture programs offering work opportunities. The Lutheran church also serves homeless people and runs homes for assaulted mothers—some of them come from the Roma community. In one of our diaconical institutions, I recently met a Roma woman who came there as a client a few years ago and now she is a member of the middle management.

Relations with Jews

The ELCH has been active in making the realities of a silenced or sometimes distorted past known to the public—even if it is painful. We want to face what Hungary and Hungarian people experienced both during the times of National Socialism and under the power of the (right-wing) Arrow

Cross movement. We encourage representatives of society and public life to look into the mirror and learn from history—so that the sins and failures of those times are not repeated. We want to show the shame of the past in the same way as the apostle Paul speaks about sins committed during the wandering in the desert, "these things occurred as examples for us, so that we might not desire evil as they did." (1Co 10:6). It means that we would like to speak not only about the past but also about the present, reacting quickly and sensitively to the social phenomena surrounding us.

I mention one example. Not long ago, we organized an exhibition of the work of a Hungarian Jewish painter, Imre Ámós who died in a concentration camp. Through that, the church also wanted to show that we despise all reactions (be they deeds, words or just hints) that classify, stigmatize or humiliate people on the basis of their descent, ethnic background, religion or sex.

In my opening speech for the exhibition, I spoke clearly about the signs of anti-Semitism in our society today. I compared them to the feelings of Cain, the brother-killer, "As long as lists are compiled about a certain kind of people—be in the Parliament or elsewhere—the mindset of Cain is still alive". (At that time a representative of the extreme right-wing party Jobbik had proposed the absurd possibility of compiling such lists.) I must say that those voices have become more subtle in recent years and there is practically no parliamentary party (either in the government or in the opposition) who would claim to be anti-Semitic.

At the same time, it is more difficult to estimate the real extent of latent anti-Semitism. Some people claim that the visual appearance of the media campaign against George Soros, a resident of the United States of Hungarian origin, resembles the anti-Semitic campaigns between the two world wars. In view of the dangers of latent anti-Semitism and xenophobia, we have zero tolerance in our congregations and church institutions of any discrimination or humiliation.

In relation to the topic, I may also mention the work of the Christian-Jewish Society where I happen to be the executive president. We try to monitor discriminatory actions against different religious communities. We also try to look at the Abrahamic religions in one framework and also point out if there are false and untruthful statements against Islam in the media or in the area of education.

The temptation of nationalism

During the 40 years of communism, showing openly nationalistic feelings in Hungary was not recommended, as the idea of internationalism dominated. Official policy did not allow the promotion of community with Hungarians living outside of the country, left on the other side of the borders drawn up by the post First World War peace treaty in 1920. This may be one reason why the expression "nation" has been used so much in the period after the sudden freedom. Many people could not however, differentiate between national consciousness and exclusive chauvinism.

Right-wing radicalism and populism are often linked to the propagation of new-Paganism. Our church is very outspoken in opposing this. Populism also often goes hand in hand with political Christianity. In many countries in Central Eastern Europe, there is an ambition to make the church the servant of politics (*ancilla politicae*). Externally this can be seen when the political power tries to heavily rely on the churches, when it tries to use them to realize its own interests. I am quite sensitive to this phenomenon myself, as I experienced how churches were deformed during the Communist dictatorship by the state demands to serve power practically without criticism. Thus, political Christianity is a combination of political interest and supposed church interest. When such a form of power leads, paternalistic church politics becomes seemingly natural. Churches—which were oppressed or marginalized earlier on—may not even notice how they flirt with the political parties. And when all this is combined with a lack of a transparent long term church financing system (that goes beyond parliamentary electoral cycles), there is a great temptation to make a deal with political power out of financial interest. Political power is tempted to maintain the financial dependency of the churches and expect them in exchange to provide a supportive liturgy for social or political events. Of course such a role of being a living political décor is not worthy of churches.

In political Christianity, the borders between nation and church become hazy. The phenomenon is described well in the title of an excellent book by Martin Schulze Wessel, "Nationalizing Religion and Sacralizing the Nation".[6]

In my church, we repeatedly underline the fact how the triple ethnic roots of our church—Hungarian, German and Slovak—enrich our community.

Even if our church has (mostly) avoided nationalistic temptations, we cannot close our eyes to what is going on in society. A decade ago, we could see the rise of an extreme right-wing party using the dubious Árpád-striped flag which had previously lost its credibility between the two world wars and the terrifying marches of the related paramilitary forces. At that time, the leadership of our church gave a statement saying: "The Evangelical Lutheran Church is troubled by the appearance of small but radical groups and refuses all action that is in the least resembles the ignoble traditions

---

[6] Martin Schulze Wessel, *Nationalisierung der Religion und Sakralisierung der Nation im östlichen Europa* (Stuttgart: Franz Steiner Verlag, 2006).

of the national Socialist and Hungaristic movements. We reject all action that offends human integrity and the identity of anyone"[7].

Readers may remember those extremist demonstrations in Hungary as pictures were widely reported in the international media. Today we can say that the quite terrifying Hungarian Guard has actually disappeared. At the same time however, reactions in society are not clear, at that time every reasonable person was against the paramilitary marches, while today the xenophobic stereotypes appear in a more domesticated attire which are attractive to a wide circle of the population. This might also be part of the nature of populism.

THE QUESTION OF REFUGEES

The refugee question—which is undoubtedly one of the biggest global issues today—offers a great variety of examples of right-wing populism. It is well-known that the present Hungarian government and media are very clearly against receiving refugees based on a quota.

As a Lutheran church, our task is to represent a special church voice—in accordance with the statements of the Lutheran World Federation and our partner churches. In Hungary the Lutheran church is quite isolated with its opinion, although there are voices—not only in smaller communities but also within the Catholic and the Reformed church—which try to promote solidarity and humanitarian solidarity in contrast to impatience and fear.

The political and media scene tend to use more and more "dreadful" term migrant instead of the word refugee—thus they intensify people's anxiety of the unknown and dangerous. The populistic approach tends to make these traumatized people responsible for the existence of predictable social problems. The media has given voice to opinions which say that strangers will not observe the laws of the country, that they will take away our jobs and they speak of an intensified risk of terrorism.

For many people, the terrorist attacks in Berlin, Brussels, London and elsewhere have been seen as proof of this connection. After that, they hailed the government and Parliament decisions to aggravate the rules for immigration and to close the bigger refugee camps. The media usually only depicts refugees if they leave rubbish after them or where we can see young men marching. Personal tragedies which would give a face to the refugee situation are nearly never presented. In conclusion, disapproval

---

[7] Full text of the declaration in Hungarian: https://zope.lutheran.hu/honlapok/nyugat/tanulmanyok/korlevelek/gardatanacsnyil2007

and anxiety has become very general—also in regions where no-one has ever seen a living refugee in their lives.

In this social context, it provoked a great wave of disagreement when in June 2017, together with Roman Catholic Bishop Miklós Beer I appeared in a video made by the UN Refugee Agency, asking people to help those coming from a war zone.[8]

After this statement, we were very strongly attacked on different online forums. The most painful is to see when aggressive hatred is combined with a reference to so-called Christian values. There are more and more voices which speak about 'Christian Hungary' and 'Christian Europe' and which are not only afraid of the spread of Islam but which use Islam and terrorism as mere synonyms.

In this situation, it is the duty of our churches to present an objective picture of the Islamic religion—underlining that the militant version does not belong to the mainstream thinking of this religion at all.

Theologians will have to analyze the intention of the political system to re-Christianize Hungary. In an overwhelmingly secular society, this intention cannot only be explained by gaining political profit or maximizing the number of votes. It is a valid task for churches to firmly and proactively enter the public/political discourse on the real content of the attribute 'Christian'.

Our further tasks include moderating prejudice and hatred by showing positive examples of integration. In this, we might rely on the Word of God: "For God did not give us a spirit of cowardice, but rather a spirit of power and of love and of self-discipline" (2 Tim 1:7).

Conclusion

This sentence leads us back to István Bibó, with whom I started my analysis. In his essay cited earlier, he wrote,

> In a state of convulsive fear and the belief that the advance of freedom endangers the cause of the nation, the benefits of democracy cannot be made use of. To be a democrat is first and foremost not to be afraid—not to be afraid of those who have a different opinion, speak a different language, and are of another race; not to be afraid of revolution, conspiracies, the unknown evil intentions of the enemy, hostile

---

[8] UNHCR Central Europe: World Refugee Day 2017, Hungary – Lutheran and Catholic bishops stand #withrefugees (published online June 19, 2017), available with English subtitles: https://www.youtube.com/watch?v=ghcBcVPfgKE [accessed 26 April 2019].

propaganda, disdain, and generally all those imaginary dangers that become real because we are afraid of them.[9]

A church living in a populistic context really has to point out how people are being scared by many imaginary threats. At the same time, we must not understate real problems at the global and local levels. The causes and possible consequences of the refugee situation must equally be studied. Causes of course include wars, poverty, climate change, human trafficking and so on.

The real problems will not be easy to resolve without a spiritual strengthening in Europe, including the conscious valuing of its Jewish and Christian heritage. In this, we have a common responsibility. It is true that in Central Eastern Europe, some elements of church life in Western welfare states are negatively overplayed, for example when in accordance with liberal thinking, they may live out their faith rather shyly or when they do not use the Christian symbols in an outspoken way. But each news item (be truthful or not) which speaks about Western Europe or Scandinavia where crosses are taken off churches in order to not insult the religious sensitivity of others, only intensifies the populistic attitude of those who would like to demonstrate their faith in a militant and exclusive manner.

In these days, 500 years after the Heidelberg disputation, it is once more significant to concentrate on the difference between the *theologia crucis* and the *theologia gloriae*. I am afraid that a church trying to conform to the spirit of the age is also tempted by the theology of glory.

We all must take on the "foolishness" of the message of the cross (1 Co 1:18). The theology of the cross is a theology of scandal. The apostle Paul represented this scandal just as Martin Luther did. In his Wittenberg theses, Luther says:

> 92. Away, then, with all those prophets who say to the people of Christ, "Peace, peace", and there is no peace!
> 93. Blessed be all those prophets who say to the people of Christ, "Cross, cross", and there is no cross![10]

Based on Jr 6:13 and Ez 13:10, Luther refers to the so-called court prophets of the Old Testament who prophesied a false peace, employing, we could say, a language of populism.

What Luther wrote in his 95 theses was only a prelude to what he developed in detail in the Heidelberg disputation on 26 April 1518, exactly 500

---

[9] Bibó, op. cit. (note 1), 151-152.
[10] Translation from http://www.luther.de/en/95thesen.html.

years ago. In his 21st point, Luther says: "A theology of glory calls evil good and good evil. A theology of the cross calls the thing what is actually is".

And in his argumentation for this point, we hear the reformatory idea of *solus Christus*, Christ alone. "He who does not know Christ does not know God hidden in suffering. Therefore he prefers works to suffering, glory to the cross, strength to weakness, wisdom to folly, and, in general, good to evil".[11]

Populism does not recognize evil, suffering, weakness or folly either.

The temptation of the way of the glory is always there—also for the church. To be on the sunny side, on the side of the successful, the eternal winners, part of the community of those insensitive to suffering. This temptation is not only there for the churches of Central Eastern Europe but also for the churches of the Western world. A church denying the cross is distanced from Christ. Jesus says quite explicitly: "Woe to you when all speak well of you..." (Luke 6:26).

If anyone is a theologian of the cross, Dietrich Bonhoeffer was. His life work serves as an example for us when looking for ways to become agents for justice and against division. I conclude with what he wrote in his *Ethics*, "The church confesses its timidity, its deviations [...] its dangerous concessions. It has often disavowed its duties [...] as sentinel and comforter. [...] The church was mute when it should have cried out, because the blood of the innocents cried out to heaven. [...] The church did not find the right word in the right way at the right time".[12]

---

[11] Translation from http://bookofconcord.org/heidelberg.php.

[12] Dietrich Bonhoeffer, *Ethics* (*Dietrich Bonhoeffer Works*, volume 6), ed. Clifford J. Green, transl. Reinhard Krauss, Charles C. West, and Douglas W. Stott (Minneapolis: Fortress Press, 2005), 138.

Public Theology, Populism, and Racism in the Post-Obama Era in the United States: A Womanist Summoning

Linda E. Thomas

I dedicate this article to my mentor, Rev. Professor Dr James Hal Cone, who died in April 2018 in New York, whose commitments I share and apply to the construction of a womanist public theology reflected in my writing as well as my actions.

Introduction[1]

My contribution is divided into four parts. First, I will describe the way I frame the production of knowledge that influences what I will say about public theology, racism and populism. In doing so, I will outline my understanding of the term womanist, and I will define the meaning of several further categories: context, culture, and racism. Second, I will describe contemporary populism, power and privilege in the United States of America. I will point out intersectional dynamics as I explore the intense upheaval

---

[1] I want to acknowledge my Black Lives Matter: Theological Anthropology and Theological Reflection on Intersectionality classes at LSTC who assisted my thinking in the writing of this lecture. Special thanks to Francisco Herrera who read drafts and offered suggestions prior to its completion. I alone however am solely responsible for its contents.

that results when these categories interact with each other. Third, I will offer a few factors that provide insight about the reasons that racism and populism in a post-Obama United States matter. Fourth, I will use an historical example from early encounters between First Nation Peoples and European settlers in New England to illustrate my thesis.

WHAT FRAMES AND INFLUENCES MY PRODUCTION OF KNOWLEDGE: WOMANIST DEFINED

The epistemological framework for my work can be described by one word: womanist. This term has been theorized and defined by novelist Alice Walker in her epic book, *In Search of Our Mother's Gardens: Womanist Prose* published in 1983. This notion set the stage for the emergence of womanist theoretical/theological reflection in the North American context.[2]

Using the term womanist as my epistemological starting point asserts that my embodied self is central to my scholarship and influences the way I work. It also asserts that my social location guides the way that I understand and produce knowledge. Making these claims is unusual for a scholar as the notion of "objectivity" still prevails among many in the academy. Anthropologists encourage and even expect each other to "name the templates" that inadvertently affect the ways they interpret or construe a given culture. They speak about reflectivity, and womanists call it subjectivity. Being a womanist anthropologist, I call it, "shared revelatory cultural knowledge" or "subjective reflectivity".

I refer to myself as a womanist constructive theologian and anthropologist because of the way I think and write about human beings across cultures and their relationship with the Divine/ God/ Higher Power as well as their interaction with other humans. The distinctive feature about the way I do my work is that I study human cultures through the lens of African American women and more. This is not to say that there is one singular view that African American women have, but rather to hypothesize that women of African descent in the United States have cultural knowledge that aligns with indigenous ways of knowing and understanding how the activity of subjugation can be generalized across time and geography; across genders, sexualities, races, ethnicities, temporarily able-bodied and differently-abled bodies. Womanists have cultural knowledges that arise as a result of being seasoned or cured like a cast-iron pan.

---

[2] See Alice Walker's four-part definition of "womanist" in Alice Walker, *In Search of Our Mothers' Gardens: Womanist Prose* (Orlando, Austin et.al.: Mariner Books, 2004).

Black women in the United States who know anything about the history of my country's interaction with black bodies, and who connect to that history and culture, have cultural knowledge that allows them to relate to others who have been dissed, as in, "kicked to the curb" or "thrown under the bus" by historically dominant people who have power and access to wealth. Therefore, I argue as a womanist constructive theologian and anthropologist that there are intersectional ways that disparate experiences of oppression have something in common. For example, I believe that women of African descent have something in common with homeless Syrian people who live in terror.

A central framework with which womanists work is "bringing our full embodied selves" into all geographies in which we find ourselves. This means I work from a hermeneutic of plurality. I am aware that the lens through which I see the world is that of an out-heterosexual, temporarily able-bodied, woman of African descent who is professionally privileged. But I most likely will not attain wealth, not because I am not industrious, but because my predecessors were enslaved, did not earn a wage, and had no pension or retirement funds to pass down intergenerationally. My ancestors' physical labor built the United States (the US Capitol, the White House, Wall Street, railroads and other structures)[3] as well as the economy of the American South. This subjectivity is the historical sociology that influences the production of knowledge in my everyday life and scholarly endeavors. Like all other people, I have a lens through which I see life and it is not neutral.

Layli Phillips' compendium of Walker's womanist ideas provides a fitting summary: womanists (black/women of color who are feminist) are anti-oppressionist across all sectors, concerned about all historically subjugated people; we are vernacular, concerned about common place and unremarkable daily life, we are group-concerned, meaning that the interests of the collective are favored over those of an individual. As such, we intentionally gather with others to explore and seek that which is in the best interests of communities related to life and culture. Finally, we are spiritualizers who offer meaning to the mundane.[4]

Expanding these notions into a theological and anthropological position, I suggest that womanists believe that the mysterious and unknowable can influence our lives. We are committed to the retrieval of buried

---

[3] Danielle Young, "6 Historic Structures in America That Were Built by Slaves," *The Root,* July 26, 2016, https://www.theroot.com/c-historic-structures-in-america-that-were-built-by-sla-1790856172 (accessed 29 July 2018).

[4] Layli Phillips (ed.), "Introduction," *The Womanist Reader* (New York: Routledge, 2006), xix-iv.

histories, narratives, stories; and we deduce, after considerable research and reflection, that disenfranchised people across the world be understood as *living breathing documents,* even after death, and recognize all *creation as sacred.* We believe that our ancestors are accessible and call upon them as needed. We value rational, logical and academic epistemologies as well as unknowable, unexplainable and intuitive ways of knowing. We resist binaries and favor both/and rather than either/or. Ultimately, we believe that there is something bigger than ourselves that makes the moon rise and the sun set every dusk. We honor the mysterious essence that provides light in wondrous darkness. We honor the beauty of the eclipse that can harm human eyes signaling humans' spacial boundedness. Finally, we favor *kairos,* rather than *chronos,* knowing the freedom, expansiveness and latitude of the former and regulation, restraint and limitation of the latter.

For the purpose of this essay, I define some further categories as follows: I define context as the setting or background that frames a milieu, environment or perspective. I define culture as recurrent behaviors providing meaning to the lives of a group of people. Culture is a vessel that holds the values, ethos, ideas, and beliefs of people across time and space.

Racism is structured, systematic and institutionalized prejudice plus power across all sectors of society that discriminate against groups of people. In the United States, racism operationalized the grounds for those who have lived intergenerationally with the negative impact of colonialism. First Nations People were colonized by Europeans who invaded this country rather than discovered it. Intergenerational white supremacy generates anti-black, brown, Muslim attitudes and behavior and is complexified when these attributes overlap creating intersecting oppressions, as articulated by Patricia Hill Collins, and intersectionality, as articulated by law professor Kimberle Crenshaw.

POPULISM, POWER AND PRIVILEGE IN THE UNITED STATES

Populism, by definition, means support for the concerns of ordinary people against the idea of the power being in the hands of an elite few. But this current movement connected to President Donald Trump specifically is populism tied to radical authoritarian nationalism that forces suppression of opposition and control of industry and commerce. One of the reasons that the polarizing populism in the United States has developed is that for many years there has been a disregard for those in underserved communities, those left out because of elitism and alienation across socioeconomic classes. This alienation of the white poor and working class has often led to blaming and attacking black and brown people as the cause of their poverty. What we call the right-wing populist narrative in the United States is led by the white elite, making it a populist movement. There is an underclass of white people in the United States who have been trained to believe that their "whiteness" elevates them over black and brown people. The Charleston church shooting in 2015, in which a white supremacist shot nine African American churchgoers, is just one example among many. Maya Angelou's autobiography, *I Know Why the Caged Bird Sings*, gives account of the effects of domination and oppression from a women's perspective.[5] The experience of discrimination and exclusion is complexified regarding those people who are lesbian, gay, bisexual, transgender, queer, intersex, asexual or allied (LGBTQIA), as could be seen in the Orlando, Florida, shooting in 2016.

While it is particularly vile currently in the United States, the intersectionality of oppression across centuries that has mangled lives in the past is constantly re-produced because culturally historically dominant groups fail to see the people of God outside their own image and purview. It is important to understand that the notion of an "historically dominant group" shifts and changes across contexts.

How do groups of peoples who have lived with the impact of white supremacy over many generations think about the democracy? How do people who dwell in the vortex of radical marginality imagine democracy? How does the witness of their daily lives interact with the values articulated about democracy? Might there be some unarticulated notions about what democracy looks like? What might the church look like if a womanist perspective of democracy was normalized?

In other words, *context, culture, racism, populism* linked with *entitlement, authority, control, and privilege*, is the place where values and power are negotiated.

To understand racism and populism in the United States, I posit that to crystalize an understanding one must critically examine and dissect the period between 1492 and 1619. Columbus is said to have discovered America in 1492, and in 1619 the first nine Africans arrived in Jamestown, Virginia, a colony established by settlers. These Africans came involuntarily and, therefore, were not free persons. They were enslaved and indentured African bodies, involuntarily torn from their land, placed as property upon ships that sailed across the great Atlantic Ocean. They were forced to step onto land stolen from First Nation Peoples by those who were sponsored and voluntarily sailed across the ocean in search of capital.

---

[5] Maya Angelou, *I know why a Caged Bird Sings* (New York: Random House, 1969).

During that period of 127 years, foundations were laid, a frame was erected and structures and systems were created for a multi-layered, many-headed institutionalized monstrosity that ran like vines across society. It was controlled by desire, privilege and wealth. These structures were visible, unambiguously attached to profit and sweeping in their power. They were logical and strategic as well as administratively managed. The highest and lowest branches of government supported these systems. Finally, they were mechanized and immoral and did not see enslaved Africans as human, but rather as means to an end. These intersectional and operationalized oppressive forces were beyond even the modern concept of race/racism. I claim that the construction of these intersectional forces amount to structural and institutionalized demonology that have continued to create delirious ramifications for black bodies. Or, as Christian ethicist Emilie Townes calls it, the "cultural production of evil."[6]

This evil spawned further iniquity across the country and its production was especially intense in the Deep South since black enslaved bodies labored to generate wealth. Thus, territories inhabited and cultivated by, and ultimately stolen from, First Nation Peoples were used to establish markets. This permitted Europeans and their descendants, who were of diverse ethnicities, but unified as white culture, to gain wealth and power. When we examine the power dynamics of this epoch (127 years), we find foundational principles of power and wealth that were planted like seeds and embedded in soil that eventually grew into toxic vines and that were re-inscribed with a vengeance in the Deep South, creating a group of people constantly at risk, subject to harm and injury, trapped in perpetual poverty and by the infringement of their rights from which future generations remain powerless to escape. We must study, understand, and come to terms with each of the tools used to construct, organize and control the dynasties of systematized demonology. It will take considerable and sustained intervention to neutralize and thwart Donald Trump's populism.

WHAT CAN THE CHURCH DO?

REMEMBER THE PAST

The more one remembers from the past, the more one can anticipate what to expect from the present. The West African philosophical concept of *Sankofa*

---

[6] Emilie M. Towns, *Womanist Ethics and the Cultural Production of Evil* (New York: Palgrave Macmillan, 2006).

is symbolized by the mythic *Sankofa* bird, who flies forwards while looking backwards while holding an egg, its future offspring. In its beak is a reminder that one must understand the past in order to move the present forward into a viable future. *Sankofa*, thus, delimits a liminal space where past, present and future co-exist and continually interact in infinite dialogue. A *Sankofa* people intentionally exercise continuity with the past to draw from the power of wise ancestors and their divinity. *Sankofa* also means recalling the moment that Africans shackled in the dungeons of Ghana's Cape Coast Castle entered the "Door of No Return" into a Middle Passage that no other people have endured. Additionally, *Sankofa* implies an element of retrieval. In fact, the Akan *Sankofa* proverb concludes with the following aphorism: "[I]t is not taboo to go back and fetch what you forgot." And, in vernacular Akan usage, *Sankofa* becomes an imperative: "Go back and fetch it." As a *Sankofa* people, African Americans are called to remember the unadulterated abuse suffered during the days of chattel slavery, and through this act of deliberate—and deliberative—retrieval, live into our eschatological determination to move forward towards the kin-dom of God.

TAKE A PAGE FROM BLACK AND WOMANIST THEOLOGIANS

The church can learn from black and womanist theology in the United States. The church can evoke *Sankofa* moments that proclaim that systematic and constructive theology for African Americans in the African American church cannot, will not and should not be a retracing of the theological lines drawn upon the Platonized philosophical canvas where the dominant culture paints the Cartesian maxim of "I think, therefore I am." In contrast to this pseudo-stoic, logocentric onto-theology and attendant "personal" soteriology, black and womanist theologians present a relational systematic theology of *différance*: "I am because we are." And *who* we are is inextricably linked with the epistemology of variegated group-ness, as in "there is no me without we"—the antithesis of the Western theo-philosophical orthodoxy. Or, in Audre Lorde's memorable formulation: "The white fathers told us: I think, therefore I am. The Black mother within each of us—the poet—whispers in our dreams: I feel, therefore I can be free." Indeed, the Western academy and white Christianity have much to gain by participating in black and womanist theological engagement of African philosophic notions whose epistemological point of departure is "we." White Christianity can grow in strength from those "we" who fought to be "free."

This African American womanist theological perspective of a variegated "we" can be a "headlight" for innovative approaches to issues of religion and culture throughout the church—and especially—in the Northern hemisphere.

The wisdom symbolically generated by the *Sankofa* bird urges us to look back and learn from our successes and failures, while moving toward a constructive theology that responds to exclusive populism across generations. Descendants of enslaved Africans who continue to be trapped in systems that have historically caused and abetted structural poverty have, throughout history, lived a version of Christianity that—through faith—gives them a have a powerful tool that aids them in dealing with the demonic.

KNOW WHO HAS THE POWER

The church is obligated to analyze the nature and structure of its institutionalized systematic demonology. Systematic demonology is not a "problem" that can be solved by educating individuals, offering explanations, or by providing information for clarification. Individuals gaining insight will not eradicate this demonic force. Systematic demonology can best be altered by analyzing power, asking who has it and how it is used. Such an analysis should go far beyond concern about individual behaviors and attitudes.

It is essential to build a shared analysis of the way demonology is perpetuated by organizational structures, processes, norms and expectations. This project requires us to move historically dominant groups to change their positions. They include, those who:

- hold visible power institutionalized positions, (i.e., judges, teachers, clergy);

- hold status ascribed by social construction, (i.e., those who identify as male versus those who identify as female; heterosexual versus LGBTQIA; white versus black (people of color); temporarily-able bodied people versus people living with disabilities.

This means they must take an active role using their institutionalized positions to properly represent the concerns of those who daily experience macro- and micro-aggressions. Their efforts must disrupt structural demonology. It is not enough for people with privilege to expect that tolerant attitudes, acceptance of difference, diversity without inclusion and equity, charity, add-ons and supplements to eradicate evil.

Stereotypes of those who have been "othered", i.e., historically subordinate people, need to be re-framed so that those who have not enjoyed equal access to food, shelter and clothing can imagine concrete and tangible power sharing and learning. Churches should be able to accept leadership from the historically subordinated people who have cultural knowledge far beyond those persons who have only theorized notions about inclusion and acceptance without having themselves been excluded because of privilege (culturally constructed identities, ascribed and achieved). Those with privilege must learn what it means to be an endangered human species because institutional and operational power sources actively sought to cause "othered" persons harm.

A womanist approach assumes that historically dominant people (across intersectionalities) and historically subordinated people have ethical duties and tasks. People with achieved and ascribed privilege, power, wealth, individually and intersectionality, need to understand how the vectors of demonology operate to give them privilege, access to resources and freedom at the expense of "othering" others. They need to know how they perpetuate demonic systems that give them advantages and grant them social subsidy, monetary subsidization and/or endowment. In other words, historically dominant groups need to know the ways they advance and keep the cancers of racism, sexism, heterosexism, Islamophobia, and other "isms" alive and metastasizing. They can become allies of many different historically subordinated people by replacing discriminatory statutes, decrees and laws that usurp power or nullify the enactment of legislation that promotes equality and equity.

The ethical duty of historically subordinated groups is to lean into the process of empowerment that involve resisting and fighting against power and control of internalized demonic oppression. A womanist approach attempts to develop models that value and build leadership in people of color while holding white people accountable for their racism. There is limited real benefit in diversity training because those with power merely acknowledge the existence of racial inequality without any intentional methods to eradicate their privilege and power, while the descendants of the enslaved continue to be traumatized by a centuries-old evil. In other words, nothing changes in the dominant/subordinate dualism. Justice necessitates a change of institutional power transactions and a reckoning of past abuses with monetary restitution. Descendants of enslaved Africans, who continue to be trapped in systems that have historically caused and abetted structural poverty, have, throughout history, lived a version of Christianity that—through faith—gives them a have a powerful tool that aids them in dealing with the demonic.

UNDERSTAND THAT THE DEFINITION OF DEMOCRACY IS CONTEXTUAL

It is critical to understand that democracy functioning in the context of intergenerational white supremacy terrifies African Americans; makes

First Nations Peoples disappear; incriminates Mexicans; dismisses and maltreats Puerto Rican citizens, as seen in the aftermath of hurricane Maria; torments Muslims; turns back gains made for transgender soldiers in the military; denigrates those with differently-abled bodies; desecrates the earth; alienates ally nations; sexually abuses women, boys and girls. The list goes on. People who have lived intergenerationally with the "articulated"[7] democracy of the words "land of the free—home of the brave" also live with "unarticulated" beliefs and behaviors by leaders sanctioned to become policies and laws by systems that contradict democracy and Christianity. Ultimately, this is what breeds the populism that produced Donald Trump.

WE MUST UPROOT THE WEEDS

The phrase "God's work—our hands" has become a motto for the Evangelical Lutheran Church in America (ELCA). The church mostly speaks of service projects when it talks this way, though many in the ELCA see this as a call to justice and activism. But as a womanist and anthropologist who is also a theologian, I ask: what does this statement have to say to leaders in the academy in these days of Donald Trump's extremely destructive brand of populism? Or more specifically, what is the work that God wants our hands to do?

For this, I turn to the Gospel of Matthew and the parable of the wheat and the weeds. In this famous parable, a farmer sows seeds in the field and tends it, but then in the night an enemy comes (take that enemy to be whoever you will) and he sows weeds among the seeds. As the crop begins to grow, then, it soon becomes clear that weeds have been mixed into the wheat—potentially complicating the growth of the wheat and troubling the harvesting process. But when the farmer's helpers ask him what to do, his response is as patient as it is practical: "Let both of them grow together until the harvest; and at harvest time I will tell the reapers, Collect the weeds first and bind them in bundles to be burned, but gather the wheat into my barn" (Matthew 13:30).

Though I do not believe that we are in any kind of end times, with the recent rise in global sexism, racism, queerphobia, xenophobia, anti-

---

[7] Angela Crowser, professor of sociology and religion at Garrett Evangelical Seminary, while guest lecturing in a Public Church class, used the notions of 'articulated' beliefs and understandings that are known, shared, and acted upon and 'unarticulated' beliefs and understandings that are known, shared, and acted upon but unspoken. Both articulated and unarticulated norms and folkways regulate communities and society and, moreover, often harm specific people, places and things, and are reinforced generation after generation.

Semitism—not to mention the continued persecution and despoilment of indigenous communities worldwide—it is now easier to tell the wheat from the weeds. Most of us know—either consciously or not—how deeply global white supremacy, sexism, ableism, trans and queer-phobia have become imbedded in the soil of the Christian church. However, it is sometimes hard to attack these demons directly because they hide so well, often possess the brightest and best people, and they know how to summon minions to their defense.

Today they are unabashed in their visibility. They are damaging people in particular cities and countries and inspiring and inciting once-timid bigots the world over to come out and strut their evil in broad daylight.

We have rallies of white supremacists, some drawing hundreds and thousands of supporters, many of whom have murder on their minds, across the United States and across the world. Governments, which once had strict but workable immigration and refugee policies, now have draconian laws, building both bureaucratic and physical walls to trap the world's most vulnerable and desperate into lives of fear. We have even seen assaults on court systems in Poland, and looming fights centered on the Supreme Court in my own country. These assaults are becoming common place, depriving the most vulnerable of sure legal protection and defense, often their very last line of defense.

Thus, this is what we must do with our hands—we are called to recognize that a harvest, though not the final harvest, is at hand and we must do everything we can to weed out destructive theologies and praxis from our midst—be it the latent racism in article submissions for journals and academic conferences, our unwillingness to change the way we teach courses like pastoral care. We want our teaching to be more attentive to the LGBTQIA community, immigrants, women, people of color, people who are differently abled, and indigenous communities. We are called especially to address the way we hire teachers and staff at our educational institutions. We have no more excuses to delay. As the world becomes more frightening to even more of "the least of these", we must do everything to make sure that the church remains a refuge of support and defense. It will only work if we use our hands to do God's work of pulling up the weeds that so often hinder us, and that will continue to hinder us until we do this work that is put before us. We must uproot the weeds. Now is the time, and for those of us who wish to give greater and richer soil to theological traditions and viewpoints that so often struggle for space and light, uprooting these weeds is one of the best ways to do so.

To ready a plot of land to take seed, you first must get your hands dirty, sometimes very dirty. Just like those who have come before us, we have a unique opportunity to confront the sins of church, not to mention the sins of our species. We can do this in ways that either lead the church forward into even greater connection to the world, into an even greater healing relationship with the people of this planet, or solidify the church's often well-earned reputation for being a hermetically sealed safe house for all of humanity's most backward looking and destructive habits—racism, queer-phobia, classism, ableism, sexism, and all of the things that keep the people of God scattered and afraid. Our call is clear. It is time to get into the fields, for the harvest is almost ready. It is time to get into the fields with Jesus and get our hands dirty.

Populist Politics in India and the Response of Churches

Roger Gaikwad

This essay begins with a discussion of the terms for populism in the Indian context, followed by a critical narration of the phenomenon of religious fundamentalism in India and its basis in *Hindutva* ideology. The paper concludes with highlighting Christian ecclesial responses.

Terms for populism in India

In the Indian context, populism could be denoted by different names such as religious fundamentalism, communalism, and nationalism. "Religious fundamentalism" is commonly understood as the strategic manipulation of religion by particular State and/or non-State actors, such as social, economic, cultural and religious organizations and movements, to gain or retain power and control and limit rights of 'others' in the society, thereby contradicting the fundamental spirit and essence of many religions: justice, equality and compassion.[1] This manipulation and control of religions is explained as follows:

---

[1] Cf. "The Impact of Religious Fundamentalisms and Extreme Interpretations of Religion on Women's Human Rights," (November 2015), briefing paper by the Association for Women in Development (AWID), the Asia-Pacific Resource and Research Centre for Women (ARROW), the Sexual Rights Initiative (SRI) and the World Council of Churches (WCC), https://www.awid.org/sites/default/files/atoms/files/rfs_cedaw_briefing_paper_nov15.pdf [accessed 1 December 2018].

Religious fundamentalists may promote themselves as representative of an authentic and historically accurate local culture, but often they introduce and impose a homogenized, rigid, singular and arguably foreign culture and attempt to export this culture to different regions in the world. While a number of distinctions exist, some common themes recur within religious fundamentalisms around the world. They tend to be absolutist, intolerant and coercive; follow a literal and singular reading of scriptures or the will of a sole religious authority or hierarchy; adhere to a supposedly 'pure' tradition; employ religious rhetoric to gain power; and are patriarchal, against human rights and particularly women's rights and freedoms.[2]

In "communalism", a particular group of people, gathered together in the name of religion or of ethnicity, caste, language, etc. may think that they share the same economic and political interests which they seek to pursue and defend together against hostile forces. This may happen when there are wide economic and social disparities in society and a group feels unjustly exploited and/ or discriminated against. This communal group may imagine itself as a nation, discovering its historical roots. Religion is a very powerful force that can weld such a group together. Such a group may fight for autonomy or independence or seek domination over other groups.

Therefore this group with a strong identity looks on other groups, not only as different, but as inimical to their interests. In a religious setting the others can be demonized, when one group thinks that God is on its side. This can lead to defensive or aggressive violence, particularly when it experiences itself as the victim of deprivation, injustice and oppression.[3]

"Nationalism" is a political, social, and economic system characterized by promoting the interests of a particular nation particularly with the aim of gaining and maintaining self-governance, or full sovereignty, over the group's homeland.[4] If the term nation is understood as a large body of people united by common descent, history, culture, or language, inhabiting a particular state or territory, I would like to clarify that India is not a nation; it is a country of many nations.

---

[2] Ibid.

[3] Lancy Lobo, "Religious Fundamentalism – A Challenge to Democracy in India," *Social Action* vol. 59 (April – June 2009), 146f.

[4] Nationalism has a number of near-synonyms, each of which carries its own distinct meaning. Patriotism is similar insofar as it emphasizes strong feelings for one's country, but it does not necessarily imply an attitude of superiority. Sectionalism resembles nationalism in its suggestion of a geopolitical group pursuing its self-interest, but the group in question is usually smaller than an entire nation. Jingoism closely resembles nationalism in suggesting feelings of cultural superiority, but unlike nationalism, it always implies military aggressiveness. cf. https://www.merriam-webster.com/dictionary/nationalism .

The biggest expression of populism in India today is that of *Hindutva*. Put quite simply, *Hindutva* is an ideology seeking to establish the hegemony of Hindus and the Hindu way of life, a political movement advocating Hindu nationalism and the establishment of India as a Hindu state. *Hindutva* deploys elements of religious fundamentalism, communalism and nationalism. In this paper therefore these terms will be used interchangeably to refer to Hindutva populism.

THE PHENOMENON OF RELIGIOUS FUNDAMENTALISM IN THE CONTEMPORARY INDIAN CONTEXT

The phenomenon of religious fundamentalism is quite complex. It is not that religion per se is responsible for fundamentalism. Rather it is the misuse of religion for communal considerations of power and privilege, guided by patriarchal, caste and hetero-normative principles that are responsible for the deplorable scenario in India today.

Excerpts from a press release which was circulated by Shabnam Hashmi, a social activist, graphically describe the complex phenomenon of Hindutva in India today.

> We members of the Indian public are deeply concerned with the grave assaults that are being mounted on the Republic. (...) As people of this vast and diverse land, affirm, we uphold and defend the constitutional values of the Indian Republic as elaborated in the preamble of the Constitution—of freedom, justice, equality and fraternity. In brutal contrast to these values, the political forces represented by the so-called *Sangh Parivar*[5] are trying to subvert our Constitution by imposing upon the whole country their ideology of majoritarian tyranny, persisting caste and gender inequality, religious intolerance, and abolition of dissent. (...) Today they have entered into a dangerous alliance with neo-liberal market fundamentalists and a section of unscrupulous capitalists and financiers who see constitutional democracy as a hurdle in the path of so-called 'development'. This alliance of religious fanatics

---

[5] The Sangh Parivar (Family of Organisations) refers to the family of Hindu nationalist organisations which have been started by members of the Rashtriya Swayamsevak Sangh (RSS), "National Volunteer Organization", or drew inspiration from its ideology. The *Sangh Parivar* represents the Hindu nationalist movement. RSS was founded in 1925 by Keshav Baliram Hedgewar (1889–1940), a physician living in the Maharashtra region of India. Hedgewar was heavily influenced by the writings of the Hindu nationalist ideologue Vinayak Damodar Savarkar and adopted much of his rhetoric concerning the need for the creation of a "Hindu nation." Hedgewar formed the RSS as a disciplined cadre consisting mostly of upper-caste Brahmins who were dedicated to independence and the protection of Hindu political, cultural, and religious interests.

and neo-liberals want nothing less than an overthrow of the state's constitutional commitment to social welfare, the public provisioning of health, education and social security, affirmative action for women, *dalits*[6] and *adivasis*[7]; the freedom of belief and worship of religious minorities; and the subversion of the criminal justice system.

Today our society is witness to increasing religious polarization and fear; and attacks on women, *dalits*, *adivasis*, religious minorities and working people; the criminal neglect of agriculture leading to an epidemic of farmer suicides; the theft of natural resources; and attacks on livelihoods and workers' rights; gender violence; the neglect of persons with disabilities; discrimination against *dalit* students in schools and universities across the country; and the persecution of people marginalized on the basis of their gender identity and sexual orientation. Worst of all, the members and allies of the so-called *Sangh Parivar* are bent upon curbing our freedoms. They tell people what to wear, write and speak; whom to love and what to eat.[8]

THE IDEOLOGY OF HINDUTVA

The term "Hindutva" emerged in late nineteenth century with the rise of communal politics in opposition to the nascent Indian National Movement. When the Indian National Congress was formed in 1885, the Muslim feudal classes and Hindu feudal classes opposed it and both articulated their own communal ideology. The ideology coming from the Hindu communal stream was vaguely called *Hindutva*. This was brought to the fore prominently by Savarkar in 1924. Savarkar also defined Hindu as one who regards this land

---

[6] Dalit, meaning "broken/scattered/crushed" is a term mostly used for the castes in India that have been subjected to untouchability. Dalits were excluded from the four-fold varna (caste) system of Hinduism and were seen as forming a fifth varna, also known by the name of Panchama.

[7] Adivasis is the collective name used for the many indigenous peoples of India. The term Adivasi derives from the word 'adi' which means 'of earliest time's or 'from the beginning', and 'vasi' meaning inhabitant or resident.

[8] The above document clearly illustrates that the sentiments of the religious identity of the majority of the Indian population are being manipulated for ulterior goals of power and benefit by fundamentalist-communal groups. Time and again one comes across statements such as that of Dharm Jagran Manch leader Rajeshwar Singh, of the Aligarh Christmas conversion programme fame, who stated in December 2014, "India's inner voice has spoken. Just wait and watch. 31 December 2021 is the last for Christianity and Islam in this country. We will finish Christianity and Islam in this country by 31 December 2021. This is our aim." Also see, John Dayal and Shabnam Hashmi (eds), *Three Hundred and Sixty-five Days Democracy and Secularism: Under the Modi Regime* (Delhi: ANHAD, 2015).

as Holy Land and Father Land, keeping Christians and Muslims out of the definition of Hindus. According to him *Hindutva* is a total Hinduness, common race (*Aryan*), culture (*Brahminic*), and the land spread from Sindhu (River Indus) to the sea. He also conceptualized *Hindu Rashtra* (State), as the goal of *Hindutva* ideology. This goal of *Hindu Rashtra* was picked up by RSS from 1925. The goal of *Hindu Rashtra* was opposed to the goal of Indian National Movement, which aimed at secular democratic India.

Excerpts from the book of M. S. Golwalkar, *We or Our Nationhood Defined* further highlight the ideology of *Hindutva*:

> Nation Concept comprises the five constituent ideas—country, race, religion, culture and language—as the necessary and indispensable ingredients, in the existence of which five in a homogeneous whole, the Nation exists and in the destruction of any one of which the Nation itself experiences extinction.
>
> If, as is indisputably proved, Hindusthan is the land of the Hindus and is the *terra firma* for the Hindu nation alone to flourish upon, what is to be the fate of all those, who, today, happen to live upon the land, though not belonging to the Hindu Race, Religion and culture?
>
> At the outset we must bear in mind that so far as 'nation' is concerned, all those, who fall outside the five-fold limits of that idea, can have no place in the national life, unless they abandon their differences, adopt the religion, culture and language of the Nation and completely merge themselves in the National Race. So long, however, as they maintain their racial, religious and cultural differences, they cannot but be only foreigners, who may be either friendly or inimical to the Nation. (....)
>
> From this standpoint, ... the foreign races in Hindusthan must either adopt the Hindu culture and language, must learn to respect and hold in reverence Hindu religion, must entertain no idea but those of the glorification of the Hindu race and culture, i.e., of the Hindu nation and must lose their separate existence to merge in the Hindu race, or may stay in the country, wholly subordinated to the Hindu Nation, claiming nothing, deserving no privileges, far less any preferential treatment -not even citizen's rights.[9]

The Constitution articulates clearly that Hindu is a religious identity and India is a national identity.[10] In contrast to the Indian Constitution, which

---

[9] M. S. Golwalkar, *We Or Our Nationhood Defined* (Nagpur: Bharat Publications, 1939).
[10] Since its inception in 1950, the Indian state did not proclaim any religion as 'state' religion. India is a union of states; it is neither Hindu Desh nor Union of Hindu States as per Constitution. We will not find the word "Hindu" in the entire Constitution. The founding fathers of the Indian Constitution preferred to call Bharat but not Hindu. The national anthem also refers to the country as Bharat. Cf. https://www.theweek.in/news/india/equality-is-the-essence-of-secular-constitution.html .

gives us the Indian identity, RSS wants to impose Hindu identity, in line with the ideology of Savarkar and Golwalkar.

Hindutva ideology, among other things, is affecting the educational curriculum. Lancy Lobo illustrates how such religion-based fundamentalism is introduced in educational institutions.[11] During the previous Bharatiya Janata Party (BJP)-led National Democratic Alliance (NDA) Government, communal ideology was promoted by Murli Manohar Joshi, then Human Resources Development Minister who not only tried to influence the school text books at the national level but also in *Saraswati Shishu Mandirs* and *Vidya Bharati* schools run by the RSS which have grown substantially in number particularly in remote and backward areas. In 1993 the total number of schools run by *Vidya Bharati* was 6,000 with 40,000 teachers and 1,200,000 students in BJP run states. With the BJP at the centre in 1998 there were 14,000 schools with 80,000 teachers and 1,800,000 students.[12]

In some of the text books used at the primary level in *Saraswati Shishu Mandirs* an extremely virulent communal view of Indian history is presented in intolerant and extremely crude style and language. So also historical 'facts' are fabricated in such a way so as to promote not patriotism, as is claimed but totally blind bigotry and fanaticism.

The intention of the *Hindutva* forces is not only to stir religious animosity through education but also to change the scientific perspective of students.[13] The inkling of this retrograde direction began with the previous BJP led NDA Government when Murali Manohar Joshi, the then Human Resources Development (HRD) Minister introduced courses like Astrology and *Paurohitya* (rituals) in Universities. In continuation with this pattern Dr. Satya Pal Singh, who is currently a minster in the Ministry of HRD, recently stated that Darwin's theory is wrong as our ancestors did not mention that they saw apes turning into humans in our scriptures. Some *Hindutva* loyalists that Wright brothers were not the first ones to invent the aeroplane, it was an Indian, Shivkar Bapuji Talpade.[14] One could cite similar other examples.[15]

[11] Lobo, op. cit. (note 3).

[12] Ibid., 153f.

[13] https://www.nationalheraldindia.com/opinion/bjp-ideology-and-future-of-scientific-enterprise-in-india.

[14] Shivkar Bāpuji Talpade (1864 – 1916) was an Indian scholar who is said to have constructed an unmanned airplane in 1895. Talpade lived in Bombay (now Mumbai) and was a scholar of Sanskrit literature and the Vedas.

[15] For instance, Y. Sudarshan, Chief of Indian Council of Historical Research, asserts that the Hindu epic *Mahabharata* can make us infer that the weapons described in them were the result of atomic fission and/or fusion. He also claims that stem cell research was there in Iron Age India.

As Ram Puniyani, a human rights activist, observes, "The twin processes involved here are to claim that all the knowledge is already there in our scriptures and that science-technology research and development should be along those lines. Second is to claim that all discoveries have their roots here in India, more so in India before the coming of Christians and Muslims. This seems to be running in parallel with identifying India with Hindus and Hinduism alone."[16]

Indeed the populism that we are witnessing is the politicization of Hindu religious sentiments, exhibiting characteristics of fascism.

RESPONSES OF CHURCHES TO HINDUTVA POPULISM

In this section, we shall briefly look at responses of churches to the existential reality of populism:

INITIATIVES OF CHURCH LEADERS

Church leaders have been taking the initiative as citizens to address the challenges of *Hindutva* Populism. For instance on 6 April 2018 the Moderator of the Church of South India wrote to fellow Indians. The abstract of his letter is as follows:

> As an Indian Citizen and the Head of the Second Largest Church in India, with more than 4.5 Million members, most of them being *dalits, adivasis*, poor farmers and fisherfolks, I hereby share the fear my people have under the rule of a Government that has become a nightmare to the poor and the minorities in India.
>
> It is a true and sad fact that the current Government that follows the *Hindutva* supremacist ideology seems to have consciously discounted what is stated in the Preamble of our Indian Constitution that declares liberty, equality, and fraternity as its ideals and assures Social, Economic and Political Justice to the citizens of India.
>
> The Government proves to be pro-corporate and unkind to the poor by waiving off loans of rich people and corporate while not waiving of the loans of the poor farmers, not giving Minimum Support Price (MSP) to them, not addressing the issues of economic distress, joblessness, price rise by forcefully implementing policies like 'Demonetization' and GST (Goods and Services Tax). In fact, corruption and scams/scandals have become a hallmark of this Government.

---

[16] https://www.nationalheraldindia.com/opinion/bjp-ideology-and-future-of-scientific-enterprise-in-india

The Church of South India demands that the Government at the centre ensures the democratic and secular fabric of India to be safeguarded instead of promoting their *Hindutva* agenda for which they demolish Churches and Mosques, vandalize religious statues and symbols, persecute Christians and Muslims, change school textbooks, insert dogmatic and pseudo-scientific religious content, ban films, books, and festivals of minorities claiming that they "offend" the Hindu nationalist sentiments.

The Church of South India not only stands in solidarity with the *Dalits* fighting for justice and equality and agitating against alleged "dilution" of the Scheduled Castes (SC) and Scheduled Tribes (ST) (Prevention of Atrocities) Act 1989, but also condemns all atrocities against the *Dalits*, tortures, rapes and brutal murders by the Hindutva extremist forces.

Church of South India also strongly demands that recommendations of the Ranganath Mishra Commission and the Sachar Committee for reservation to Dalits of Christian and Muslim minority communities be implemented.

On this day on April 06, 1930, at the end of the 'Salt March', Mahatma Gandhi raised a lump of mud and salt and declared, "With this, I am shaking the foundations of the British Empire". Today, on April 06, 2018, I urge my fellow citizens in India to unite together and shake the foundations of another empire being built by the corporate fascists.[17]

Open letters have also been written to the Prime Minister of India on various occasions by the NCCI, particularly by the General Secretary.[18]

The National Council of Churches in India (NCCI) and Catholic Bishops Conference of India (CBCI)

The NCCI, which is a fellowship of Reformation and Syrian Christian Church Traditions, and CBCI have been observing 10th August every year as Black Day, because it was on this day that a discriminatory Presidential Order was promulgated in 1950. Paragraph 3 of the Presidential Order denies equal rights for affirmative action benefits to Christians and Muslims of *Dalit* origin on the basis of religion. This is contrary to and violative of the fundamental rights assured by the Constitution of India to all citizens.

---

[17] http://ncci1914.com/2018/04/09/an-open-letter-from-bishop-most-revd-thomas-k-oommen-moderator-church-of-south-india-to-the-fellow-citizens-of-india/
[18] http://ncci1914.com/2017/04/14/open-letter-prime-minister-india; http://ncci1914.com/2014/07/02/an-open-letter-to-the-prime-minister-of-india/; http://ncci1914.com/2017/08/14/independence-day-2017-open-letter-to-the-prime-minister-of-india; http://www.christiantoday.co.in/article/ncci.demand.action.against.kathua.and.unnao.rape.case/18552.htm

NCCI and CBCI along with churches and Christian NGOs and Muslim friends have been holding protest rallies every year in Delhi when the Parliament is in session. The protestors include bishops, nuns, priests, and leaders of different church traditions.

A Public Interest Litigation case was filed in the Supreme Court of India in 2004 (Civil Writ Petition No.180/2004) challenging the validity of the 1950 Presidential Order. The NCCI and CBCI have been pursuing this matter.

THE NATIONAL UNITED CHRISTIAN FORUM COMPRISED OF THE NCCI, CBCI AND THE EVANGELICAL FELLOWSHIP OF INDIA

On 17 March 2015, members of the National United Christian Forum came together for a National Consultation on *"Upholding Constitutional Rights of Minorities, with Special Reference to Christians"* and sent a statement to the government.

Around 40 representatives of the National Council of Churches in India, Catholic Bishops Conference of India and Evangelical Fellowship of India Council of Churches met together on March 15, 2017 at the Delhi Bible Institute, New Delhi as part of a National Conference organized by the National United Christian Forum.

Discussions were held on three important topics which the Christian communities are currently facing, that is, the *Uniform Civil Code*, the *National Education Policy* & the *Juvenile Justice Act*. It was decided to make a joint response about these concerns to the Government and to the Churches.

NCCI AND CIVIL SOCIETY: WIDER ECUMENICAL RESPONSE

NCCI initiated a study (2013-15) on "Discrimination and Violence against Christians and Muslims in India". The researchers did an in-depth study gathering data from all possible governmental and non-governmental agencies and covering all states of our country. The study recommended:

IMMEDIATE MEASURES

- Unity among denominations, sectarian groups, religious minorities against threats of violence

- Secure justice for victims of physical violence through legal mechanisms within State laws.

- Minorities should be aware of the legal provisions in the Constitution.

- Minorities need to be active in social and political engagements from local self governance to the Union government.

- Minority communities should approach, apart from NMC, the Human Rights Commission, National Commission for Women, National Commissions for Scheduled Castes (SC) and Scheduled Tribes (ST).

- Minorities should take initiative in the promotion of secularism.

MEDIUM TERM MEASURES

- The perception of the majority about Religious Minorities as 'outsiders', 'non-Indian' or 'aliens' should change.

- Inter-faith conversations should happen to remove the misunderstandings about each other's religious precepts and practices.

- Understanding and acceptance of the principle of equal opportunity.

- Transparency in political-legal systems should be instilled

- Minorities should be aware of international laws and provisions.

- Reformation inside churches needs to be undertaken—specifically among youths

- Minorities to create new forums to address the concern on Freedom of Religion and Minority Rights in India.

- Recommendations to the Universal Periodical Review of India at the UNHRC Meeting in 2017

- Repeal all the anti-conversion laws (promulgated as the 'Freedom of Religion Acts).

- The Presidential Scheduled Caste Order, 1950 should completely delink the Scheduled Castes status from religion. *Dalit* Christians & *Dalit* Muslims should be able to avail the "SC/ST Prevention of Atrocities Act".

- Enact legislation on the *'prevention of communal violence'*, so that state machinery may effectively work & initiate transparent actions on the perpetrators.

- Enact a special *'witness protection'* law to protect the lives of witnesses involved in cases of communal incidents.

- Amend the *'Whistle Blowers Protection Act, 2011'* to include human rights defenders & Right to Information (RTI) activists.

- Ratify 'UN Convention against Torture (CAT)' & enact domestic legislations. Put in place an *'equal opportunities'* commission to eliminate discrimination of vulnerable sections & minorities.

- Provide more autonomy, power and resources to the human right bodies such as National Human Rights Commission (NHRC), National Commission for Minorities (NCM) etc.

- Strengthen human rights training in all educational institutions focusing on religious harmony & pluralism.

- Maintain disaggregated data on caste and religion related discriminations and ensure its access to citizens.

- Invite 'UN Special Rapporteur on Freedom of Religion or Belief' to provide constructive suggestions.

CONCLUSION

The rise of populism is assuming alarming expressions and proportions as time passes by. The 2019 General Elections in India are also drawing near. The Church, Religious Communities and Civil Society at large have to stand up for a Sovereign Socialist Secular Democratic Republic of India, which secures to all its citizens: Justice, Liberty, Equality and Fraternity, as asserted by the Indian Constitution.

Churches as Agents for Justice and against Division. Justice and Reconciliation as a Fundamental Mission of the Churches in Rwanda after the genocide

Pascal Bataringaya

Introduction

People cry for peace almost every day, and through the media, these cries can be heard in places far away from the original contexts of violent conflicts. In the midst of conflicts and wars in the world, Christians have been and are still challenged to view peace as their central task. Christians are also called to be peacemakers because the gospel is peace and Christ himself is peace. Jesus came to bring about peace between humans and God and this kind of peace extends to peace among humans and between humans and nature. So the task of Christians as far as peace-building is concerned, has both vertical and horizontal dimensions. Christians work towards horizontal political and social peace because they are strengthened by the deep vertical peace of faith.

But political and social peace without reconciliation is not possible and in the case of Rwanda where we had a tragic history of genocide against the Tutsi in 1994, the difficult process of reconciliation challenges Christians to take reconciliation and peace seriously as their message and mission. That is why the churches in Rwanda have to play a central role in the process of social and political reconciliation. This reconciliation calls also for justice.

In the face of justice and as a pre-condition of their peace-building mission, the churches need to acknowledge their complicity in the genocide against the Tutsi in Rwanda. Rwanda has gone through a history of political violence that culminated in 1994 in genocide against the Tutsi.[1] It is estimated that more than 1 million people were killed in a period of 100 days. Besides the loss of human lives, the genocide caused considerable damage to socio-economic structures, properties, family and community cohesion. Social relations were destroyed, the sense of community was not taken into consideration, and the cultural orientation was without meaning as the genocide was committed.

For this reason, healing is a complex process that has to deal with historical trauma both on the collective and the individual levels, with current injuries after oppression, violence, wars and genocide, and with their more indirect consequences. In this case justice is also a priority.

Stephen D. Lowe describes the complicity of the churches in the following way:

In 1994, most observers considered Rwanda to be the most Christian country of all the African nations. Some 90% of the population self-identified as Christian and of this number 65% self-identified as Roman Catholic (based on 1991 census data). [...] According to African Rights, "more Rwandese citizens died in churches and parishes than anywhere else." [...] The genocide revealed the saint and sinner in everyone involved, including Christians in general and clergy specifically".[2]

Documentation is scarce, but among the verified places of the genocide are the church buildings in Nyamata, Nyange, Kibuye and Nyundo. In the aftermath,

---

[1] A historical overview on the political situation before, during and immediately after the genocide can be found here: John Eriksson et al., *The International Response to conflict and Genocide: Lessons from the Rwanda Experience* (OECD: Joint Evaluation of Emergency Assistance to Rwanda, 1996), online accessible: https://www.oecd.org/countries/rwanda/50189495.pdf (last accessed August 25, 2018). Cf. Linda Melvern, *Ruanda: Der Völkermord und die Beteiligung der westlichen Welt* (Kreuzlingen/München: Hugendubel, 2004). A succinct overview on African decolonization history since the mid-1950s and its political repercussions can be found here: Martin Meredith, *The state of Africa. A history of fifty years of independence* (London: Simon & Schuster, 2006).

[2] Stephen D. Lowe, *Genocide and reconciliation in Rwanda: from complicity to credibility* (online resource: Forum in Public Policy/The Free Library, 2008), https://www.thefreelibrary.com/Genocide+and+reconciliation+in+Rwanda%3a+from+complicity+to+credibility.-a0218606516 (last accessed 25 April 2019). The quote within the quote is from: [No author named], *Rwanda: Death, Despair, and Defiance* (London: African Rights, 1995), 865.

the Christian churches lost any credibility they had before the genocide in terms of being peace-building and justice-seeking institutions because of their complicity in that atrocity. As Tom Ndahiro said: "The church has failed in her mission, and lost her credibility, particularly since the genocide. She needs to repent before God and Rwandan society, and seek healing from God."[3]

More than ten years after the Genocide (in 2005), the South African Council of Churches led an interfaith delegation to visit Rwanda to discuss the role of faith communities in facilitating national justice and reconciliation. The visit coincided with the Day of Reconciliation in Kigali organized by the South African embassy. The delegation met with the Minister of Foreign Affairs and Cooperation, Gacaca court officials, the National Unity and Reconciliation Commission, and church leaders.

Stephen D. Lowe sums up the conclusions of the delegation's visit in 2005: "The delegation reported that their 'meetings with Rwanda's faith communities were the least satisfying and hopeful aspect of the experience'. [...] The delegation reached the conclusion that the churches in Rwanda 'have lost their credibility'."[4] There was a big need of justice and reconciliation.

The question of complicity of the churches must be set in the context of a divided church.[5] The churches were far from neutral in their sympathies. Another complicity was the failure of many church leaders to disassociate themselves from the regime's human rights violations (there was a close collaboration between churches and the government).

The internal complexities for the churches in dealing with the consequences of the genocide are very important, yet the churches should never lose view of the wider context, the grave consequences of the genocide on Rwanda's society at every level. On the basis of the churches' task of peace-building and socio-political reconciliation, the focus needs to be both internal and external. From this viewpoint, while there are numerous consequences of the 1994 genocide in Rwanda, the major consequence is that the genocide fractured families, business partnerships, government coalitions, neighborhoods, civic organizations, churches, friendships, social relations and even marriages. That is why justice and reconciliation

---

[3] Tom Ndahiro, "Genocide and the role of the Church in Rwanda," (online resource: Pambazuka News, 2005), https://www.pambazuka.org/human-security/genocide-and-role-church-rwanda (last accessed 25 April 2019).

[4] Lowe, op. cit. (note 2). The quotes in the quote refer to a news item from 2005 on the South African Church Council's website that is no longer accessible.

[5] On the role of the churches during the genocide, cf. Tharcisse Gatwa, *Rwanda Églises: Victimes ou Coupables. Les Eglises et l'idéologie ethnique au Rwanda 1900-1994* (Yaoundé/Lomé: Ed. CLE/HAHO, 2001). A broad overview on the history of the churches in Sub-Saharan Africa can be found here: Klaus Hock, *Das Christentum in Afrika und dem Nahen Osten* (Leipzig: Evangelische Verlagsanstalt, 2005).

work which begins with personal relations between people and smaller communities is so very necessary. It is a mission of the church and the base of the life in this country where about 200,000 people were in prison on suspicion of participating in the genocide.

The basis for any public and social engagement of the churches is theological reflection and analysis. The concept of reconciliation has its origins in the Bible and in Christian theology. In particular, it has its origins in Old and New Testament theology (it is the central message of the Bible and the Gospel) and especially the theology of the Apostle Paul. Karl Barth defined the Christian doctrine of reconciliation as "the restitution, the resumption of a fellowship which once existed but was then threatened by dissolution."[6] Dietrich Bonhoeffer drew attention to the connection between reconciliation with God and reconciliation (including justice) in sociality.[7]

The Christian concept of reconciliation refers to how humanity is reconciled to God through the death and resurrection of Jesus Christ. Paul understood reconciliation as both a restoration of a broken relationship between God and humanity and a "ministry of reconciliation" (2 Cor 5:18) that attempted to bring human enemies together and to create a state of sustainable peace. Paul understood the vertical reconciliation offered through Christ that brings the possibility, the power and hope for a social reconciliation between estranged and divided groups. It shows us the effectiveness of reconciliation across divisions of nations, cultures, religions and classes.[8]

WORKING TOWARDS SOCIAL RECONCILIATION IN RWANDA

While there are government and church reconciliation efforts underway in Rwanda including the creation of Gacaca courts and the Unity and Reconciliation Commission, there is a role for the church in Rwanda to bring

---

[6] Karl Barth, *The Doctrine of Reconciliation* (Church Dogmatics 4:1), transl. Geoffrey W. Bromiley and Thomas F. Torrance (London/New York: T&T Clark, 2005), 22. Quoted by Lowe, op. cit. (note 2).

[7] For Bonhoeffer's understanding of reconciliation, cf. Dietrich Bonhoeffer, Éthique, transl. Ernst Fuchs and Dieter Müller (Genève: Labor et Fides, 1997) and Martin Heimbucher, *Christusfriede-Weltfrieden. Dietrich Bonhoeffers kirchlicher und politischer Kampf gegen den Krieg Hitlers und seine theologische Begründung* (Gütersloh: Gütersloher Verlagshaus, 1997).

[8] On the theology of reconciliation from a Roman-Catholic liberation theology perspective, cf. Hildegard Goss-Mayr, *Wie Feinde Freunde werden. Mein Leben mit Jean Goss für Gewaltlosigkeit, Gerechtigkeit und Versöhnung* (Freiburg: Herder, 1996) and Hildegard Goss-Mayr and Jean Goss, *Évangile et lutte pour la paix* (Paris: Les Bergers et les Mages, 1989).

about reconciliation. Stephen D. Lowe writes, "The church's role in Rwandan reconciliation may need to begin with a humble admission of moral failure and complicity in the genocide where appropriate. [...] Achieving substantial reconciliation is possible only when there is honest admission of fault and a commitment to restitution and restoration of broken relationships."[9] In their efforts towards reconciled sociality, the churches can learn much from the work of the Gacaca courts. All Rwandans have accepted and supported Gacaca courts as a good method and a way to achieve justice and reconciliation.[10]

For more than twenty-four years, Rwanda has been and still is embarking on the way of reconciliation after many decades of divisionism which culminated in the Genocide against the Tutsi. Even though our past tragedy has passed, Rwandans have to heal the trauma of the past. They have to do more in rebuilding the needed social cohesion and renewal of human values.

The reconciliation process in Rwanda focuses on reconstructing Rwandan identity, as well as balancing justice, truth, peace and security. The Constitution now states that all Rwandans share equal rights. Laws have been passed to fight discrimination and genocide ideology. The churches are also very involved and very committed for the justice and reconciliation work, including the Presbyterian Church, the church of which I am a member.

THE ROLE OF RWANDAN TRADITION AND CULTURE IN THE PROCESS OF JUSTICE AND RECONCILIATION

Primary responsibility for reconciliation efforts in Rwanda rests with the National Unity and Reconciliation Commission, established in 1999.[11] Its most influential instrument on the grassroots level are the Gacaca courts. In the face of the overwhelming number of perpetrators and victims, and the need for concrete measures towards social justice, it was decided during the national consultations that it was necessary to conceive of an alternative approach in addition to the International Criminal Tribunal for Rwanda and the national court system. The aim was to provide justice for the people during their natural lifetime. It was concluded that the Rwandan

---

[9] Lowe, op. cit. (note 2).
[10] Cf. Arthur Molenaar, Gacaca: Grassroots justice after genocide. The key to reconciliation in Rwanda? (Leiden: African Studies Centre, 2005), 161-162.
[11] Cf. UN Department of Public Information, *Background Information on the Justice and Reconciliation Process in Rwanda* (online resource, 2014), http://www.un.org/en/preventgenocide/rwanda/about/bgjustice.shtml (last accessed August 25, 2018).

Gacaca process should be applied and complemented by the necessary laws in order for its proceedings to be conducted as judgement.

The process resulted in a law rehabilitating, structuring and giving mandate to the pre-colonial tradition of Gacaca tribunals. Gacaca became a combination of the traditional community court system and the modern legal system. It was established formally as a voluntary process set up in all villages across the country for a limited period of time.

Most of the work was done on the local level where the genocide was committed. Nine judges were elected by the population of a village among people of integrity (Inyangamugayo). They were trained to distinguish between the case categories of three of the four categories of the perpetrators of the genocide and to pronounce judgment. A day per week was set apart to allow the villagers to attend the Gacaca. The law provided provision for the community work of those who confessed and requested forgiveness. Many suspects started to give testimonies about genocide and about where they put the bodies of the victims. Thousands of prisoners have now been released from prisons and reintegrated to their communities after repentance, punishment and reeducation. The goal of Gacaca courts was not only to punish but also to reconcile people for peace and the future of the country. The Gacaca courts officially closed in 2012 after dealing with thousands of cases which would have taken 200 years in normal courts.

For making and keeping peace, there is also a program called Ingando which focuses on peace education. It aims to clarify Rwandan history and the origins of divisions among the population, promote patriotism and fight against genocide ideology. Another important program we have is called "Itorero". Established in 2007, the Itorero program is a leadership academy to promote Rwandan values and cultivate leaders who will help for the development of the community (the justice and reconciliation process included). Third, an education strategy of Seminars was established offering training for political and ecclesiastical leaders, political party leaders, youth and women in different areas such as trauma counseling, conflict mitigation and resolution. National summits have been organized on topics related to justice, peace, reconciliation, good governance, human rights, national security and national history.[12]

Although the churches' complicity eroded trust in them and the denominational landscape has changed noticeably, the churches remain a strong influence in Rwandan society, as Christine Schliesser describes: "Since the genocide, the Catholic Church has lost about one third of its members. In contrast, the Protestant denominations have had a steady increase in membership. From 19% in 1990, they have doubled to 38% in 2015 [...].

---

[12] Cf. Ibid.

Within the Protestant denominations, it is the Pentecostal branch that has gained particular momentum [...] While there have been substantial shifts within the institutionalized Christian faith, the overall adherence to Christianity has remained stable and strong at 90% of the population."[13]

The churches in Rwanda are fully committed to the process of social and political justice and reconciliation. The churches have been involved in developing teaching the word of God on justice, confession, repentance and forgiveness as a way to reconciliation and peace. Different churches have worked hard to bring about confession, repentance and forgiveness, and in this way they aim to take up their responsibility for the reconstruction of a reconciled Rwandan society. The first step was to reconstruct the basic structures and to provide the basic necessities, including justice and reconciliation. Churches needed to find ways for reconciliation by active participation in the life of society. Consequently, church initiatives have been tools in justice and peacemaking, in the promotion of constructive dialogues, at all levels, among parties involved in violent conflicts in the country. The churches in Rwanda are better equipped than any other single actor to consolidate the current peace gains through a reconciliation process.

Churches have played the role of capacity builders in education, especially through involvement in ethics education. Today churches have increased their awareness and capacity about the decisive role they can play in justice and peace building. Using their extensive education institutions (60% of schools in Rwanda belong to the churches) and training centers, churches are, more and more, better equipped in analyzing and understanding the causes of conflicts and their dynamics. The education of young people is the key to the future of a country where the population is renewed rapidly. It is the duty of the churches to educate children and young people in the values of the Gospel which will be, for them, a compass to show them the way. It is necessary for them to learn to be active members of the church and society in promoting justice, reconciliation and peace, as the future is in their hands.

With these wide-spread endeavors the churches in Rwanda are building the capacity of their members and the society at large to prevent violent conflicts and sustain peaceful interactions among their believers and among all Rwandans. The churches accept their social and political responsibility

---

[13] Christine Schliesser, "From "A Theology of Genocide' to 'ATheology of Reconciliation'? On the Role of Christian Churches in the Nexus of Religion and Genocide in Rwanda," in *Religions* 9:2 (2018), 1-14: 7 (doi:10.3390/rel9020034). Schliesser refers to statistics by the National Institute of Statistics of Rwanda from 2015 that are available online: http://www.statistics.gov.rw/publication/rphc4-thematic-report-socio-cultural-characteristics-population.

for justice and peace—not only in the vertical dimension, but also in the horizontal dimension.

Challenges and recommendations for reconciliation work by the churches

The first challenge is to set up adapted post-genocide pastoral work for peace-building rooted in basic moral values, memory purification and reconciliation with our past. Research in Christian theology is useful to develop the means that can lessen the influence of ethnic stereotypes on personal and communal relations, and strengthen the awareness of a universal bond between Christians in baptism. All churches must have the programs of genocide commemoration in their liturgy so as to enable their full and active involvement in both preparation and implementation of non-religious communal and individual commemoration actions as a way of trauma healing. In addition, we recommend to church members to participate actively in commemoration actions, especially young people. That will support the commitment of the Presbyterian Church in Rwanda formulated and expressed in the "Never again".

The Presbyterian Church in Rwanda—with about 300,000 members one of the oldest churches in the country—joined the first official church confession of guilt, the "Confession of Detmold" of 1996 [14] and has formulated its own confession of guilt during the General Synod of December 1996. In order to face the challenges of the consequences of the genocide against the Tutsi, the Presbyterian Church in Rwanda has established the "Commission of Unity, Reconciliation and Fighting against Genocide Ideology" which has implemented important activities in the domain of social unity and reconciliation. The general objective of this Commission was to analyze the causes and the consequences of genocide and to think about the contribution of the church in the commemoration of the 1994 genocide against Tutsi to justice, unity and reconciliation. Its specific objectives are (1) to promote justice, unity and reconciliation among people who were traumatized by the Genocide against the Tutsi in 1994, (2) to identify the causes of genocide and to try to find solutions to them and to the challenges of aftermath,(3) to identify various understandings of genocide commemoration and explore its significance in Rwandan society

---

[14] Schliesser, op. cit. (note 13), 8. She continues: "For twenty years, it would remain the sole public confession of a church." (ibid.). *The Confession of Detmold* can be found online here: http://kirchenkreis-saarost-butare.chapso.de/confesson-ofdetmold-s200320.html [last accessed 1 December 2018].

of today, and (4) to establish the impact of the church in communicating the message of justice, unity and reconciliation to the social relationships in the post genocide country.

In short, the commission aims to clarify Rwandan history and the origins of divisions amongst the population, to promote justice, unity, reconciliation and peaceful cohabitation but also to fight against genocide ideology. Its responsibility was also to point out a link between justice and reconciliation, and to generate recommendations for the reconstruction of the Rwandan family and society. In its responsibility there is also the task of continuing and encouraging ways of genocide commemoration that allow us to learn from the past in order to prepare our future well. That is the global objective of commemoration as a part of reconciliation is the sense of a restoration of friendly relations, conciliation or rapprochement. Remembering means speaking, talking about the situation and facilitating a renewal of relations, a renewal of social and individual life that has come to terms with the past. Forgetting, on the other hand, means silence and death; it severs the community from its painful past, thus bringing a momentary semblance of solace, but by merely anaesthetizing the pain, it prevents true healing as well as individual or social renewal.

Through the activities of that Commission, the Presbyterian Church has started to organize memorial sites where all bodies that were found are buried. It has also been involved in developing the teaching of the word of God on justice, confessing, repentance and forgiveness as a possible way to reconciliation and peace. Twenty-four years after the tragic situation, justice, reconciliation and healing of memories remain without doubt the priority of the public witness of the churches in Rwanda. Repentance, forgiveness and reconciliation might seem impossible from a human point of view after so much suffering. The churches' witness and work takes its initiative, however, from the vertical aspect of peace and reconciliation, even as they embrace their social and political responsibilities. Social and political reconciliation is like a gift to receive from Christ, based on reconciliation with God. Jesus Christ has entrusted Christians with the ministry of reconciliation for God's creatures. Based on reconciliation with God, justice and reconciliation take concrete forms in social practice and communal life in the following ways: a "zero tolerance" attitude towards impunity, listening to the stories of others, sympathizing with suffering and striving to alleviate it, sharing emotions with deep respect; respecting the personal experiences of others, and accepting different views of the importance of historical identity.

The work and the role of the Commission of Unity and Reconciliation has shown that Justice and Reconciliation in Rwanda are possible. But it is a long way and a process and especially in the case of genocide. The work organized and done by churches is key for the Healing of Memories that is needed to achieve good peaceful relationships. It is in this way that human beings find security and personal direction for their lives.

Social justice and reconciliation belong together. There can be no forgiveness and no reconciliation if there is no justice. That justice, repentance, forgiveness, reconciliation and peace belong together is an interpretation of the teaching of the Bible. But it is important to understand that reconciliation is a process, because it can seem like it is a long way but it is the center of life in a country like Rwanda. The justice and reconciliation process must be supported by many people in order to effect significant social change. The majority of the population in Rwanda has expressed their willingness to accompany this process through the Gacaca Courts. For that reason, political and religious education about reconciled relationships is well anchored in Rwandan society, and play an important role.

Churches in Rwanda have restored confidence between people. They have played an important role in the good progress of the Gacaca courts, strengthening and inspiring the Gacaca courts by supporting them publicly and by interpreting their court work in the light of God's Word.

The Kinyarwanda concept of Gacaca is one of the culturally rooted strategies of justice and reconciliation in neighborhood contexts. The term means "the grass around the residences in villages, where people would gather to listen to different parties involved in the conflict, to let themselves be organized by the most trustful elders of the community for finding solutions to the problem"[15].

The Gacaca Courts process was initiated with the following objectives: identifying truth about what happened locally during the Genocide, speeding up the justice about the genocide, fighting against the culture of impunity, contributing to the national unity, reconciliation and peace process, and demonstrating the capacity of Rwandans to resolve their own problems and conflicts through their culture and tradition. Only once fair justice was seen to be administered within Rwandese society, so broken by the genocide, could reconciliation and unity be possible.

Gacaca served to promote justice and reconciliation by providing a means for victims to know the truth about the death of their family members and relatives. It also gave perpetrators the opportunity to confess their crimes, to show a feeling of remorse and to ask for forgiveness in front of their community. Desmond Tutu's praise of the Gacaca courts connects aspects from political ethics and from theology:

---

[15] Cf. Sebastian Friese, *Politik der gesellschaftlichen Versöhnung: Eine theologisch-ethische Untersuchung am Beispiel der Gacaca-Gerichte in Ruanda* (Stuttgart: Kohlhammer, 2010), 59ff.

As an approach, Gacaca shows courage, daring and originality on the part of the Rwandan society. By adopting a strategy that is based on its own historical and cultural values, Rwanda has set a new standard. [...] In this way a new chapter in thinking about conflict resolution is written. [...] Especially for the African continent, Gacaca can provide important lessons, because too many African societies share the problems of civil war and its aftermath. However, these societies also share these informal, accessible and restorative legal traditions that are incorporated in communities and whose main goal is to reconcile conflicting parties. For these reasons, Gacaca's relevance goes beyond the borders of this small country. [...] [Through the reconciliation process] God wants to show that there is life after conflict and repression—that because of repentance and forgiveness there is a future. [...] To work for reconciliation is to want to realize God's dream for humanity—when we will know that we are indeed members of one family, bound together in a delicate network of interdependence.[16]

Finally, the use of justice, repentance and forgiveness for reconciliation and healing of memories means the reconciliation with oneself, with God and with the others. That was the way used by the Commission of Unity and Reconciliation and the Churches in Rwanda to develop a faith characterized by justice, trust, brotherly love, peace and that overcomes the fear of the other. 24 Years after Genocide we hope that will continue to help us in order to achieve our goal. And together in communion and in Mission it will be possible because united we are capable to do it.

In my contribution, I have tried to show how even after the disruption of human communion by the genocide in Rwanda, the church's mission for justice and reconciliation is not only necessary but also possible. It is the mission of the churches in Rwanda individually, but they also need to combine their respective individual efforts in order to accomplish this mission. Considering the challenges that the work of social and political reconciliation is facing today as a result of conflicts, violence and wars, the churches responsibility for concrete social engagement comes ever more to the fore.

---

[16] Desmond Tutu, *No future without forgiveness* (New York: Doubleday, 1999), 274-282.

ANALYSING THE POLITICS OF POPULISM

Radical Right-Wing Populism and Nationalized Religion in Hungary

Zoltán Ádám & András Bozóki[1]

The relation between right-wing politics and religious worldviews in Central and Eastern Europe in general and in Hungary in particular has been the subject of recent academic research.[2] This inquiry fits into the long-standing research interest in religious interventions into politics and the role of the church in shaping policy decisions.[3] In this paper we argue that although in Hungary the relationship between right-wing populism and religion is only of secondary importance in setting the right-wing political agenda, historical Christian churches do have a hand in providing legitimacy for right-wing populism.[4] The governing Fidesz party, and its right wing opposition Jobbik, that are both considered to be radical right-wing populist parties,[5] make religious references to signal their traditional social values

---

[1] An earlier version of this text was published as "Right-wing Populism and Nationalized Religion in Hungary," in *Intersections. East European Journal of Society and Politics* 2:1 (2016), 98–122.

[2] Andrea L. P. Pirro, *The Populist Radical Right in Central and Eastern Europe* (London: Routledge, 2015).

[3] Karrie J. Koesel, *Religion and Authoritarianism: Cooperation, Conflict, and the Consequences* (Cambridge: Cambridge University Press, 2014). Anna Grzymala-Busse, *Nations under God: How Churches Use Moral Authority to Influence Policy* (Princeton: Princeton University Press, 2015).

[4] "Right-wing" in East Central Europe is defined by cultural rather than economic terms. It usually contains (ethnic) nationalism, social conservatism, elements of religious traditions and historical references to patriotism. Herbert Kitschelt, "Formation of Party Systems in East Central Europe," in *Politics and Society* 20:1 (1992), 7–50.

[5] We agree with Cas Mudde who argues that Fidesz is not a moderate center-right conservative party any more due to its political radicalization driven by party

and identification with the societal mainstream. While Jobbik tends to mainstream extremism, Fidesz radicalizes the mainstream.

As Hungary has been fairly secularized, right-wing populist parties cannot afford to appear to the electorate as political representatives of churches or religious values. Yet, both Fidesz and Jobbik tend to refer to religious values and to seek church support as we will show. As a result, a link between right-wing populism and religion has been created in Hungarian politics over the past 25 years, in line with long-standing historical patterns originating from the interwar period. Meanwhile, liberal and left-wing parties have rather promoted secular ideologies. Thus the divide between leftist/liberal-centrist versus anti-communist parties has appeared to follow the classic secular versus confessional cleavage.[6]

We begin this article by presenting our understanding of political populism. Secondly, we will discuss the rise of right-wing populism in Hungary and its dominance since the end of the 2000s. Thirdly, we will look at the role of religion in right-wing politics and the relation between churches and right-wing parties. Fourthly, before some conclusions, we will discuss the phenomenon of right-wing nationalism as a surrogate religion.

POPULISM AS POLITICS OF UNDER-INSTITUTIONALIZATION

We see populism as an anti-elitist political ideology, sentiment, and movement that contrasts the interests of the "pure people", often presented as oppressed and innocent, with the oppressive, corrupt elite and its foreign allies. Populists favor "the people" over any other options,[7] just as they consider "the people" as homogeneous in using them in their fight against political pluralism.[8] As Edward Shils famously observed, "according to populism the will of the people enjoys

---

president and prime minister Viktor Orbán. Cf. Cas Mudde, "Is Hungary Run by the Radical Right?," in *Washington Post*, August 10, 2015.
[6] Seymour M. Lipset, and Stein Rokkan, *Party Systems and Voters' Alignments* (New York: The Free Press, 1967).
[7] Margaret Canovan, *Populism* (New York: Harcourt, Brace, Jovanovich, 1981). Also: Hanspeter Kriesi and Takis Pappas, "Populism in Europe during Crisis: An Introduction," in *European Populism in the Shadow of Great Recession*, ed. Hanspeter Kriesi and Takis Pappas (Colchester: ECPR Press, 2015), 1–22. Also: Cas Mudde, *Populist Radical Parties in Europe* (New York: Cambridge University Press, 2007)—and: Cas Mudde and Rovira Kaltwasser, *Populism: A Very Short Introduction* (Oxford: Oxford University Press, 2017).
[8] William A. Galston, *Anti-pluralism: The Populist Threat to Liberal Democracy* (New Haven: Yale University Press, 2018) and Jan-Werner Müller, *What Is Populism?* (Philadelphia: University of Pennsylvania Press, 2016).

top priority in the face of any other principle, right, and institutional standard. Populists identify the people with justice and morality".[9] The people's justice, independently from its substance, is regarded more important than the rule of law.

When electorally successful, populist parties come to power and form governments. As they initially represent an anti-elitist and anti-institutional stance, their administrative performance may well run into difficulties, and they often under-deliver on promises. Yet, the Fidesz administration in Hungary since 2010 has demonstrated that populist parties can be successful in power, and their administrative performance might well be sufficient to get reelected. Fidesz managed to combine anti-elitism, nationalism and an anti-EU stance with a pragmatist approach in most policy areas, presenting a charismatic leadership, allegedly defending the national interest and those of ordinary people.

Populism does not have a particular and permanent ideological content but rather an anti-elitist approach to politics that seeks political mass-mobilization and mass-participation in the political process.[10] In this sense, populism (as a minority group) makes use of democratic structures and decision-making processes even though it fails to live up to (or openly rejects) the constitutional norms of liberal democracy. While engaging in mass-mobilization, populist parties tend to manipulate the public discourse by using mass media outlets and advocating their own (often ideologically defined) world views. This ideological content may be nationalistic, xenophobic, anti-gay, anti-liberal, anti-western or, anti-Semite, anti-Arab, anti-Muslim or, for that matter, even neoliberal: the only criteria is that along the particular ideological content populist political protagonists must be able to perform top-down mass-mobilization. Once this requirement is attained, populism can serve various ideological purposes: It can be nationalist, socialist, semi-fascist or even neoliberal.[11] Populism may amplify any of these ideas as the unifying and homogenizing idea of the nation, and so can be described "as the militant use of political partisanship for the sake of overcoming pluralism in partisan views and creating a unified opinion, that is to say, by making one partisan view representative of the whole people".[12]

Populism in power can be understood as a way of governance in which power is personalized and its execution organized along lines of personal relations. This relates to permanent mass-mobilization as a means of popular legitimation. For-

---

[9] Edward Shils, *The Torment of Secrecy* (London: W. Heinemann, 1956), 97.

[10] Ernesto Laclau, *On Populist Reason* (London and New York: Verso, 2005).

[11] András Bozóki, "The Illusion of Inclusion: Configurations of Populism in Hungary," in *Thinking Through Transition: Liberal Democracy, Authoritarian Pasts, and Intellectual History in East Central Europe after 1989*, ed. Michal Kopecek and Piotr Wcislik (Budapest and New York: Central European University Press, 2015), 275–311.

[12] Nadia Urbinati, *Democracy Disfigured: Opinion, Truth, and the People* (Cambridge, Mass.: Harvard University Press, 2014), 109.

mal political and administrative institutions need to be sufficiently fluid to allow for mass participation in politics, the organizing principle of power is personal authority—just as in pre-democratic history. Thus, such populist legitimation processes typically take place under (semi-)authoritarian conditions that ensure the continued power of the ruling populist party of government, while curtailing the opposition's chances to raise an effective electoral challenge.

This (semi-)authoritarian rule is, however, not always easy to maintain if policies are harmful for some part of the electorate, especially in the context of developed democratic structures.[13] In fact, the loss of popularity in case of populist governments easily turns into loss of legitimacy, the loss of unanimous approval and of the popular belief that those in government justifiably exercise "the will of the people". Populist governments thus typically try to maintain their popularity even at very high long-term economic cost. Given the type of legitimacy populist governments seek, such—in the long run self-defeating—economic policies can still make sense politically in the short run.[14] This was mainly a characteristic of left-wing populism that sought popular legitimation through the inclusion of under-privileged social classes. Neoliberal populism, in turn, pursued market reforms and maintained sustainable economic policies.[15]

However, whether left or right wing, populism tends to rely on charismatic, personalized rule, in contrast to the impersonalized, rational bureaucratic legitimacy characteristic of industrialized western societies.[16] Traditional and charismatic legitimacy in a Weberian sense do not require any formal act of mass-approval of power. Populism, on the other hand, is based on formal approval of governance by people, and populist political regimes in this sense belong to the tradition of modernized, secular power. As a result of weak political institutions and civil society, rational bureaucratic legitimacy is typically not sufficient to preserve political stability in relatively less developed societies. Therefore, charismatic legitimacy continues to play a dominant role, along with formal

---

[13] For the consequences of under-institutionalization in authoritarian regimes see: Jennifer Gandhi, *Political Institutions under Dictatorship* (Cambridge: Cambridge University Press, 2008).

[14] Rudiger Dornbusch and Sebastian Edwards, "Macroeconomic Populism in Latin America" in *Working Paper* No. 2986 (Cambridge, Mass.; National Bureau of Economic Research, 1989). Also: Jeffrey Sachs, "Social Conflict and Populist Policies in Latin America," in *Working Paper* No. 2897 (Cambridge, Mass.: National Bureau of Economic Research, 1989).

[15] Edward L. Gibson, "The Populist Road to Market Reform. Policy and Electoral Coalitions in Mexico and Argentina," in *World Politics* 49:3 (1997), 339-370.

[16] Max Weber, *Economy and Society*, transl. Guenther Roth and Claus Wittich (Berkeley: University of California Press, 1978 [German original: 1922]).

mass-approval of power.[17] Hence, populism in a Weberian context can be labeled as an attempt to rationalize, and thus justify, charismatic rule, in which political leaders themselves become institutions and power tends to be personalized.

In other words, populism is a shortcut for establishing the missing element of rational, impersonal institutions. In the absence of sufficiently strong civil societies and political institutions, populism makes up for the missing element of bureaucratic legitimacy.[18] However, a political regime based on a personalized way of governance, lacking rationally organized bureaucratic institutions remains predictably unstable.[19] This fits our conceptual framework: As personal authority in populism tends to substitute for institutional authority, the loss of popularity of leaders tends to create systemic crises, while the transfer of power from one leader to another is typically a great challenge.

To avoid systemic crises, populist leaders are tempted to rely on the infrastructure of the Church in order to substitute the missing links in the "infrastructural power"[20] of the state. Populist leaders can pragmatically "outsource" this infrastructural power to the Church while maintaining their power over the remnants of state institutions which perform the function of coercive power.

Finally, modern democratic populism in the post Second World War era can be seen as the substitute of totalitarian politics in a period of mass democracies. Modern democratic populism originally appeared in South America where illiberal politics was less discredited than in Western Europe. Modern populists, such as Argentina's Juan Perón, managed to combine popular participation with the oppression of the political opposition. As an observer put it, "populism emerged as a form of authoritarian democracy for

---

[17] To be sure, charismatic and traditional legitimacy play a crucial role in mature liberal democracies as well. Identification with particular politicians, their personal characteristics and capability to represent a set of "sacred values" in a particular society remain to be decisive elements of democratic political life. Cf. Dean Williams, *Leadership for a Fractured World: How to Cross Boundaries, Build Bridges, and Lead Change* (Oakland, CA: Berrett-Koehler, 2015) and Geert Hofstede, Cultures and Organizations – Software of the Mind (USA: McGraw-Hill, 1997).

[18] In line with this observation, the critique of technocratic, impersonalized power in modern societies emphasizes the positive role of populism in making society once again the dominant political actor instead of professionalized technocratic elites. Cf. Laclau, op. cit. (note 9).

[19] Joel Horowitz, "Populism and its Legacies in Argentina," in *Populism in Latin America*, ed. Michael L. Conniff (Albuquerque: University of New Mexico Press, 1992), 23–47.

[20] For distinction between infrastructural and coercive power and a detailed analysis of dimensions of state power see: 1986) Michael Mann, "The Autonomous Power of the State: Its Origins, Mechanisms and Results," in *European Journal of Sociology* 25:2 (1984), 185–213 and ibid., "Societies as Organized Power Networks," in *The Sources of Power* (Vol. 1), ed. Michael Mann (Cambridge: Cambridge University Press, 1986), 1–33.

the post-war world; one that could adapt the totalitarian version of politics to the post-war hegemony of democratic representation. While it curtailed political rights, populism expanded social rights; and at the same it put limits to the more radical emancipatory combinations of both".[21]

Hence, populist governments are typically "democratic" in the sense of seeking mass-approval of power, but they build "illiberal democracies" in which governments are not constrained by the rule of law, and impose a majoritarian approach to governance, systematically exploiting political minorities, and ensuring their own reelection by using public resources. They approximate Robert Dahl's "inclusive hegemony" that allows for (limited) participation but curtails contestation for political power.[22] Left-wing populists usually tend to use plebiscitarian mass support in order to transform established institutions into more "flexible" ones. They concentrate power in the hands of the president, limit debates, strike at opponents, and tend to use state resources and state apparatus for campaigning. They seek to deconstruct democratic accountability by eliminating safeguards against arbitrary rule. Right-wing populists favor the market economy, but push for constitutional changes and embrace an increasingly personalist leadership style and the practice of rule by "emergency" decrees.

Leaders in both camps tend to dismantle checks and balances, intimidate the opposition, attacking the privately-owned media, co-opt civil society organizations and try to build new "civic" organizations from the top down.[23] They selectively disregard the norms and procedures of liberal democracy. In Europe, Viktor Orbán's hybrid, semi-authoritarian regime is a prime example of such politics.[24]

---

[21] Federico Finchelstein, "Returning Populism to History," in *Constellations* 21:4 (2014), 467–482: 467.

[22] Robert A. Dahl, *Polyarchy: Participation and Opposition* (New Haven: Yale University Press, 1971).

[23] Cf. Sebastián L. Mazzuca, "The Rise of Rentier Populism," in *Journal of Democracy* 24:2 (2013), 108–122 and Kurt Weyland, "The Threat from the Populist Left," in *Journal of Democracy* 24:3 (2013), 18–32.

[24] For analyses of the Orbán regime see András Bozóki, "Occupy the State: The Orbán Regime in Hungary" in *Debate: Journal of Contemporary Central and Eastern Europe* 19:3 (2011). 649–663. Ibid., "Broken Democracy, Predatory State, and Nationalist Populism" in *The Hungarian Patient: Social Opposition to an Illiberal Democracy*, ed. Péter Krasztev and Jon Van Til (Budapest and New York: Central European University Press, 2015), 3–36. Ibid., "A Párttól a Családig: hatalmi rendszerek és befolyási modellek" (From Party to Family: Systems of Domination and Models of Influence) in *Magyar polip: A posztkommunista maffiaállam* 3. (Hungarian Octopus: The Postcommunist Mafia State 3.), eds Bálint Magyar & Júlia Vásárhelyi (Budapest: Noran Libro, 2015), 223–259. Also: Tamás Csillag and Iván Szelényi, "Drifting from Liberal Democracy: Traditionalist / Neoconservative Ideology of Managed, Illiberal, Democratic Capitalism in Post-Communist Europe" in

The populist takeover of Hungary

Strengthening right wing populist and extreme nationalist movements across Europe have puzzled democratic theorists and worldwide observers alike, seeming to be incompatible with the purportedly liberal democracies in which they are taking root. In the nearly three decades since the collapse of communism in the former Soviet bloc, countries in East Central Europe have struggled to create a democratic legacy and propel their societies towards democratic futures. In Hungary—although the Roundtable Talks of 1989 led to a democratic arrangement and nonviolent transition from communism to a market economy and democracy[25]— many Hungarians became disillusioned with their post-transition situation. A sense that democracy was "stolen" from Hungarians has arisen, and that a new transformation must be undertaken if Hungary is to be truly vindicated from centuries of indignity under various imperial powers and then of communism.

A 2009 Pew Research report measured public opinion of democracy and the current state of affairs in post-communist states. Tellingly, 77 per cent of Hungarian respondents indicated their frustration with the way Hungarian democracy had worked in the time period 1991-2009, and 91 per cent of Hungarians thought that Hungary was not on the right track.[26] Approval of democracy in Hungary immediately following the fall of communism was at 74 per cent, whereas by 2009 this figure had fallen eighteen percentage points to 56 per cent.[27]

In 2010, shortly after these survey results were published, Orbán's nationalist Fidesz party won the elections by absolute majority, which was translated, due to the disproportionate electoral rules, into a two-thirds

---

Intersections: East European Journal of Society and Politics 1:1 (2014), 18–48. János Kornai, "Számvetés" (Taking Stock), in *Népszabadság* (January 6, 2011) – and ibid., "Hungary's U-turn," in *Capitalism and Society* 10:1 (2015), article 2, accessible online: https://journal.capitalism.columbia.edu/content/past-issues [last accessed 23 April 2019]. Bálint Magyar, *Post-Communist Mafia State: The Case of Hungary* (Budapest/New York: CEU Press, 2016) – plus ibid. and Júlia Vásárhelyi (eds.), *Twenty-five Sides of a Post-Communist Mafia State* (Budapest/New York: CEU Press, 2017). And Rudolf Ungváry, *A láthatatlan valóság: fasisztoid mutáció a mai Magyarországon* [The Invisible Reality: Transmuted Fascism in Today's Hungary] (Bratislava: Kalligram, 2014).

[25] András Bozóki, ed., *The Roundtable Talks of 1989. The Genesis of Hungarian Democracy* (Budapest and New York: Central European University Press, 2002).

[26] For more details see "Two Decades after the Wall's Fall: End of Communism Cheered but Now with More Reservations," *The Pew Global Attitudes Project* (Washington, D.C.: Pew Research Center, 2009), accessible online: https://www.pewglobal.org/2009/11/02/end-of-communism-cheered-but-now-with-more-reservations [last accessed 23 April 2019].

[27] Ibid.

parliamentary supermajority. Not insignificantly, Jobbik took 17 per cent of the vote in addition to Fidesz's 53 per cent, representing a noteworthy increase in radical right wing representation in Hungarian elections.

Using its two-thirds parliamentary majority, Fidesz altered the constitutional system. They did not only introduce a new constitution, but changed electoral rules and fundamental laws, governing the relationship among government bodies and between the government and citizens.[28] The authoritarian turn was carried out by the two-thirds parliamentary majority itself, without any meaningful concession to the opposition and without a referendum or other institutionalized way of popular approval of the new Fundamental Law that replaced the Constitution of 1989. The Fundamental Law suffers a critical lack of legitimacy, and hence will be relatively easy to modify by a future liberal democratic majority.[29] However, perhaps the most shocking aspect of the Fidesz takeover from a liberal democratic viewpoint has been the fact that even this restricted legitimacy seems to represent a larger, more extensive popular political appeal than the pre-2010 liberal democratic regime did. In this sense, the right-wing populism of Fidesz that is in many ways based on exclusionary policies appears to be more successful—and for some key electoral groups more inclusive—than the left-wing populism of previous center-left coalitions had been. Whereas Fidesz exercises authoritarian rule and exerts strict state control over society and economy, center-left governments maintained liberal democratic institutions and pursued inclusive policies through providing economically unsustainable social provisions.[30] Whereas Fidesz built an economic clientele, the center-left let multinational companies run the economy. By introducing a flat personal income tax, Fidesz increased the taxation of lower incomes and reduced that of higher ones. It also provided large tax allowances for high earning middle class families—and in real terms much smaller ones for low earners. Hence, it redistributed money from the relatively poor to the relatively rich, relying on the political support of the latter, but also gaining popularity among the former as a nationalist government providing law and order after the "two chaotic decades of transition."

Increasing economic problems after 2006 were widely associated with the failure of liberalism and the political left. The fact that left-wing governments privatized national assets both in the 1990s and the 2000s—

---

[28] Bozóki, *Occupy the State* (op. cit., note 23).

[29] János Kis, "From the 1989 Constitution to the 2011 Fundamental Law," in *Constitution for a Disunited Nation. On Hungary's 2011 Fundamental Law*, ed. Gábor Attila Tóth (Budapest/New York: CEU Press, 2012).

[30] On economic policies prior to 2010 see Zoltán Ádám, *Why Hungary? A political economic assessment of the Hungarian post-communist economic transition* (Debrecen: University of Debrecen Dissertation, 2015) (in Hungarian).

according to right-wing parties, allegedly benefiting former communist oligarchs—pushed the right-wing electorate to adopt simultaneously anti-communist and anti-capitalist attitudes. The visible rise in foreign direct investment reinforced their perception of liberal elitism and cronyism between a "comprador bourgeoisie", made up by former communists and multi-national capital. In short, the economic crisis of the 2000s alongside the unsustainability of populist economic policies played a major role in the de-legitimization of liberal democracy.[31]

At the June 2009 European parliamentary elections, center-right Fidesz gained 56 per cent of popular votes whereas far right Jobbik received 15 per cent. Then in the April 2010 national elections, Fidesz received 53 per cent and Jobbik got 17. Due to the disproportional electoral system, Fidesz' victory was transformed into a two-thirds parliamentary majority. Left-wing and centrist parties together gained less than 20 per cent of parliamentary seats. The takeover of the populist right was completed politically and ideologically[32] and a new, anti-liberal regime was established. Liberal democracy was replaced by an illiberal one, and later on, after the unfair elections of 2014, by a hybrid regime, a mix of democratic and autocratic practices.[33]

RADICAL RIGHT POPULISM AND PAGANIZED CHRISTIANITY

Historical Christian churches had been traditionally strongly affiliated to right-wing politics in interwar Hungary, providing popular legitimacy for the Horthy regime[34] that relied on the so called "Christian national middle class," and considered itself anti-liberal, anti-Semitic and strongly national-ist. "Christian" in this context first of all meant non-Jewish: reducing the economic, social and cultural influence of the generally highly assimilated

---

[31] Umut Korkut, *Liberalization Challenges in Hungary: Elitism, Progressivism, and Populism* (New York: Palgrave Macmillan, 2012), 60.

[32] On Hungarian populism see Bozóki, *The Illusion of Inclusion* (op. cit., note 10) and Zsolt Enyedi, "Plebeians, Citoyens and Aristocrats or Where is the Bottom of Bottom-up? The Case of Hungary" in *European Populism in the Shadow of the Great Recession*, eds Hanspeter Kriesi and Takis Pappas (Colchester: ECPR Press, 2015), 242–257.

[33] For the definition of hybrid or mixed regime see: Steven Levitsky and Lucan A. Way, *Competitive Authoritarianism: Hybrid Regimes After the Cold War* (Cambridge: Cambridge University Press, 2010) and Valerie Bunce and Sharon Wolchik, *Defeating Authoritarian Leaders in Postcommunist Societies* (Cambridge: Cambridge University Press, 2011).

[34] Miklós Horthy was Regent of Hungary in 1920–1944. For an historical assessment of the Horthy regime, see Krisztián Ungváry, *A Horthy-rendszer mérlege* [An Evaluation of the Horthy Regime] (Budapest: Jelenkor & OSZK, 2012).

Hungarian Jewish community was a primary ambition of the regime. Hence, Hungary introduced a cap on the number of Jewish university students as early as 1920, which is considered the first anti-Jewish Act of 20th century Europe.[35] As a historian of the interwar period explained:

> The regime also had its own official ideology, known as 'Christian nationalism'. The latter blamed liberal legislation during the period prior to 1918 for weakening the 'spiritual unity' of the Hungarian nation, something it claimed could only be guaranteed by Christianity. Therefore, after 1920, Church and State were indissolubly linked to the whole of the regime and took on a 'Christian character', implying a complete sharing of interests between the historical Christian Churches and the Hungarian State.[36]

Fidesz and Jobbik are in many ways successors of interwar political parties. In a classic authoritarian fashion, Fidesz has hijacked the entire state and made it its own political and economic asset, refusing the principles of limited government and the system of constitutional checks and balances, curtailing the prerogatives of the (otherwise already diluted) Constitutional Court and undermining the institutional autonomy of the judiciary system. Finally, the new voting system has given Fidesz an even larger electoral advantage than a dominant party had enjoyed in the 1990-2010 electoral system, resembling the structural political conditions of the interwar period at an increased level of participation.

Jobbik, in turn, represents the far-right opposition of the ruling party, following the tradition of the Arrow Cross movement that ruled Hungary in 1944-1945 during the Nazi occupation. It rejects the social and political principles of the European Union, campaigns for a strategic alliance with Russia and other eastern powers, and mobilizes against the Jewish and Roma minorities. Fidesz and Jobbik have both sought to build a mass movement around themselves. Whereas Fidesz created the network of "civic circles", Jobbik built a uniformed paramilitary group, the Hungarian Guard.

Fidesz and Jobbik both operate outside the realm of liberal democracy. They both campaign for the extreme right vote, resulting in a strongly nationalist populism in both cases.[37] This meant Fidesz had to adopt increasingly illiberal

---

[35] M. Mária Kovács, Törvénytől sújtva. *A numerus clausus Magyarországon 1920-1945* [Down by law. The numerus clausus in Hungary 1920-1944] (Budapest: Napvilág, 2012).
[36] Csaba Fazekas, "The Roman Catholic Church and Exterme Right-Wing Ideologies in Hungary, 1920-1945," in *Catholicism and Fascism in Europe 1918-1945*, eds. Jan Nelis, Anne Morelly and Danny Praet (Hildesheim: Georg Olms Verlag, 2015, e-book), 367–378.
[37] János Dobszay, "Egyet jobbra, kettőt jobbra" [One Step to the Right, Two Steps to the Right], in *HVG* (*Heti Világgazdaság* – Hungary's leading economic and political

policies in order to maintain its political dominance and a parliamentary supermajority since 2010. (Fidesz kept its two-thirds parliamentary majority at the 2014 general elections, labelled as free and fair, but lost it a year later as a result of a local by-election.) Consequently, the political center shifted further to the right, polarizing left and right and making it more difficult for political moderates to appeal to a mass electorate.[38]

One of the most intriguing questions from our point of view is whether the politicization of religion has played a significant role in this further right shift. Our answer is no: Hungarian right-wing populism, performed by Fidesz and Jobbik in an increasingly similar ideological fashion, has used limited religious references in the post-1989 era. The most important reason for this, we argue, is the limited role of churches and religion in the Hungarian society.

Although Hungary is certainly not a particularly atheist society, a clear majority refuses to follow churches and to participate in institutionalized religious activities. Whereas there was a revival of churchgoing after 1989, a large part of society is still distant from churches and religious references. Hence, any particular party appearing to be overly devoted towards religion and churches may alienate a substantial part of the electorate.

As representatives of current right-wing populism, neither Fidesz nor Jobbik define themselves through a religious identity, although in party manifestos both of them claim to be "Christian". Yet, Christianity in this context rather signifies a degree of social conservatism and traditional nationalism than expressing any substantive religious reference.

As for Fidesz, party leader Orbán though a member of the Hungarian Reformed Church, regularly participates in the festive Catholic processions, known as *Szent Jobb Körmenet* (Sacred Right March) held each year on the 20 August anniversary of the foundation of the Hungarian state. In the meantime, he openly identifies his own political camp with "the Nation" and takes his opponents as the ones who serve "foreign interests". The turn from their original anti-clericalism in the late 1980s and the

---

weekly) (May 9, 2015), 6-9. Also: Péter Krekó and Gregor Mayer, "Transforming Hungary – Together? An Analysis of the Fidesz-Jobbik Relationship," in *Transforming the Transformation? The East European Radical Right in the Political Process*, ed. Michael Minkenberg (London: Routledge, 2015), 183–205. Cf. Mudde, op. cit. (note 4).
[38] This is by no means a new phenomenon in Hungarian politics. Polarization had been a characteristic of Hungarian politics since about the mid-1990s: Gergely Karácsony, "Árkok és légvárak. A választói viselkedés stabilizálódása Magyarországon" [Frontlines and illusions. The stabilization of voting behavior in Hungary], in *A 2006-os országgyűlési választások. Elemzések és adatok* [The 2006 elections. Analyses and data], ed. Gergely Karácsony (Budapest: Demokrácia Kutatások Magyar Központja Alapítvány/Budapesti Corvinus Egyetem, 2006) 59–103.

early 1990s to their openly positive stance towards religion never played a highly important role in the history of Fidesz. A recent book on the history of the party—published by a semi-official publishing house of Fidesz—does not even discuss the role of religion in the formation of party ideology.[39]

The new Fundamental Law adopted in 2011 was the result of a unilateral governmental process, which did not reflect at all a national consensus. This Law, voted by Fidesz MPs, refers to Hungary as a country based on Christian values. The text increases the role of religion, traditions and "national values". In contrast to the Constitution of 1989, the Fundamental Law of 2011 serves as expression of a secularized national religious belief system: a sort of paganized, particularistic understanding of the universalistic spirit of Christianity. The signing of the Fundamental Law by the President of the Republic took place on the first anniversary of Fidesz' electoral victory falling on Easter Monday, April 25, 2011, and included the blasphemous claim of a bizarre parallel between the resurrection of Jesus and the adoption of the new Fidesz-constitution.[40]

Fidesz uses religious symbols in an eclectic way in which references to Christianity are often mentioned together with the pre-Christian pagan traditions. This refers to the idea of "two Hungarys": the Western Christian and the Eastern pagan, tribal one. In Viktor Orbán's vocabulary, the Holy Crown of Saint Stephen, the first Hungarian king, who introduced Christianity to Hungary, can easily go together with the Turul bird, a symbol of pre-Christian, ancient Hungarians. The concept of political nation gave way to the ethnic idea of national consciousness. On inaugurating the monument of "National Togetherness", Orbán voiced his conviction that the Turul bird is the ancient image into which the Hungarians are born:

"From the moment of our births, our seven tribes enter into an alliance, our Saint King Stephen establishes a state, our armies suffer a defeat at the Battle of Mohács, and the Turul bird is the symbol of national identity of the living, the deceased, and the yet-to-be-born Hungarians".[41]

He conjectures that, like a family, the nation also has a natural home – in this case, the Carpathian Basin – where the state-organized world of work produces order and security, and one's status in the hierarchy defines authority. The legitimacy of the government and the Fundamental Law is not only based on democratic approval, but it is approved by God, and features the spirit of Hungarians represented by the Turul. All these concepts

---

[39] Edith Oltay, *Fidesz and the Reinvention of the Hungarian Center Right* (Budapest: Századvég, 2012).

[40] Bozóki, *Broken Democracy* (op. cit., note 23).

[41] Viktor Orbán, "Minden magyar a turulba születik [All Hungarians Are Born Into the Turul Bird]," in *Népszabadság* (September 29, 2012).

have replaced an earlier public discourse whose central categories were liberal democracy, market economy, pluralism, inalienable human rights, republic, elected political community, and cultural diversity.

As for Jobbik, research shows that its pro-Christian stance simply indicates that the party should be interpreted as "non-Jewish".[42] By using this discourse, Jobbik creates an easily identifiable reference to its anti-Semitism. Jobbik's ideology is that of a radical right-wing party "whose core element is a myth of a homogeneous nation, a romantic and populist ultra-nationalism directed against the concept of liberal and pluralistic democracy and its underlying principles of individualism and universalism".[43] In addition to this nationalist rhetoric there is an underlying economic appeal that blames globalization for Hungary's troubles.

Pirro identifies Jobbik by its clericalism, irredentism, social-nationalist economic program, and by its anti-Roma, anti-corruption, and anti-EU stance. The party believes that "national morality can only be based on the strengthening of the teachings of Christ", and Jobbik promotes the spiritual recovery of Hungarians through returning to the traditional communities: the family, the churches, and the nation.[44] Jobbik was particularly militant against the Roma and against the European Union (burning an EU flag and throwing another one out of the window of the Hungarian parliament).[45] It was also vehemently pro-Christian in installing large wooden crosses at several squares of Budapest.

Although Jobbik enjoys the support of certain members of both the Catholic and the Calvinist Church neither church in general approves Jobbik and most church leaders tend to distance themselves from it. Despite its manifestly Christian self-identification, Jobbik is seen by many of them as representing an essentially pagan, anti-Christian cultural tradition. This might not be accidental. In fact, despite Jobbik's self-definition as Christian party, Jobbik voters are the *least* religious of all in Hungary.

It is among Fidesz voters that church adherents represent the highest share, though even here this is only 22 per cent, followed by 15 per cent among Socialist voters. Again, followers of churches represent a conspicuously low 6 per cent among Jobbik voters. At the same time, explicitly

---

[42] Political Capital Institute: *Research on religion and right-wing politics* (Budapest: Political Capital Institute, 2011).

[43] Online resource: "About Jobbik. Movement for a Better Hungary," http://www.Jobbik.com/ [accessed 1 December 2018] the 2006 document is no longer online.

[44] Pirro, op. cit. (note 1), 71.

[45] On the anti-Western stance of Jobbik: Emel Akcali and Umut Korkut, "Geographical Metanarratives in East-Central Europe: Neo-Turanism in Hungary," in *Eurasian Geography and Economics* 53:5 (2012), 596–614: 602.

non-religious people have the highest share among Jobbik voters (41 per cent), and their share, interestingly enough, is lower among Socialist voters (21per cent) than among the Fidesz electorate (22 per cent). Fidesz has probably been the most preferred political party by Christian churches since at least the beginning of the 2000s, and Prime Minister Orbán has at numerous occasions identified himself as a Christian believer. Fidesz also established a strategic alliance with the Christian Democratic People's Party (KDNP), a historically dominantly Catholic party, since 2002.

Although certainly not disliked by the Catholic Church, Fidesz probably has closer ties to the Reformed Church, Hungary's second largest confession. Orbán himself is Reformed and one of his closest political confidents, Minister of Human Capacities, Zoltán Balog was a Reformed pastor before taking up professional politics. Orbán likes to attend religious ceremonies and to deliver semi-public speeches in churches. Correspondingly, Fidesz's relation to churches is friendly but not strongly institutionalized. Yet, Christianity in general serves as a broad ideological reference, this becomes more concrete at certain politically prominent moments. For instance, in the new "Memorial of the German Occupation of 1944-45" on Szabadság tér, a central square in Budapest, Hungary is represented by the Archangel Gabriel and is being attacked by the German imperial eagle. This highly controversial new memorial seeks to modify the public discourse on Hungary's role in WWII, depicting the country as a victim rather than a perpetrator. Nevertheless, Fidesz typically refrains from directly advocating entrenched religious ideas that may alienate people. One explanation for this is that Fidesz is a large umbrella organization, "the party of power", and its voters typically do not nurture strong religious identities. Therefore, while using religion to justify its populist policies, Fidesz have to keep a delicate balance.

CHRISTENDOM AS SACRALIZATION OF THE NATION

Whereas neither Fidesz nor Jobbik can be considered to be the political representatives of specific churches or particular religious values, radical right-wing populism itself can be understood as a kind of surrogate religion. Hungarian right-wing populism uses Christianity as a reference, but its political content often appears to be in contrast to Christian values. Instead it advocates a highly nationalistic surrogate-religion in which the nation itself becomes a sacred entity and national identification carries religious attributes. It rather refers to Christendom than Christianity. This kind of surrogate religion is able to draw a sizeable number of followers in Hungary as it does in other countries. It has little to do with actual religious beliefs, even if it uses religion in general and Christianity in particular as a source of political endorsement.[46]

The nation as a sacred collective entity is a crucial element of both Jobbik's and Fidesz's political ideology, and large historic Christian churches typically subscribe to this. The dominant attitude of the Roman Catholic and the Reformed Churches—Hungary's two largest Christian denominations—approves it, and only smaller Christian churches, notably the traditionally more liberal Lutherans and some evangelical communities, tend to distance themselves from it.

The role of churches is important precisely because of the lack of rationally operating social and political institutions that integrate the nation as a political community. Instead, churches provide ideological resources to support right-wing populism, essentially playing a propaganda role for the regime. In exchange for this, a growing share of publicly financed services in education and healthcare are being administered by the historical Christian churches. This makes institutional relations between churches and secular authorities increasingly vital for both the churches and the state: church-run schools, hospitals and even universities are quite generously financed by the government but in exchange they need to fulfill certain administrative operational criteria. Another way of the institutionalized participation of churches in everyday life is the incorporation of religious studies into the national curriculum of elementary schools that the Fidesz government introduced from 2013.[47]

Religious conflicts, such as the opposition to Islam or other religions have not so far played a major role in the creation of political identity. Unlike their radical Western European counterparts, the Hungarian populist right did not display any strong anti-Islam stance, which was probably due to its traditional anti-Semitism. This attitude changed recently due to the increasing number of migrants to Hungary from the Middle East. In the summer of 2015, the Hungarian government built a wire netting fence on the border between Serbia and Hungary to prevent mass migration. It also took the opportunity to raise its popularity by conducting a hate campaign against immigrants, which was, however, based on ethnicity rather than religion.

To demonstrate the state of mind of the Hungarian radical right on the migration issue, it is worth quoting Péter Boross, a former Prime Minister

---

[46] Cf. Tamás Szilágyi, "Quasi-Religious Character of the Hungarian Right-Wing Radical Ideology. An International Comparison," in *Spaces and Borders. Current Research on Religion in Central and Eastern Europe*, eds. András Máté-Tóth and Cosima Rughinis (Berlin/Boston: De Gruyer, 2011), 251–264: 252.

[47] Non-religious students can elect to take ethics instead.

of Hungary and former advisor to Viktor Orbán, who has been close to both Fidesz and Jobbik:

Rome was wise back then. They left the conquered provinces in peace and officially adopted some of their gods in Rome. Washington does the opposite. It wants to impose its own God, Democracy, on the conquered countries.[48]

An influential father figure in shaping the ideas of the Hungarian right, Boross suggests that each nation has a right to create its own state, its own political regime (whether it is democracy or autocracy is less relevant), and also to choose its own God. While he wants to defend Europe, he displays strong anti-EU sentiments. Boross' views embrace ethnic nationalism in its crudest form:

> Today nobody dares to say that immigration is not a problem of culture and civi-
> lization, but an ethnic problem. [...] It is very important that it is not only their
> culture that is different, but their instincts, as well as their biological and genetic
> properties. [...] Cultural integration has not yielded anything good. Unfortunately,
> if this has not been a successful process in the case of the gypsies living with us,
> then there is not much chance that this is possible with the hordes of Muslims
> crossing the green border. [...] The European Union should not be thinking in
> terms of its own refugee quota system, but in forming its own armed forces".[49]

While Fidesz interprets Christianity within the framework of nationalism, Jobbik frames it as part of its nationalism *and* anti-Semitism. In this sense, Hungarian right-wing populism does not have to rely on religious affilia-tions, nor does it place a particular emphasis on mobilizing them: They are simply parts of their fundamentally nationalist world views without any substantive religious references. Although religious identities are mobilized by the right, they are merged with nationalistic world views and ideologies.

Finally, one should note that Fidesz in government has insisted on approving the status of churches on political grounds. In a high-profile case, the Fidesz government in 2012 introduced a restrictive regime of registering churches, making it the prerogative of parliament to recognize a religious community as a church. Yet, both the Constitutional Court (in 2013) and the European Court of Human Rights (in 2014) judged the new provisions unacceptable, forcing the parliament to repeatedly revise it.[50]

---

[48] Péter Boross, "Americans Are Intellectually Unsuitable to Lead the World," in *Budapest Sentinel*, August 2015.

[49] Ibid.

[50] The Constitutional Court in 2013 and the European Court of Human Rights in 2014 considered the deprivation from the status as a church and recognition by

The new provisions obviously sought to extend government control and to differentiate between "accepted" and "non-accepted" churches. This way, the Fidesz government attempted to alter the relations between the state and churches and to strengthen its strategic alliance with the politically preferred large historical Christian churches.

CONCLUSIONS

Hungarian right-wing populism, represented by the governing Fidesz party and its semi-opposition Jobbik party, has dominated the Hungarian political scene since the end of the 2000s. The Hungarian populist Right has in many ways followed the historical patterns laid down in the interwar period by the then governing conservatives and their extreme right opposition.

We considered populism as an anti-elitist, anti-pluralist, and anti-institutional political behavior that identifies with "the people", and enhances their "direct" participation in the political process as opposed to representative government. Populism has an ideological character but in itself does not have a particular ideological content. Rather, it is a pattern of discourse and behavior that can be filled by both left- and right-wing ideologies. We also argued that in a post-totalitarian historical era, populism should be seen as the political manifestation of illiberalism, especially in (semi-)peripheries such as Latin America and Eastern Europe. Such an understanding of populism can be easily reconciled with the Dahlian concept of inclusive hegemony: a form of government based on popular participation without public contestation for power.

Both Fidesz and Jobbik have strong tendencies towards such a restrictive notion of democracy and they both manifestly dismiss the principles of liberal democracy. Although neither of them appear before the electorate as a deeply religious political party, both of them portray themselves as socially conservative, "Christian" nationalists. This includes a form of institutionalized cooperation between them and large historical Christian churches. Whereas the political right gains political support and legitimacy from churches, the latter are commissioned to run educational, health

---

Parliament as a rights violation, while the existence of two kinds of statuses for religious groups was considered discriminatory. Eötvös Károly Policy Institute, Hungarian Helsinki Committee, Hungarian Civil Liberties Union, and Mérték Médiaelemző Műhely, *Disrespect for European Values in Hungary 2010-2014. Rule of Law – Democracy – Pluralism – Fundamental Rights* (Budapest: 2014), online resource: http://helsinki.hu/en/disrespect-for-european-values-in-hungary-2010-2014 [last accessed 23 April 2019]).

and social care institutions on government-provided budgets. In addition, politically well-received churches have been given official church status with all its benefits, whereas their politically less obedient counterparts have been stripped of it.

However, in a substantially secularized country, such as Hungary, actual religious values play a limited role in policy-making. No rational political party would risk to represent a primarily religious agenda to win elections. Christianity is an important political asset, but it is not enough to carry elections and gain majority political support. To maximize electoral votes and to avoid the breakdown of the state, Viktor Orbán used the infrastructural power of the Church to outsource certain functions and responsibilities of the state to the Church while maintaining his own exclusive control over the coercive power of the state. Within the realm of politics, the "vision of 'the people' as a united body implies impatience with party strife, and can encourage support for strong leadership where a charismatic individual is available to personify the interests of the nation".[51] As a charismatic leader Orbán claimed full sovereignty over the political process and used populism as a shortcut to reach his political aims.

The Orbán regime also demonstrates that radical right-wing populism employs a quasi-religious ideological construction through which it attempts at mobilizing a wider social spectrum: ethno-nationalism. This surrogate religion offers a nationalist and paganized understanding of Christianity and elevates the concept of ethnically defined nation to a sacred status. Thus, religion is "nationalized". "Nationalized Christianity" also provides legitimacy for the "rationalized charismatic rule" of authoritarian leaders, who represent exceptional characteristics but are nevertheless popularly elected. This rule is illiberal and anti-democratic even though it relies on (often manipulated) elections and other forms of centrally controlled "national consultations". Within the European Union, Viktor Orbán's Hungary is the closest approximation of this type of governance.

---

[51] Margaret Canovan, "Trust the People! Populism and the Two Faces of Democracy" in *Political Studies* 47:2 (1999), 2–16: 5.

Populism and an ethic of intellectuality and catholicity. Reflections from South Africa

Nico Koopman

This paper argues that populism might also be described as a logic and idea. This logic and idea underlie and are interwoven with various expressions of populism. Populism as a logic and idea is an anti-intellectual flight from complexity. This anti-intellectual flight from complexity provides fertile soil for the growth of absolutism and annihilation, for relativism and nihilism, and for various manifestations of populism to flourish. An ethic of intellectuality and an ethic of catholicity are proposed as appropriate public theological responses to populism.

AN INFLATED CONCEPT

Populism is an inflated concept with a plurality of meanings. Some view it as a popular force for the mobilization of the common people. In Latin American societies such as Argentina, populism is a liberating political force. There, it is also viewed as a socio-economic approach to be employed to accelerate the redistribution of wealth and to bring about more government spending for social transformation. It is also a political strategy and approach, with a charismatic leader who enjoys the support of the masses. Populism is famously viewed as an approach involving a certain kind of political rhetoric. Populism is also used in an ideological sense. It is used as a world view that appeals to people by dividing them and history into homogeneously good people who should be praised, and a homogeneously evil elite who should be opposed.

There are more subtle, so-called thinner ideological positions, which, in the end, also advance this simplistic division between the one-sidedly bad and one-sidedly good, albeit in more subtle forms.[1]

A LOGIC AND IDEA

This brief contribution simply discusses populism as a logic, a way of thinking, of interpreting, of understanding the world; and as an idea, a way of looking at the world and of picturing and forming the world. Populism as a logic and as an idea is, in various ways, underlaid and interwoven with multiple understandings of the notion of populism.

AN ANTI-INTELLECTUAL FLIGHT FROM COMPLEXITY

Populism as logic and idea is a flight from complexity. It functions with an anti-intellectualism that fails to recognize or deal with the complexity of life and the various challenges that human beings have to deal with in all walks of life, from the most intimate to the most public, global and cosmic.

THE FERTILE SOIL OF ABSOLUTISM

The anti-intellectual flight from complexity nurtures a logic of absolutism, which is expressed in the stereotyping, stigmatization, demonization and annihilation of those whose viewpoints differ from theirs, and who are different in terms of identity. This absolutistic logic is fertile soil for populism in various modes.

THE FERTILE SOIL OF RELATIVISM

The anti-intellectual flight from complexity is also expressed in a logic of relativism, where "everything goes", and more dangerously, of *acedia*, apathy, carelessness, hopelessness, melancholy, inertia, and nihilism. Such melancholy and nihilism are fertile soil for populism in various modes. Simplistic, politi-

---

[1] For helpful discussions of these diverse uses of populism today, see Cas Mudde and Cristóbal Robira Kaltwasser, *Populism. A very short introduction* (Oxford: Oxford University Press, 2017); Jan-Werner Müller, *What is populism?* (Pennsylvania: University of Pennsylvania Press, 2016).

cal and socio-economic solutions for poverty, inequality and unemployment might thrive in a context of collective melancholy and nihilism.

TOWARD AN ETHIC OF EMBRACING INTELLECTUALITY

Developing an ethic (a vision, habitus and practices) that helps to embrace the Christian practice of loving God with one's mind just as much as one's heart is one crucial response to populism. St. Anselm articulated this well in his classic formulation that Christian faith is a faith that seeks understanding, *fides quarens intellectum*. It is a faith that calls to be made, as far as possible, intellectually accessible to those inside and those outside the faith community; and it is a faith that helps its adherents to make intellectual sense of the world. Where there is a commitment to intellectuality, to loving God with all of one's mind as well, absolutism and relativism can be resisted; complexity can be dealt with constructively. Complexity has many faces and shapes.

Complexity implies the plurality of voices, opinions and perspectives on various challenges. These voices are manifold and more than often contradictory. An ethic of intellectuality accepts this plurality and deals constructively with it through exposure of differing views through dialogue and the search for consensus, or even peaceful co-existence and continuous deliberations in the case of incommensurable positions.

Ambiguity, another manifestation of complexity, refers to the fact that the same phenomenon or reality can be described in different and even contradictory ways by different people and in different contexts. Ambiguity also refers to the shifting meanings of words, sentences and concepts. Travelling on the road of ambiguity requires wisdom, courage and patience. It also demands the ability to communicate very sophisticated positions in clear and intellectually accessible ways. Ambiguity should not be confused with unclarity and vagueness.

We also need to live with duality, the capacity to live with the notion of *both and*, and not only with the more famous *either or*. We need to say "yes" to more than one thing simultaneously, even though it might look as if these things contradict each other. An ethic of intellectuality assists us to live simultaneously with more than one "yes" to contradictory questions.

An ethic of intellectuality teaches us to live with paradoxes, i.e. with apparent but not real contradictions, which permeates human existence. South Africans in general and the churches in particular need to say "yes", there are good things happening in South Africa—otherwise we will become discouraged, melancholic, apathetic, *acedic* and unfaithful to our God-given calling. And we need to say "yes", there are still bad things happening in South Africa—otherwise we will become unrealistic and naive, and we will be insensitive to the pain and anger in our society.

111

An ethic of intellectuality also advances the notion of proximity amongst people. The logic of the three articles of the Belhar Confession is that visible, concrete, experienced unity, where people develop sympathy, empathy, interpathy and solidarity (Article 1), stands in service of reconciliation (Article 2) and of justice (Article 3).[2] Reconciliation and justice grow where people do not live outside of hearing distance, but where they hear each other, see each other, feel each other, understand each other, participate and share in each other's lives, joys and sorrows, in guilt and shame, in anger and pain.

A last dimension of an ethic of intellectuality has to do with a logic that seems to be absurd, ridiculous and foolish. For reconciliation and justice to materialize, we need forgiveness. Forgiveness opens the door for recognition of guilt, contrition, remorse, confession of guilt, reparation, restitution and restoration. Inspired by this logic, Archbishop Emeritus Desmond Tutu calls his famous book *No Future Without Forgiveness*.[3]

TOWARD AN ETHIC OF EMBRACING CATHOLICITY AND COSMOPOLITANISM

To overcome populism, we need to develop an ethic that helps us to rediscover and embrace catholicity and cosmopolitanism. According to Robert Schreiter, three dimensions of catholicity are of importance, namely wholeness (the physical extension of the church throughout the world in time and place), fullness (orthodoxy in faith), as well as exchange and communication.[4] Confessing and embodying catholicity as wholeness demands that churches pay attention and acknowledge where the triune God is at work in the world outside the church. Schreiter pleads that we recognize the hidden treasures outside the church.[5] Confessing and embodying wholeness implies solidar-

---

[2] The Belhar Confession online: *Die Belydenis van Belhar,* https://belydenisvanbelhar. co.za/wp-content/uploads/2011/11/Belydenis-van-Belhar.pdf (Afrikaans original, last accessed September 11, 2018); English translation: Confession of Belhar, ed. Presbyterian Church (U.S.A.), https://www.rca.org/resources/confession-belhar (last accessed September 11, 2018).

[3] See Desmond Tutu, *No Future Without Forgiveness* (London: Rider, 1999). For a very helpful explication of this logic see Dirkie Smit, "Confession – guilt – truth – and forgiveness in the Christian tradition," in *Dirkie Smit, Essays in Public Theology*, ed. Ernst M. Conradie (Stellenbosch: Sun Press, 2007).

[4] See Robert Schreiter, *The new catholicity: Theology between the global and the local* (Maryknoll: Orbis Books, 2002), 128.

[5] For a traditional perspective on the work of the spirit in individuals, the church as well as in broader society, see the ecumenical document published by Faith and Order, *Confessing the one faith* (Geneva: WCC Publications 1991).

ity with those who are marginalized and wronged in a glocally fragmented world. The line of fragmentation, compartmentalization and division between rich and poor runs through continents, northern and southern countries, and through individual countries and cities in both the North and South.[6]

In African contexts, the notion of catholicity as wholeness is related to the concept of *ubuntu*. *Ubuntu* entails the elements of community and restorative justice.

To confess and embody fullness, integrity and authenticity of faith implies addressing various concrete challenges. It entails participation in this world from the position of faith. In making interventions in glocalized societies, the church drinks from her own wells. Christian theologians make theological contributions. They do not act as social scientists with a religious interest. Catholicity implies a wholeness and fullness that is eschatologically materialized in the coming kingdom or reign of God.

For Schreiter, catholicity today implies that the church communicates her contribution to a greater extent in the world, that she goes public more explicitly with theological convictions. In this regard, Leander Keck's three-fold plea for communication is helpful. First, Keck pleads for the development of an informational apologetics, which implies that churches "overcome what they have mastered—the art of talking to themselves."[7] Churches are therefore challenged to revisit the rich tradition of rhetoric as well as the modern sources of communication.[8]

Second, Keck argues that communication also entails the cultivation of a positive disposition among the public about Christian convictions.[9] In this process, television, various types of music and art, should be utilized. Although he criticizes televangelism, he refers to research that indicates that these televangelists are experienced by the public in different social strata as people who are more concerned about human needs, hurt, loneliness and meaninglessness.

Finally, he states that communication implies commending the gospel more confidently and compassionately. He reckons that the attempts in mainline churches, especially since the nineteenth century, to make the gospel presentable to modern societies have had two negative consequences:

On the one hand, by making the substance of the faith continually more palatable to the increasingly secular mind, the hearty gumbo of the Christian faith has

---

[6] See Schreiter, op. cit. (note 4), 131-132.
[7] Leander E. Keck, *The church confident: Christianity can repent, but it must not whimper* (Nashville: Abingdon Press 1993), 108.
[8] Ibid., 110.
[9] Ibid., 110-114.

been thinned so often that there is little nourishment left. On the other hand, by concentrating on how one *can* be a Christian and a modern person at the same time, something vital has been lost: the conviction that one *ought to be* a Christian. Unless the mainline recovers its confidence in the gospel enough to commend it heartily, the future of these churches will be bleak indeed.[10]

An ethic of catholicity might come to expression as an ethic of cosmopolitanism. Kwame Anthony Appiah employs the notion of cosmopolitanism, which is a helpful way of expressing the idea of a maximalist identity.[11] He explains that his use of the notion of cosmopolitanism, which literally means citizen of the world, does not suggest an abstract universalism, which is actually the imperialism of western liberalism, i.e. one parochialism that is advanced at the expense of other parochialisms, which are all oppressed. Neither is cosmopolitanism for Appiah mere adherence to principles of moral universalism, i.e. moral cosmopolitanism, or adherence to the values of the world traveler, who takes pleasure in conversation with exotic strangers, i.e. cultural cosmopolitanism. His life as the son of a black African father and white English mother, i.e. his life as a hybrid, has taught him that one can live with more than one loyalty at a time. He states: "Our community was Asante, was Ghana, was Africa, but is also (in no particular order) England, the Methodist Church, the Third World: and ... my father insisted that it was also all humanity."[12] For Appiah, a constructive understanding of cosmopolitanism entails that a commitment is made to both the universal and the particular.[13]

A tenable cosmopolitanism, in the first instance, must take seriously the value of human life, and the value of particular human lives, the lives people make for themselves, within the communities that help lend significance to those lives. This prescription captures the challenge. A cosmopolitanism with prospects must reconcile a kind of universalism with the legitimacy of at least some forms of partiality.

An ethic of catholicity and cosmopolitanism entails communing with and embracing people of all places, people of all times, people of all perspectives in the search for the truth of Luke 2:14, which is expressed in the song of the angels when the birth of our Lord, Jesus Christ, is announced: "Glory to God in the highest heaven, and on earth peace to those on whom his favor rests."

---

[10] Ibid., 116.
[11] Kwame A. Appiah, *The ethics of identity* (Princeton: Princeton University Press, 2005), 214, 222. Cf. his *Cosmopolitanism. Ethics in a world of strangers* (New York/London: W.W. Norton & Company, 2006).
[12] Appiah, *The ethics of identity* (note 11), 214.
[13] Ibid., 222–223.

Populism, People and a Task for Public Theology

Rudolf von Sinner

This contribution is written within the contemporary Brazilian and Latin American contexts, where there are different understandings of populism, including positive ones. [1] Populism, as an inter-contextual concept, has to be understood from a wide variety of perspectives. Theologically speaking, I suggest that it is necessary to look closely at the notion of people as *ochlos* rather than *demos* or even *laos*, for which there is a tradition within liberation theologies in Latin America and around the world, and, of course, in biblical witness. Churches would then, in the first place, have to be agents of dialogue among the people and the forging of horizons of meaning oriented towards a common good. I shall expose this in three steps: (1) through a contextualization from two recent events that point to challenges of popularity and, potentially, of populism or populisms; (2) through a discussion of the concept of populism, especially in dialogue with Ernesto Laclau; and (3) through a theological reflection on foundations and activities needed for a meaningful public theology in this context, focusing on the concept of "people".

---

[1] See, for instance, Fernando Perlatto, "Adeus ao populismo? Reviravoltas de um conceito e de uma política no Brasil do tempo presente", in Fernando Perlatto and Daniel Chaves (eds), *Repensar os populismos na América do Sul: debates, tradições e releituras* (Macapá/Rio de Janeiro: Editora da Universidade Federal do Amapá/ Autografia, 2016), 70-94.

CHALLENGES OF POPULARITY AND POPULISM

In mid-August 2017, former human rights government minister and now federal deputy Maria do Rosario of the Workers' Party accepted an invitation from our Institute of Ethics at Faculdades EST in São Leopoldo, Brazil, and gave a lecture on the human rights situation in Brazil. Not surprisingly, she had a full house in front of her and presented a very worrying picture of the human rights situation in the country. She valued very much the contribution of churches and theology towards the practice and theory of human rights. A boy from a slum gave a moving witness during the discussion and said, crying, that it was the Worker's Party, under then president Lula and with Rosario as minister, that had given him strength and hope to become a hip-hop artist. Their presence and politics were, one could say, able to light a flame of hope in the midst of despair. Shortly after the event, a video with part of Rosario's speech was posted on her Facebook page. Thousands of reactions immediately poured in, most of them offensive and related to her person—and what, to many, she represents—and in no way to what she had said. That she was "disgusting" [nojenta] was about the "nicest" thing they could write about her. The wider context is probably illuminating: only two days earlier, Rosario had won her case before the High Court against her fellow deputy Jair Messias Bolsonaro who, during a session in Congress, had said "she did not deserve to be raped" because she was "very ugly". The judges unanimously understood this meant, effectively, to declare that rape was a kind of benefit to the victim, and judged it to be an "evil expression" that "despises the dignity of any woman".[2] At Rosario's lecture, we commemorated the victory, which is the victory of many women she represents, a victory, indeed, for human dignity and human rights, especially women's rights. And yet, despite Bolsonaro showing at every moment he stands for a clearly racist, misogynous, homophobic and authoritarian attitude, even invoking the death penalty and the legitimacy of torture, he has been elected president and—he is highly popular. One could call this populism: the focus on a state leader with a messianic appeal to the masses.

On his part, former president Luis Inácio Lula da Silva, a highly charismatic leader, has fallen into public disgrace. What happened to him, a politician who left office at the beginning of 2011 with the approval of 80 percent of the population? What happened to him who, some would say, was

---

[2] https://g1.globo.com/politica/noticia/stj-mantem-condenacao-de-bolsonaro-por-ofensas-a-maria-do-rosario. ghtml, acessed on 3 June 2019.

a populist, and a very successful one?[3] Why is somebody portrayed as the incarnation of evil before he is elected, then becomes a kind of messiah and now, for many, the incarnation of evil again, without reasonably balancing his successes and failures? Some make it seem as if he was the only corrupt person in the country. At the same time, there is no material proof of his having received as a bribe the three-story apartment in the Guarujá resort he was convicted for, and photos circulating on websites showing a luxurious *intérieur* were proven to be forged and had to be taken off the web.[4] In using Lula as a type of scapegoat, all the traditional oligarchies in politics and the economy want, so it seems, to cover up their own wrongdoings. But beyond that, why is there so much aggressive energy, so much hatred against a president under whose direction thirty-six million people left the poverty zone?[5] It seems to be the old political messianism in reverse: either the president is the country's savior or the devil himself.[6] Congress, which includes some thirty parties in 2019 that are not tied directly to the elected president, acts on its own grounds and appears to waive any responsibility for the government and its policies. Some would say such a sway is the result of populism—either the president's or the others'. The tide can turn quickly, especially when power constellations change.

Lula himself said in his speech, before turning himself in to the federal police and starting to serve his sentence after being convicted, that he never was just a person, but was, rather, "an idea". Even in custody, what he represents for the transformation of Brazil and the dreams and hopes he continues to kindle go far beyond a single person—although they depend on this person as representation of the idea. This is one way to understand why it was so difficult for his followers at the trade union's headquarters to let him walk over to the federal police officers who then took him to jail. It is

---

[3] Perlatto, op. cit. (note 1), 71, names as elements for populism in its recent, critical key: "the presence [...] of charismatic and personalistic leaders, the excessive control of the market through a hypertrophied State and the orientation for the execution of social policies that are considered to promote assistencialism [a patronizing, giving aid rather than a help to be self-sustaining] and clientelism" (usually applied to Lula and Dilma in Brazil, Morales in Bolívia, Correa in Ecuador, the Kirchners in Argentina, Vasquez and Mujica in Uruguai, Chavez and Maduro in Venezuela).
[4] http://cartacampinas.com.br/2018/04/x-noticias-falsas-sobre-o-triplex-do-guaruja-contribuiram-para-a-condenacao-sem-provas-de-lula/, accessed on 3 June 2019.
[5] See Cláudio Carvalhães and Raimundo Barreto, "A coalition to impeach: How evangelicals helped oust Brazil's president", *The Christian Century* 33/23 (2016).
[6] On the history of such messianism see Marilena Chauí, "Raízes teológicas do populismo no Brasil: Teocracia dos dominantes, messianismo dos dominados", in Evelina Dagnino (ed.), *Os anos 90: Política e sociedade no Brasil* (São Paulo: Brasiliense, 1994), 19-30.

no mere coincidence that before the political act that included Lula's speech that there was a religious ceremony that showed the historical partnership of the Roman Catholic Church, but also of sectors of other churches, with the trade unions, landless worker's movement and the Workers' Party. It is safe to say that this religious-political partnership made possible the emergence of a new civil society towards the end of the military regime.[7] Officially, the ecumenical ceremony presided over by Bishop emeritus Dom Angelico Sandalo Bernardino, a long-standing friend of Lula's, was in memory of Lula's deceased wife, Marisa. Bishop Angelico and his fellow celebrants tried hard to guarantee silence and a spiritual attitude for this religious moment. Of course, no strict separation between religion and politics was possible, not even intended, but Bishop Angelico managed to maintain a reasonable respect for someone and something bigger than politics: God and faith. And so, he could even, for a moment, silence the many cries of "*não te entrega* (do not turn yourself in)" that emerged from the public. As an ecumenical voice, Rev. Lusmarina Campos Garcia, a Lutheran pastor in Rio de Janeiro who formerly served in Geneva, spoke. Her voice recalled the traditional Brazilian and Latin American joinder of the struggle for citizenship and ecumenical engagement. To be ecumenical meant to struggle for justice, and Christians struggling for justice considered themselves, with pride, ecumenical.[8] Campos Garcia made clear that, even with Lula imprisoned, the values and struggle he stood for could not be imprisoned. The cause is wider, and the political and religious support for it is wider. Her words were an important part of helping Brazilians to understand Lula's imprisonment as a victory rather than just the incarceration of an outlaw. Yes, Lula is much more than a person, but it is only his person that had the legitimacy to proclaim the continuation of the struggle and, at the same time, to comply with the law. He could have opted for fleeing or fighting, but he stayed in order to not endanger the democratically legitimized rule of law, even as he continued to affirm there was no proof against him and that he was innocent. A great, a necessary, and an effective speech, I would say. Some would certainly say it was populist.

Let us now look more closely at a challenging Latin American understanding of populism developed by Ernesto Laclau (1935-2014).

---

[7] See Rudolf von Sinner, *The Churches and Democracy in Brazil: Towards a Public Theology Focused on Citizenship* (Eugene, Or.: Wipf & Stock, 2012).

[8] See Magali do Nascimento Cunha, "Limits and Possibilities for the Ecumenical Movement Today. A Latin American View", in Raimundo Barreto, Ronaldo Cavalcante and Wanderley P. da Rosa, (eds.), *World Christianity as Public Religion* (Minneapolis: Fortress, 2017), 33-48.

Another view on populism: Ernesto Laclau

Laclau, an Argentinian political philosopher, lived since the 1970s in England, where he taught at the University of Essex. He is known, together with his life partner, Belgian political scientist Chantal Mouffe, as a post-Marxist, post-foundational defender of what they call radical democracy. Both are particularly interested in the discursive and militant articulation of popular movements. Their thinking served as an inspiration for the Spanish political popular movement *Podemos* and the Greek *Syriza* movement. Although they have different emphases, both Laclau and Mouffe defend a post-foundational view, seeking to avoid both pre-figured and eschatologically pre-set foundations[9] They are informed by Antonio Gramsci's theory of hegemony, Lacan's psychanalytic theory of the subject and post-structural semiotic theory, among other resources.[10] They also strongly resist the traditional way of despising the people as mere masses prone to manipulation.[11]

For Laclau, this means moving from the universalism of the absolute to the universalism of the particular.[12] He takes up the Gramscian distinction between *plebs* as particularity and *populus* as an abstract universality hegemonically constituted. There is *populus* only as incarnated in the *plebs*, so it is not a pre-established given. The people and social order are not created by preconceived concepts, institutions or even a charismatic leader, but emerge performatively through discourse in difference and constant struggle, dispensing a non-discursive reference as foundation.

Such position comes in opposition to what he sees as a liberal, formal, technocratic and pragmatic occupation of politics and democracy, valuing excessively politics over "the political" as a space of articulation and hegemony of the people. Rather than any pre-political foundation on which to build, there is, for Laclau, an "empty signifier" to be filled according to the hegemonic forces. Applying this to the above case, we could say that

---

[9] Marius Hildebrand and Astrid Séville, "Populismus oder agonale Demokratie? Bruchlinien der theoretischen Symbiose von Laclau und Mouffe", *Politische Vierteljahresschrift* 56/1 (2015), 27-43, here 28.

[10] See, for instance Ernesto Laclau and Chantal Mouffe, *Hegemony and Socialist Strategy. Towards a Radical Democratic Politics* (2nd edition, London: Verso, 2014).

[11] See, for instance, Julián Molina and Vedia Grosser, "La construcción del 'pueblo', según Laclau", *La lámpara de Diógenes: Revista de Filosofia* 16/17 (2008), 137-157.

[12] Ernesto Laclau, Emancipación y diferencia (Buenos Aires: Ariel, 1996), 43-68, as mentioned by Nicolás Panotto, "Mediaciones analíticas em o trabalho de ernesto laclau: uma relectura crítica desde la antropología política", *Pléyade* 16 (2015), 235-259, here 239. I would like to thank Nicolás for the important subsidies he has made available to me for this section, and for his critical reading of a first draft.

Lula as "idea" fills the place of such an "empty signifier". It is to a certain extent contingent that it be Lula who is the signifier of the popular struggle. However, it is certainly his person and what he represents that makes him so important for many. Another example of this phenomena is Nelson Mandela, whose person and name represented the concrete struggle of black people in South Africa and beyond, as well as more broadly the principles of equality, freedom, solidarity and justice.[13]

The 2013 protests in Brazil offered an example of an emerging popular stance, with non-traditional protest groups taking to the street and complaining about the presence of traditional pressure groups. It was certainly a popular manifestation, and a very diverse and amorphous one at that—triggered by the rise in price of bus tariffs, but then exacerbated by a host of different and divergent demands. While there was some debate and discourse, there was little articulation or strategic planning, and so this important movement had no sustainability and no lasting, concrete, effect. In the meantime, there has been political protest and social critique both defending and critiquing Lula, with nationalists demonstrating against corruption and for the imprisonment of Lula. As such, popular debate, including taking to the streets, is positive for democracy, with various groups articulating their demands and fighting for hegemony. However, there is, generally, no dialogue between the two groups, no debate with at least a common goal, just rhetoric, where one is characterized as friend or foe. Brazil is, I contend, in dire need of a culture of dialogue and a reasonably common vision—and such vision should indeed emerge from below. This can be nurtured by the churches, as I shall argue in the third section.

For his part, Laclau develops, in his *On Populist Reason*[14], a theory of populism in which he describes as normal rather than as a pathology or dangerous deviance from democracy. However, this approach is more descriptive than normative and, at least theoretically, leaves open the possibility of all kinds of hegemonies. Mouffe is more normative in her agonistic theory of democracy. Rather than creating opposition between insiders and outsiders, friends and enemies, she talks about struggling in a pluralistic democracy that has as its goals freedom and equality. Rather than friend or foe, there are legitimate adversaries. A culture of conflict—not of violence or false harmony—is certainly something that should be part of our conviviality and our construction of a just society.

---

[13] Cf. Hildebrand and Séville, op. cit. (note 9), 32, who cite Oliver Marchart, "Zum Verhältnis von Kulturtheorie, Diskurstheorie und politischer Theorie", in: Frauke Berndt and Christoph Brecht (eds), *Aktualität des Symbols* (Freiburg: Rombach, 2005), 245-268, here 267.

[14] Ernesto Laclau, *On Populist Reason* (London, New York: Verso, 2007).

It is important to note that while liberation theologies and philosophies in Latin America tend to stress, even more so in their post- and decolonial mode, the overcoming of essentialist and prefigured rationalities, modernities, democracies and even religiosities, authors like Enrique Dussel connect with normative and externally established elements such as the preferential option for the poor or victims. For Dussel and others, following Emmanuel Lévinas, the messianic irruption of the other becomes tantamount.[15] While Laclau shares such anti-totalitarian ontology, he does not adopt the ethical interpellation of the other. Following Dussel's logic, I would suggest that, beyond the emergence of a popular drive from below, we need ethical interpellation and references for just procedure and for a reasonable definition of what democracy is to be, precisely in order to hear the voices of the excluded and marginalized and not succumb to sheer power, rhetorical or otherwise, of one group coming to dominate the rest. What is, then, the opportunity and task for a Public Theology? I come to my third and last part.

THE CENTRALITY OF THE PEOPLE— TASKS FOR A PUBLIC THEOLOGY

As we have seen, populism is a polysemic, ambiguous and often vague concept. In Latin American political theory, it traditionally meant the closeness of the single, charismatic leader to the masses that bypassed the elites and the established order. However, the supposedly uniform masses, seen as incapable of transformation and subjectivity by both the right and the left, came, in Laclau's redefinition of populism, to be discovered as people—not in a nationalistic sense, but, first and foremost, in a social sense. The people are the oppressed, the downtrodden, the excluded, the marginalized as Liberation Theology taught us. Hugo Assmann, one of the most radical liberation theologians in the 1970s and 1980s, later questioned many of his own presuppositions and came to see the people, not as only being in want or in need of something they lack, but as bearers of wishes, of desires. Their subjectivity and embodiment came into focus. At the same time, Assmann articulated the need for an education that pre-eminently included the development of solidary, competence and sensitivity.[16]

---

[15] Enrique Dussel, *Ethics of Liberation: in the Age of Globalization and Exclusion* (Durham: Duke University Press, 2013).

[16] Hugo Assmann and Jung Mo Sung, *Competência e sensibilidade solidária. Educar para a esperança* (3rd ed. Petrópolis: Vozes, 2010).

Laclau, then, inverts the meaning of populism from a manipulation of the masses by a leader to a way of performative, discursive and pluralistic articulation of subjectivities that on acquiring hegemony emerge as people, the *plebs* creating the *populus*. Theologically, this is relevant because populism, in this sense, focuses the attention on the people, or we could say on the priesthood of all believers. From the standpoint of Latin American Liberation Theology, the freeing from bondage in Egypt led to political and social liberation and a new configuration of the oppressed people of God.[17] I can only register here that such a view neglects the fact that liberation from Egypt was followed by the occupation of the land with nefarious consequences, including new oppressions that last to this very day. For Liberation Theology, the interest for the people is intrinsically linked to the option for the poor, seeking their emancipation both in society and in the church.[18] Within the urgency of situations in which the people found themselves massively oppressed, the notion of the "crucified people" was introduced, a kind of historical soteriology that links the concrete suffering of the people to Jesus Christ's salvific work.[19] The "people" or "people of God" generally refer to the Greek *laos [theou]*.[20] In a further radicalization of Korean Minjung, i.e. people's theology, the term "people" can also echo the Greek *ochlos*, the common people, a term used by Philo and Josephus and many others in a derogatory way, but portrayed positively in "a close relationship to Jesus" especially in the Gospel of Mark.[21]

Theologically, one is part of God's people through baptism, but practically comes to understand and adopt such a condition on a daily and continuous learning basis. Baptism is a given, a moment, but also a process. To be a Christian is, then, something constantly in the making within the constant horizon of the scandal of the cross and resurrection of Christ. Similarly, being a "people" is not a given, but part of a continuous process.

---

[17] Here I draw freely on my "Volkskirche und Kirche des Volkes: Einsichten der Befreiungstheologie", in David Plüss, Matthias D. Wüthrich and Matthias Zeindler (eds), *Ekklesiologie der Volkskirche. Theologische Zugänge in reformierter Perspektive*, *Praktische Theologie im Reformierten Kontext* Bd. 14 (Zürich: TVZ, 2016), 372-383.
[18] See Gustavo Gutiérrez, *The Power of the Poor in History* [1979] (Eugene, OR: Wipf & Stock, 2004).
[19] Ignacio Ellacuría, "Das gekreuzigte Volk", in Ignacio Ellacuría, Jon Sobrino (eds), *Mysterium Liberationis. Grundbegriffe der Theologie der Befreiung*, vol. 2 (Luzern: Exodus, 1996), 823-850.
[20] See the call for a laocracy from both a theological and democratic-theoretical point of view, and, thus, not only focused on the church, but on society in Jörg Rieger, Jung Mo Sung and Nestor Míguez, *Beyond the Spirit of Empire* (London: SCM, 2009).
[21] *Volker Küster, Jesus und das Volk im Markusevangelium. Ein Beitrag zum interkulturellen Gespräch in der Exegese* (Neukirchen-Vluyn: Neukirchner, 1996), 59.

From the amorphous mass emerges the people, the *populus* from the *plebs*, the People of God from the human species, the city of God from within the earthly city. The people, in general, and the people of God are, then, not a given, but a process, an "event" rather than an institution, as underlined in their specific ways in Leonardo Boff's "ecclesiogenesis" and Vitor Westhelle's "Church Event".[22] People are, therefore, not simply a representation of a reality but a programmatic concept. The people of God, as embodied subjects, have as their dynamic, not predefined and yet within the horizon of the incarnation, the embodiment of God in Jesus Christ. Such embodiment shows God assuming vulnerability, a vulnerability typical of the reality of most people in most contexts. Also in Jesus' practice, the people he was sent to were not simply a given, but modified and reconstructed by Jesus' presence, Jesus' words and deeds. In and through Jesus, the best and worst of humanity became visible—the generosity of the "sinful woman" that anointed Jesus (Luke 7:36-50) as well as the brutality of those who condemned and crucified him. As Luther insisted, believers are simultaneously justified and sinners, justified *in spe*, in hope, and sinners *in re*, in fact. To live with such uncomfortable, but realistic ambiguity is not easy, but necessary to be able to constructively contribute to the church's edification and the construction of a just society.

A close look at who and where the people are is, then, needed. In Brazil and Latin America, it has become common to state that "while Liberation Theology opted for the poor, the poor opted for the Pentecostals", a statement I first heard from José Comblin, an eminent Belgian-Brazilian liberation theologian. So the people can be found in settings where they theoretically might not be, because they lack the correct discourse. Indeed, there is little explicit consciousness of citizenship and much less discourse on citizenship, social justice and transformation in most Pentecostal churches.[23] And yet, many of those churches are the most efficient in giving people a sense of being people, and articulating community. This has to be understood by theology and, not least, a public theology, as a contribution to the emergence of a people. Public theology must be a listening theology; it has to be a learning theology; and from there, an articulating, networking, conflictive, agonistic theology. With concrete bodies, concrete subjects thus being

---

[22] Leonardo Boff, "Was bedeutet theologisch 'Volk Gottes' und 'Kirche des Volkes'", in *Und die Kirche ist Volk geworden. Ekklesiogenesis* (Düsseldorf: Patmos, 1987), 47-84, here 64. He can call the masses "Non-People", with reference to Hos 1:6.9 und 1 Petr 2:10. See also Vítor Westhelle, *The Church Event: Call and Challenge of a Church Protestant* (Minneapolis: Fortress Press, 2010).

[23] See Rudolf von Sinner, "Pentecostalism and Citizenship in Brazil: Between Escapism and Dominance", *International Journal of Public Theology* 6/1 (2012), 99-117.

heard and perceived in the public sphere, their voice and contribution will emerge. That does not mean that it is automatically always edifying. We cannot escape ambiguity even within the church, and the church is part of the world's ambiguities. Ideally, the church can provide a space where the concrete anxieties, needs and desires can be uttered and articulated. This is what we need today more than ever in Brazil and, I presume, in many other contexts. As such a space, the church, beyond all public statements it may make, becomes a strong witness to society by its sheer presence and endurance—of the people, by the people and through the people.

POPULISM IN AMERICA: THE DURESS-PRODDED PERVERSION OF THE COVENANT

Marcia Pally

My task in this short essay is to offer some insights into why populist/neo-nationalist movements are persuasive. Towards this end, I will look at a few features common to many such movements. Beyond these few, investigations of populism/neo-nationalism must drill down into the historico-cultural matèrièl of the society in which the populism/neo-nationalism is situated. In particular, into the historico-cultural matériel grounding *beliefs about what society* (who's in, who not) *and government* (its size and roles) *are*. It is from this matériel that populism/neo-nationalism draws its world view, narratives, and solutions for societal problems. As a case study, I will look at the United States of America. To understand populism/neo-nationalism, we need to avoid a typology of the *vox populi* where it is "democracy" if we like it and "populism" if we don't. Indeed, depending on who is written into the *populus,* populism/neo-nationalism can be a corrective to unresponsive government (as the Bernie Sanders's 2016 presidential campaign illustrates).

First, commonalties among many populisms/neo-nationalisms:

1. Populism is a program of solutions to economic and sense-of-place duress. It is a response to threats to one's sense of "the ways things ought to go," to a "decent" place in society that gives one a sense of purpose, of knowing what is fair, what is due you and what is due others.

1.1 Both economic and sense-of-place duress may be sudden or accumulated over time. They may be present and active or anticipated fear of duress for me or my children.

2. *Populist solutions aim to answer the questions:* (a) who is under unfair duress—what Andre Gingrich calls the "emotionalized us"[1], (b) why and how "we" have been wronged, (c) by whom—"them."

3. *Populist questions and answers are binary in form: not any school, work, or other community but my community, the people, in struggle against others, "them".*

4. Criteria for understanding and assessing a political movement/party include: who precisely is "us" in struggle against "them", how sharply constructed is the binary between "us" and "them", how are "we" and "they" treated. To what extent is there a notion of a "worthy opposition," where "them" is understood as part of the legitimate *vox populi* with sufficient standing in society to influence policy and with whom one's own group negotiates.

4.1 *Greater binarity suggests less inclusion of "them" in the distribution of resource and opportunity and in political and civil society negotiations.*

5. *In order to "feel right" and be thought effective, populist/neo-nationalist solutions must be understandable.* While new proposals are not precluded from understandability, the most easily understood solutions are familiar, drawn from society's historico-cultural matériel. This matériel provides the pool of ideas from which populism draws its ideas and proposals. In turn, because these ideas and proposals are drawn from long-standing cultural matériel, they resonate with and are understandable to its audience.

THE AMERICAN CASE

Following these commonalities, populisms in the U.S. are responses to economic[2] and sense-of-place duress. The Public Religion Research Institute and *The Atlantic* report that, among the populist "base" of white working-class voters, fears about immigration and cultural displacement

---

[1] Andre Gingrich, "Neo-nationalism and the reconfiguration of Europe," in *Social Anthropology* 14:2 (2006), 195-217: 199

[2] Federal Reserve Bank of St. Louis, "The Bigger They Are, The Harder They Fall, The Decline of the White Working Class," 2018, https://www.stlouisfed.org/household-financial-stability/the-demographics-of-wealth/decline-of-white-working-class (accessed Oct. 8, 2018).; Joseph Stiglitz, *The Price of Inequality: How Today's Divided Society Endangers Our Future* (New York: W.W. Norton, 2013).

were more powerful factors than economics in their support for Donald Trump as president.[3]

In positing solutions, both left and right populisms suggest an "us" and "them" but diverge on who "we" and "they" are. For left-populism, "they" are the wealthy that take an unfair share of societal resources and resist a fair share contribution to the common good. The "we" is relatively pluralistic: "ordinary hardworking Americans" including "older immigrants" (those in the U.S. for two or more generations, who speak English) *and* newer immigrants, blacks, and importantly, national government. Though government may contain corrupt politicians, it is seen overall as the people's representative, able to create programs that boost broad-based opportunity.

Right-wing populists report greater sense-of-place duress in the fear that immigration is unraveling the values that "we" understand as making the best person and society. It sees national government, new immigrants, and sometimes blacks as the sources of this unraveling who should therefore be constrained. Sixty percent of white working-class Americans believe the country needs a leader who will break the rules, a frequent government-wary, populist stance.[4] Americans who fear their culture is in danger from foreign/immigrant influence were 3.5 times more likely to prefer Trump than those who do not share this fear.[5]

BELIEFS ABOUT SOCIETY AND GOVERNMENT: THE HISTORICO-CULTURAL GROUND—COVENANTALISM, REPUBLICANISM, LIBERALISM

Importantly, left and right populisms draw not on divergent ideas about society and government but on shared ones. Most relevant for this discussion are covenantalism, republicanism, and liberalism. American covenantalism begins

---

[3] Emma Green, "It Was Cultural Anxiety That Drove White, Working-Class Voters to Trump," in *The Atlantic* (May 9, 2017), online: https://www.theatlantic.com/politics/archive/2017/05/white-working-class-trump-cultural-anxiety/525771/ (last accessed August 30, 2018).

[4] Maria Perez, "White Americans Feel They Are Victims of Discrimination, a New Poll Shows," in *Newsweek* (October 24, 2017), online: http://www.newsweek.com/white-americans-feel-they-are-victims-discrimination-new-poll-shows-691753 (last accessed August 30, 2018).

[5] Daniel Cox, Rachel Lienesch, Robert P. Jones, "Beyond Economics: Fears of Cultural Displacement Pushed the White Working Class to Trump," in *Public Religion Research Institute/The Atlantic Report* (May 09, 2017), online: https://www.prri.org/research/white-working-class-attitudes-economy-trade-immigration-election-donald-trump/ (last accessed August 30, 2018).

with Reformed Protestant political theory, which, building on the Hebrew Bible, saw covenant as a *reciprocal* commitment between parties where each gives for the flourishing of the other yet retains her unique identity and value. Johannes Althusius (1563-1638) held that persons have a "symbiotic" nature so that we live in covenant with God and each other.[6] The "fundamental law" of the commonwealth "is nothing other than certain covenants by which many cities and provinces come together and agree to establish and defend one and the same commonwealth by common work, counsel, and aid."[7]

Covenantal political theory had foundational influence on American beliefs about society and government. John Winthrop's "A Model of Christian Charity" (1630) held that community hangs together by "mutual consent"[8] in bond with God and among persons "*so that,*" echoing Althusius, "every man might have need of others." To ensure that no power overtake these bonds, Massachusetts enacted the Body of Liberties in 1641, establishing protections of the common good against the rich and politically ambitious. As for them, Winthrop explains, "The care of the public must oversway all private respects."

A second ground for American notions of society and government is the Aristotelian republic, which too understands human beings as social both to survive and to achieve our fullest development by *participating* in the *polis*. As with Althusius and Winthrop, the unjust person is one who shirks responsibilities to the commons and grabs undue benefits. Thus, a republic is successful insofar as it educates citizens in civic virtue, enabling them to contribute to governance, overturn unjust laws, and care for the common good.

By mid-eighteenth century, America had melded together covenantal and republican thinking. Protection of this covenanted republic from oppressive government was precisely the concern of the U.S. Declaration of Independence, the checks and balances of tri-partite government, and American federalism, granting much political power to the local states and "We, the People."

A third grounding for ideas about society and government was liberalism, which sees the individual not so much networked as free to leave the

---

[6] Johannes Althusius, *The politics of Johannes Althusius. An abridged translation of the third edition of Politica methodice digesta, atque exemplis sacris et profanis illustrate,* transl. Frederick S. Carney (Boston: Beacon Press 1603/1964), Chapters 1, 3-4.
[7] Althusius, ibid., paragraph 49. https://oll.libertyfund.org/titles/althusius-politica/simple (accessed May 19, 2019).
[8] John Winthrop, *A Model of Christian Charity* (1630) (San Francisco: Internet Archive, n.d.), online: https://archive.org/stream/AModelOfChristianCharity/AModelOfChristianCharity_djvu.txt (last accessed August 30, 2018).

polis to pursue opportunity. The idea of the separable individual got a loud hearing in America owing to (a) the Protestant emphasis on individual Bible reading and individual inner faith and (b) the conditions of immigration and settlement. As many early Americans were fleeing persecutory states, their flight reinforced the advantages of separability. The uprooting experience of immigration and rough conditions of the frontier boosted the advisability of individual and *local* self-reliance. With remarkable trust in the individual, preachers of the First Great Awakening (1730s-1740s) declared the "absolute necessity for every Person to act singly".[9] The most well-known story of American liberalism, however, is political: the substantial protections for individual belief and action.

These foundations over time yielded America's hybrid, liberal covenanted republic, protecting individual liberties within the framework of the common good for the well-being of both.

FROM THE HYBRID LIBERAL COVENANTED REPUBLIC TO "ALTHUSIAN" AND "TOCQUEVILLIAN" POLITICS

At least two important socio-political streams emerged within America's liberal covenanted republic. One, following Althusius, sees government as *of* the covenanted community, itself understood as broadly inclusive, following the biblical covenant as a "blessing of all the nations" (Genesis 12:3, 26:4, 28:14). In this tradition, the outsider and needy are *written into* covenant, republic, and government responsibilities. They must be cared for politically and economically. That is, granting rights and providing economic assistance are *both* means of societal inclusion. This inclusivity was at work in the religious freedom granted by the Rhode Island Charter (1663) and in Winthrop's economics, in which "every man afford his help to another in every want or distress". It was at work when President Dwight Eisenhower (Republican) wrote (1954), "Should any political party attempt to abolish social security, unemployment insurance and eliminate labor laws and farm programs, you would not hear of that party again in our political history. There is a tiny splinter group, of course, that believes you can do these things [...] Their number is negligible and they are stupid."[10]

---

[9] Gordon S. Wood, "American religion: The great retreat," in *New York Review of Books* 53:10 (June 8, 2006), 60-63: 61.

[10] Dwight D. Eisenhower, *The Papers of Dwight David Eisenhower*, vol. 15, ed. by Louis Galambos and Daun van Ee (Baltimore: Johns Hopkins University Press, 1996) ch. 13, 1386.

Althusian ideas about society and government are prominent in the pool of materièl from which many American left-wing populisms draw their worldview and policies. The "emotionalized us" is a diverse population of older and newer immigrants, blacks, and all those losing out to monied interests, "them." Government is seen as able, along with civil society, to relieve duress by returning resources to a broad-based "us".

A second socio-political stream—"Tocquevillian," for Tocqueville's admiring description of it—draws the covenanted community more closely. Faraway national government and other alien groups—new immigrants, blacks—were not so readily seen as part of the community but as potentially disruptive outsiders.

Tocquevillian localism has prodded much the best in America, including a democratic critique of central authority and the vibrancy of civil society. But under *duress* (sudden or accumulated, present or anticipated), as people find solutions in binarized world views, (a) community may be reconfigured into community-in-struggle-against-others, who should be constrained or expelled and (b) suspicion of *oppressive* government may become suspicion of government *per se*, which should be kept small and limited in funds—except to implement (a), keeping foreign people and products out.

A few examples help illustrate right-wing populist wariness of government, beginning with motives for gun rights. David French explains in the influential *National Review* that, "an assault-weapon ban [...] would gut the concept of an armed citizenry as a final, emergency bulwark against [government] tyranny".[11] In December 2017, Trump opened protected land to business development, presenting the change as freeing Americans from government interference: "Some people think that the natural resources of Utah should be controlled by a small handful of bureaucrats located in Washington [...] They're wrong."[12] When eleven states brought suit against Obama's health insurance reform (Obamacare), they wrote to the court that it "rests on a claim of federal power that is both unprecedented and unbounded".[13] By contrast, Speaker of the House Paul Ryan said, under the

---

[11] David French, "Assault Weapons Preserve the Purpose of the Second Amendment," in *The National Review* (February 21, 2018), online: https://www.nationalreview.com/2018/02/assault-weapons-preserve-the-purpose-of-the-second-amendment/ (last accessed August 30, 2018).

[12] Julie Turkewitz, "Trump Slashes Size of Bears Ears and Grand Staircase Monuments Image," in *The New York Times* (December 4, 2017), online: https://www.nytimes.com/2017/12/04/us/trump-bears-ears.html (last accessed August 30, 2018).

[13] United States Supreme Court, Case Number 11-398: United States Department of Health and Human Services Et Al. v. State of Florida Et Al., Brief for State Respondents on the Minimum Coverage Provision (February 6, 2012), 1, online: http://www.americanbar.org/content/dam/aba/publications/supreme_court_preview/briefs/11-398_resp_state.authcheckdam.pdf (last accessed August 30, 2018).

Republican plan "People are going to do what they want to do with their lives because we believe in individual freedom.".[14]

Arlie Hochschild describes "the deep story" in which *both* government and other "outsiders" are suspect: "outsider" minorities and immigrants are "cutting in line" (for jobs, resources, opportunity) ahead of "us"–and worse, cutting in with the help of government that gives outsiders aid.[15] Thus "we," who have worked hard and deserve fair reward should remove these outsiders: shrink government social services (for education, health care) and regulations (on business and finance), reduce taxes and return the money to "we, the people," and close borders to alien people and products.

So persuasive is this "deep story," that Americans vote against government programs they use and need. Those who, under the Republican replacement for Obamacare would have lost at least $1,000 in government subsidies voted for Trump by seven percentage points. Those who stood to lose $5,000 or more voted for Trump by fifty-nine to thirty-six percentage points.[16] Binyamin Applebaum and Robert Gebeloff concluded their research saying that "as more middle-class families like the Gulbransons land in the safety net [...] They are frustrated that they need help, feel guilty for taking it and resent the government for providing it.".[17]

Concluding thought

Addressing populism/neo-nationalism requires, as a first step, understanding how the world looks to those who find populism/neo-nationalism persuasive. From there, solutions must be worked out to address the undergirding duresses. For people will not forego the solutions they have unless there is a real possibility of alternatives.

---

[14] CBS News, *Face the Nation Transcript* March 12, 2017, online: http://www.cbsnews.com/news/face-the-nation-transcript-march-12-2017-ryan-paul-sanders/ (last accessed August 30, 2018).

[15] Arlie Russel Hochschild, *Strangers in Their Own Land: Anger and Mourning on the American Right* (New York: The New Press, 2016).

[16] According to the Cooperative Congressional Election Study and Kaiser Family Foundation data as quoted in: Nate Cohn, "Trump Supporters Have the Most to Lose in the G.O.P. Repeal Bill," in *The New York Times* (March 10, 2017), online: https://www.nytimes.com/2017/03/10/upshot/why-trump-supporters-have-the-most-to-lose-with-the-gop-repeal-bill.html (last accessed August 30, 2018).

[17] Binyamin Applebaum and Robert Gebeloff, "Even Critics of Safety Net Increasingly Depend on It," in *The New York Times* (February 11, 2012), online: http://www.nytimes.com/2012/02/12/us/even-critics-of-safety-net-increasingly-depend-on-it.html (last accessed August 30, 2018).

STATE THEOLOGY AND POLITICAL POPULISM IN SOUTH AFRICA? A KAIROS CRITIQUE

Dion A. Forster

This article reflects on political and religious populism in South Africa and considers both political and church discourses. Situated within the context of growing concerns of state corruption, the slow pace of transformation, and the re-emergence of identity politics in South Africa, it draws on the South African Kairos Document (KD) of 1985 for contemporary theological orientation. The Kairos document's notions of "church theology", "state theology" and "prophetic theology"[1] offer valuable tools for critiquing religious political populism in South Africa at present.

SOUTH AFRICAN POLITICAL AND RELIGIOUS POPULISM UNDER APARTHEID

South Africa has a complex history regarding the power relationships between the church(es), the state and "the people". The relationship between the South African Nationalist government and the Dutch Reformed Church in South Africa during the apartheid era is perhaps the most widely

---

[1] Kairos Theologians, *Challenge to the Church: A Theological Comment on the Political Crisis in South Africa* (Johannesburg: Kairos Theologians, 1985), http://www.sahistory.org.za/archive/challenge-church-theological-comment-political-crisis-south-africa-kairos-document-1985 [accessed 1 December 2018].

considered of these relationships.[2] It led to the contamination of both the mandate of the nation state and the witness of the church. Both institutions failed the South African people. In particular, this corrupt political and theological relationship resulted in theological heresy[3] and religiously sanctioned human rights abuses on a mass scale.[4]

During the years of the apartheid struggle some South African Churches, in various forms witnessed in words and deeds against both the heresies of the apartheid state supporting churches, and the systematic human rights abuses of the apartheid state itself.[5] This witness was also international and, for example, led the Lutheran World Federation (LWF) at its 1977 Assembly in Dar es Salaam to "appeal to our white member churches in southern Africa to recognize that the situation in southern Africa constitutes a *status confessionis*." At its 1984 Assembly in Budapest—a year before the publication of the Kairos document—the LWF suspended the membership of white member churches in South Africa and South West Africa, as they had not "publicly and unequivocally" rejected the system of apartheid.[6]

In this sense, one could argue that some churches, ecumenical bodies, denominations, local congregations, communities, and individual members represented the will of the people, and their desire for social and political justice. Notable examples of populist religious leaders from different Christian churches are Archbishop Desmond Tutu of the Anglican Church, Dr Beyers Naudé of the Dutch Reformed Church, Bishop Peter Storey of the Methodist Church of Southern Africa, and Rev. Dr Allan Boesek from the Uniting Reformed Church of South Africa. These men played a significant role in the deconstruction of apartheid theology and practice. They are examples of religious political populism that had a positive effect on society and strengthened the witness of the churches.

---

[2] Cf. Richard Elphick and T. R. H. Davenport, *Christianity in South Africa: A Political, Social, and Cultural History (*University of California Press, 1997); John W. De Gruchy, The Church Struggle in South Africa (Minneapolis: Fortress Press, 2005).2012

[3] Cf. John W. De Gruchy and Charles Villa-Vicencio, *Apartheid Is a Heresy* (Grand Rapids, MI: William B. Eerdmans Publishing Co., 1983), 81–85.

[4] De Gruchy op. cit. (note 3), 46, 52, 97, 145, 256.

[5] The use of the term church in these three forms stems from Dirk J. Smit, *Essays in Public Theology: Collected Essays* 1 (Stellenbosch: AFRICAN SUN MeDIA, 2007), 61–68. It is here used as adapted by Forster. Cf. Dion A. Forster, "What Hope Is There for South Africa? A Public Theological Reflection on the Role of the Church as a Bearer of Hope for the Future," in *HTS Teologiese Studies* 71:1 (2015), 1–10.

[6] Ralston Deffenbaugh, *The Lutheran World Federation and Namibia* (LWF, Geneva, 2017) 15-16, https://www.lwfassembly.org/sites/default/files/resources/12A-LWF-and-Namibia.pdf [accessed 1 December 2018].

SHIFTS IN RELIGIOUS AND POLITICAL POPULISM
AFTER THE 1994 DEMOCRATIC ELECTIONS

After 1994, the social actors of power in South African society changed from the National Party and the apartheid sanctioning Dutch Reformed Church to the first democratically elected political party, the African National Congress (ANC). The mainline, largely English speaking, multiracial, churches (such as the Methodist Church of Southern Africa, the Anglican Church, and the Catholic Church) came to occupy the positions of social prominence.

However, while the political and religious actors changed after 1994, a relationship of concern exists between many of these churches and the state, once again challenging the witness of the church as well as the credibility of the government in South Africa. The church is now facing the threat of becoming embedded in the actions and intentions of the national state.[7] It is extremely dangerous, and indeed a denial of the high calling of the church, when it subjugates its work and witness to support political tendencies, or nationalist ideologies.

Hence, this section seeks to highlight how problematic religious and political populism can become when the church chooses to use its social capital and the trust of its members to gain social and political prominence from a corrupt and unjust state. This is most clearly exemplified at present by the relationship between the Methodist Church of Southern Africa (MCSA) and the governing party in South Africa, the ANC. I will give two examples of problematic religious and political populism. Then I shall critique current religious political populism from the perspective of the 1985 Kairos Document.

In the lead up to the last South African national elections (2014), there was increasing rhetoric of a religious nature intended to sweep up populist support in the speeches of ANC politicians. ANC aligned clergy supported these religious overtones. This is not surprising as 84.2% of South Africans self-identify as Christian.[8] Moreover, most politicians have some church affiliation by virtue of their own faith. The last parliamentary census

---

[7] Denise Ackermann warned the South African churches and their leaders in 2012 to "engage, but not be embedded" in political parties and the aims of the state (Edwin Arrison in Ernst M. Conradie and Miranda Pillay, *Ecclesial Reform and Deform Movements in the South African Context* (Stellenbosch: AFRICAN SUN MeDIA, 2015), 12).

[8] General Household Survey 2013, Statistical Information, General Household Survey (Pretoria, South Africa: Statistics South Africa, 2014), http://www.statssa.gov.za/publications/P0318/P03182013.pdf [accessed 1 December 2018].

showed that 65% of current parliamentarians said that they are members of the Methodist Church of Southern Africa.[9]

The most public displays of religious political populism were the activities of the Rev. Vukile Mehana, the Chaplain General to the ANC at the time, and a senior minister in the MCSA, serving on the denomination's executive, holding the portfolio of human resources management. Rev Mehana defended President Jacob Zuma's statement that persons who voted for the ANC would go to heaven, while those who voted for other parties could go to hell.[10] Here is what President Zuma said,

> I start from basic Christian principles. Christianity is part of what I am; in a way it was the foundation for all my political beliefs.... When you vote for the ANC, you are also choosing to go to heaven. When you don't vote for the ANC you should know that you are choosing that man who carries a fork ... who cooks people.[11]

This claim is clearly politically motivated and holds little theological credibility by any standards. Yet Rev. Mehana defended Mr Zuma's claim saying the following:

> While the popular Christian understanding of heaven is equated to a physical place, theologically heaven can also mean the presence of God. When the President urged citizens to vote for the ANC, equating that with heaven, he meant that voters—theologically may miss the opportunity of being in the presence of God if they do not vote for the ANC.[12]

Mehana is employing what the Kairos theologians identified as a form of "state theology", by providing theological sanction for an inappropriate expression of political power by the head of state and the leader of the governing political party.[13]

---

[9] Dion Forster, 'A State Church? A Consideration of the Methodist Church of Southern Africa in the Light of Dietrich Bonhoeffer's "Theological Position Paper on State and Church"', *Stellenbosch Theological Journal* 2:1 (2016), 61-88: 70, doi:10.17570/stj.2016.v2n1.a04.

[10] Vukile Mehana, 'Zuma's Remarks Explained – ANC Chaplain General', 7 February 2011, http://www.politicsweb.co.za/politicsweb/view/politicsweb/en/page71639?oid=220386&sn=Detail&pid=71639 [accessed 1 December 2018].

[11] Jacob Zuma, quoted by: Gareth Van Onselen, "The ANC, Religion and "the Truth"," in *www.Inside-Politics.Org*, 17 August 2015, https://inside-politics.org/2015/08/17/the-anc-religion-and-the-truth/ [accessed 1 December 2018].

[12] Mehana, op. cit. (note 10).

[13] Cf. John De Gruchy, "From political to public theologies: the role of theology in public life in South Africa," in *Public Theology for the 21st Century: Essays in Honour*

A second example comes from just before the 2014 elections when Mehana encouraged pastors in Cape Town to solicit votes for the ANC. He said to a group of gathered clergy, "[y]ou cannot have church leaders that speak as if they are in opposition to government ... God will liberate the people through this (ANC) government".[14]

Such examples of religious political populism are particularly troubling when one considers the social power dynamics of populist movements. As Louise Vincent points out, the ANC had been facing a loss of public confidence. She notes that leading up to the elections there was a "disillusion with politicians who seem far more concerned with in-fighting than with addressing [the needs of] citizens".[15] She suggests that this was a trend in the ANC's overly confident style of politics after winning the 1994 elections so convincingly.

> After 1994, popular mobilisation came to be pathologised in favour of a version of democracy that was more about elite pacting [building economic and political pacts] than about mass participation in politics.[16]

Such action creates stark social divisions in society along the lines of class, culture, and identity. Trying to recapture their image of being "the people's party", the ANC engaged in shallow forms of identity politics. While failing to keep its own house in order, it began to blame social failures on the Black and White economic elites, thereby demarcating "the people" in opposition to these "others" who were identified as the primary source of South Africa's struggles.[17]

> While this [class binaries and race binaries] may be true as a rough description, it avoids addressing the government's failure to tackle this issue [...] What it silences for the listener and the reader is complexity, process, and class dynamics. What it confirms is race populism.[18]

---

of Duncan B. Forrester, ed. by William Storrar and Andrew Morton (London: A&C Black, 2004), 45-62: 50–51; Allan Aubrey Boesak, *Kairos, Crisis, and Global Apartheid: The Challenge to Prophetic Resistance* (London: Palgrave Macmillan, 2015), 15.

[14] Bekezela Phakathi, 'Pastors Will Not Help ANC Win Votes, Says DA', 6 February 2014.

[15] Louise Vincent, "Seducing the People: Populism and the Challenge to Democracy in South Africa," in *Journal of Contemporary African Studies* 29:1 (January 2011), 1-14: 2; doi:10.1080/02589001.2011.533056 [accessed 1 December 2018].

[16] Ibid.

[17] Gerhard Maré, "Race, Democracy and Opposition in South African Politics: As Other a Way as Possible", *Democratization* 8:1 (2001), 85-102: 97, doi:10.1080/714000182 (last accessed September 1, 2018).

[18] Ibid.

This is what Laclau understood as the "class character" of populism, "the people" are constructed as a homogenous power bloc of opposition to whatever is considered, in overly simplistic terms, to be the problem.[19]

Louise Vincent thus comments that if "the populist leader can claim to be the voice of the people then it stands to reason that those who offer a different political or social vision are not simply political opponents but much more damningly, opponents of the people."[20] This describes the strategy of leaders such as Jacob Zuma and the clergy who support him precisely.

Conclusion: The church and political populism? A Kairos critique

In 2015, the 30th anniversary of the South African Kairos document (KD)[21] was celebrated. Drafted during the darkest period of apartheid, this document confronted the churches in South Africa to consider how they hindered transformation and supported injustice[22]. The churches were challenged to move away from a theology that upholds the aims of nationalist apartheid power ("state theology"), or theologies that retreated from society ("church theology"). The Kairos theologians advocated for a "prophetic theology", and a "prophetic church", that would witness to God's will in the church and in society at large.[23]

The Kairos challenge to the church remains as important today as it was 30 years ago. Then as now, it reminds both the church and the state that each has a specific role within God's will for society. What makes

---

[19] Cf. Ernesto Laclau, 'Universalism, Particularism and the Question of Identity', in *The Politics of Difference: Ethnic Premises in A World of Power*, ed. Edwin Wilmsen and Patrick McAllister (Chicago, Il: University of Chicago Press, 1996), 49; John Saul, 'The Dialectic of Class and Tribe', in *The State and Revolution in Eastern Africa* (New York, NY: Monthly Review Press, 1979), 401.

[20] Vincent, op. cit. (note 15), 6. As ANC politician Julius Malema said in 2009: Those who oppose the ANC are "suffering from a serious [mental] illness". Quoted by Quinton Mtyala, "ANC wants three-thirds majority, says Malema," in *IOL News* (April 16, 2009), online: https://www.iol.co.za/news/politics/anc-wants-three-thirds-majority-says-malema-440111 (last accessed September 1, 2018).

[21] Kairos Theologians, op. cit. (note 2).

[22] Ibid., 15–17. Cf. De Gruchy, op. cit. (note 13), 51.

[23] For the use of the term 'public', cf. Dirk Smit, "What does 'Public' mean? Questions with a View to Public Theology," in Public Aims, Methodologies, and Issues in Public Theology, ed. by Christian L. D. Hansen (Stellenbosch: SUN Press, 2007), 11–46., as well as John de Gruchy, "Public Theology as Christian Witness: Exploring the Genre," in International Journal of Public Theology 1:1 (2007), 26–41.

the Kairos document important is that it not only criticized the state but passed prophetic judgement upon it.[24]

John De Gruchy notes that the apartheid state sought to counter the contentions of the Kairos theologians by working "in tandem with right wing religious organizations".[25] In other words, parts of the South African churches had become agents of the unjust state, expressing support for its views and acting as a social shield to deflect criticism. Captured by nationalistic ideas, they listened to the voices of political leaders rather than the voice of God. As was noted above, there is a fear that this is taking place once again.

The Kairos theologians emphasized the responsibility to be both a pastoral and a prophetic church.

Both the church and the state fail God and the people (God's will and the common good of the citizens) when the relationship between the church and the state is compromised for the sake of political or religious expediency. Such negative religious political populism harms society and dishonors God. The church and the state each have a responsibility to safeguard the role and function of the other. When one oversteps its bounds, both are in error (one for committing the error, and the other for allowing it to take place unchallenged).

Populism is a complex social phenomenon. In South Africa's past, it served the good of the people as "prophetic" churches and church leaders worked for justice and peace. However, at present, a destructive form of populism has emerged. This current form of religious political populism seeks to divide society, supporting the unjust and corrupt actions of the state while offering moral and religious sanction to its leaders. Such a populist state theology is not in the interest of the churches, the state, or the people of South Africa. It is an offence to the nation, to the intention of God, and it jeopardizes the common good of South Africans.

---

[24] De Gruchy, op. cit. (note 3), 198.
[25] Ibid., 197.

Church Institution and Ethnonational Mythology: The Case of Ex-Yugoslavia

Branko Sekulić

Introduction

This paper summarizes a delicate and complex problem arising from the relationship between church hierarchy and the ethnonational politics in the former Yugoslavia, which has taken an ethnoreligious form. I will briefly present the main points of this issue and explain the kinds of socio-religious problems with which we are dealing.

Distinction between the Church and the Churches

In order to be precise and clear in this analysis, it is critical to understand that such a thing as the church—as one fully and completely defined body—does not exist, for the church is not one, but many, which means that it consists of a group of local churches. Every social context in the world where Christianity is present has its own kind of theological peculiarities—they emerge from the shared corpus of Christ's message, but are framed according to local cultural and historical circumstances.[1]

---

[1] See Edward Schillebeeckx, "Forward", in: Robert J. Schreiter, *Constructing Local Theologies* (Maryknoll, NY: Orbis Book, 1999), ix.

I always keep separate the notion of church as an institution that abides in a specific context, ethnic or national group, and the church as a heritage of Jesus Christ. This differentiation is the best method to approach certain socio-religious problems in a proper way. This does not mean that the church institution as a temporal value and Jesus' heritage as eternal value are divided against each other. The distinction prevents the possibility of falling into the trap of criticizing Jesus' praxis instead of the aberrations of certain church officers or church hierarchies in a specific social context.

The logic of some church fathers such as St. Ambrose, St. Augustine and St. Jerome, illustrates this dichotomy, for they criticized the *habitus meretrius* (vice of prostitution) of the church institution, which resulted in a depiction of the church as the *casta meretrix* (chaste whore), a phrase that includes two aspects of its being: heavenly brightness and worldly dirtiness.[2] Its heavenly brightness is related to the legacy of Jesus Christ as an inexhaustible source of holiness. The worldly dirtiness is related to church institutions in concrete local situation as something that partly depends on the nature of people who form a community of believers in that place, whether they are priests or laity.

This whorish part of the church is something which is taken into consideration when it is necessary to give contextual observations around the state of the church, for, in comparison to the legacy of Christ, the church is perishable. However, the problem does not lie in Christianity in itself, but in the understanding and practicing of it by certain church institutions and their members. We should beware of generalization, for each problem has its own name.

In that context, I focus on the so-called phenomenon of ethno-religion in the former Yugoslavian territory as a junction between the church institution and ethnonational mythology.

ETHNONATIONAL MYTHOLOGY

A political myth is defined as a kind of ideological narrative that, by offering a vision of the past, present and future in a certain social group, is recognized as a truth.[3] The political myth does not only give a kind of theoretical definition of the world, but provides practical conditions to

---

[2] See Leonardo Boff, *Francis of Rome and Francis of Assisi: A New Springtime for the Church* (New York: Orbis Book, 2014), 18f.

[3] See Henry Tudor, *Political Myth: The Political Uses of History, Tradition and Memory* (London: Macmillan Publishers, 1972), 138. Christopher G. Flood, *Political Myth: A Theoretical Introduction* (New York/ London: Routledge, 2002), 42.44.

change that world according to its own criteria, and that effort is usually expressed through the dramatic form.[4]

With this dramatic form, the mythopoeic, a process of myth-making, draws people more effectively into the concerned content by creating a sense of personal involvement and responsibility for what is being talked about.[5] But when the mythopoeic process starts from the perspective of a certain ethnic and national group, then an ethnonational mythology is born and an ethnonational political myth becomes a kind of foundation of a new reality for the community in question.[6]

THE CHURCH INSTITUTION AND ETHNONATIONAL MYTHOLOGY

Ethno-religion, which is the term used for this new junction between the church institution and ethnonational mythology, results when political myth in an ethnic form finds its expression within the religious narrative of a certain church institution. The transformation of political myth into ethnonational myth is just a part of this issue, for it entails only the secular side of the story. Religion gives a full, sacral, dimension to it.[7] Only when the political myth of one ethnic group also takes on a sacral dimension does it receive the strength necessary for a social transformation. In addition to this sense of distinctiveness that creates a political and ethnic myth, we must add the sense of being chosen that undergirds a religion. There, one ethnic or national group looks upon itself, not just as an important factor on the historical level, but on the eschatological level also. For ethno-religion, it is not enough that it just convinces someone of something, but that it strive toward a complete transformation of a person's state of mind.

The structures of the church institution that stands behind such an effort have a tendency to do two things: to give to their own struggles a sort of sacred characteristic (savior of the nation); to provide to the community which they represent a certain socially acceptable or special status (chosen people). It is exactly these two elements—seeing itself as a savior of the nation and chosen people—that, when incorporated into the base of ethno-religious policy, tend to integrate it in a certain social context as its

---

[4] See Tudor, op. cit. (note 3), 16.
[5] See Flood, op. cit. (note 3), 43f. Tudor, op. cit (note 3), 16f.61.
[6] See Tudor, op. cit. 15–17.31.61.
[7] See Emilio Gentile and Robert Mallett, "The Sacralisation of Politics: Definitions, Interpretations and Reflections on the Question of Secular Religion and Totalitarianism", *Totalitarian Movements and Political Religion* 1, no. 1 (2007), 21–26.

raison d'être. In addition, they are then supported by ethnical myths that generate collective feeling, for mythical instinct changes the things in the way they were supposed to be, not as they were or should be.[8]

THE CHURCH INSTITUTION AND ETHNONATIONAL MYTHOLOGY IN THE FORMER YUGOSLAVIA: THE CASE OF THE ROMAN CATHOLIC CHURCH IN CROATIA[9]

A good example of this appears in the jubilee movement, the so-called Thirteen Centuries of Christianity among the Croats (1975-1984), with which the Roman Catholic Church in Croatia, tentatively speaking, celebrated more than 1,300 years of the alliance between the Croatian people and the Roman Catholic Church.[10] This jubilee, according to the words of the late Bishop Frane Franić (1912-2007), was a celebration that intended "[t]o give thanks to God for the baptism of Croats, when from the river Jadro, 'the Croatian Jordan', the first baptismal water was trickled down the Croatian forehead", which happened, according to the bishop, during the time of Croatian Duke Porin (Borna) at the end of the ninth century.[11] In this statement, we find answers to three questions—when it appears, where it appears, and who were the founders of a particular ethnic group or nation—that constitute the basic myth surrounding the origin[12] of the Croatian ethnic group as Christian.[13] Very soon, it will become obvious

---

[8] See David Lowenthal, *The Past Is Foreign Country* (Cambridge: Cambridge University Press, 1985), 324.

[9] This is just one of the several myths in the case of the Roman Catholic Church in Croatia that I have chosen to briefly present for this occasion, with the remark that a parallel can also be drawn with the Serbian Orthodox Church, but, due to practical considerations, they will not be mentioned here.

[10] See Stanko Josip Škunca, "Papa Ivan IV. Zadranin I Misija Opata Martina 641. Godine," *Radovi Zavoda Za Povijesne Znanosti HAZU U Zadru* 48 (2006), 187-98.; Trpimir Vedriš, "Pokrštavanje I Rana Kristijanizacija Hrvata," in *Nova Zraka U Europskom Svjetlu. Hrvatske Zemlje U Ranome Srednjem Vijeku (Oko 550 - Oko 1150),* Povijest Hrvata, Sv. 1, ed. Zrinka Nikolić Jakus (Zagreb: Matica Hrvatska, 2015), 173-200.

[11] See Frane Franić, *Putovi Dijaloga* 2 (Zagreb: Grafok, 2001), 407.

[12] See Anthony D. Smith, *The Ethnic Origins of Nations* (Oxford: Blackwell, 1995), 192.

[13] There is also a legend about five brothers (Klukas, Lobel, Kosenc, Muhlo, Hrvat) and two sisters (Tuga and Buga), who came to Dalmatia and started the story of the Croatian people. However, this story, such as it is, remains within the framework of classical mythological narrative, while in this case, we are talking about the mythological concept that has moved from the literature into the political program.

that under the term Christianity, the Roman Catholic Church in Croatia actually means Catholicism.

QUESTIONABLE ASSUMPTIONS

This analysis illustrates two completely questionable assumptions. First is the assumption that the Croatian people was always deeply connected with Christianity. This actually means that Croatians are deeply connected with Catholicism instead of Orthodoxy, even when the line between East and West was just a line between Rome and Byzantium's jurisdictions, and not a collision between two different worlds as it is usually interpreted in the political imaginarium of Croats and Serbs.

The second assumption is that Croatian people, as a nation, are more than thirteen centuries old, which actually means that they were in former Yugoslavian territory before any other nation, regardless of the fact that it is very clear that before the nineteenth century this people had not developed a national consciousness. So, they just took a certain people (Slavic tribes) who had lived in the territory where today's Croatia is, and uploaded them in their own ethnical and national history.

Thus, when we put all ideologies and national dreams aside, we get a basic tendency, which in this case aims to emphasize that Croats, who are Roman Catholics, are completely different people from Serbs, who are Orthodox, while the Serbian ethnonational mythology claims, for instance, that all people in the former Yugoslavia are Serbs who a long time ago were violently separated from their Serbian ethnical body by the efforts either of Rome (Croats-Catholics) or of Constantinople (Bosniaks-Muslims).

In other words, this case of ethno-religion is actually rooted in an idea of hostility toward other ethnic, national, confessional or religious groups that should be assimilated, banished or eradicated, while the ethnonational mythology and religious elements are just a kind of foreplay to the politics of ethnical cleansing and genocide. This especially comes to the fore if we take into consideration the fact that after the Cold War, religious and ethnic conflicts appeared as the greatest threat to world security.[14]

---

[14] See Jonathan Fox, *Ethnoreligious Conflict in the Late 20th Century* (Lanham: Lexington Books, 2002), 143.

CONCLUSION

The serious challenge is obvious. We are dealing, not only with some aberrations in the relationship between the church institution and politics, but with the aberration itself, that kind of phenomenon whose existence has gone beyond the church and political framework and created a new form of life and identification—an ethno-religious one. To the follower of ethno-religion, the difference between the religious values and ethnonational mythology simply does not exist. In the context of the former Yugoslavia, if one is Croat, one must be Roman Catholic also, and if one is Serb, one must be Orthodox, there is nothing between. That is the real challenge to Christianity in the former Yugoslavian territory.

Standing up against right-wing populist movements. Common ecumenical tasks in the context of shrinking civil space and the global crisis of democracy

Dietrich Werner

From its early inception in 1959 in Berlin—almost 60 years ago—Bread for the World, the national development organization of Protestant churches in Germany, raised its voice for the support of the marginalized and those excluded from freely determining the fate and quality of their lives. Bread for the World believes in the crucial role of civil society organizations, of churches, faith-based organizations (FBOs) and non-government organizations (NGOs) to enhance work for the alleviation of poverty, human rights and ecological transformation throughout the world. This is particularly important today as states get weaker or cannot function properly, and as the number of such fragile states is multiplying. Strengthening civil society actors has been one of the primary objectives of Bread for the World over the past few years, while supporting partner organizations in more than 90 countries worldwide. But this work—despite ambitious political goals and common agreements like the United Nations Sustainable Development Framework (UNSDF)—has not become easier in recent years. On the contrary, partners of Bread for the World are increasingly sharing stories about restrictions they face in operating in public space. Rigid forms of state surveillance, complex registration procedures, direct discriminatory practices, including sanctions against foreign money transfer or explicit legal means of suppression against civil society organizations, are on the increase. Such measures threaten the very survival of certain partners in countries where the voices of human rights activists are most needed. There are alarming trends for what we would call a "global crisis in democracy". Let me illustrate this by reviewing data from recent reports.

Bread for the World showed in its recently published "Atlas der Zivilgesellschaft"[1], which is based on the CIVICUS Monitor[2] Reports, that only two percent of people worldwide live in countries where public space for civic activism is truly open. Seven of eight states worldwide narrow, repress or close the space of actors such as human rights defenders, journalists or NGOs (or 173 states in total). As Bread for the World is a development actor, the report also examined the correlation of development and freedom. Looking at the Human Development Index and the CIVICUS data, we can see that the more open a society is, the more likely it is to achieve human, social and economic development.

Similar trends of shrinking space were recently outlined in the "Freedom in the World Report 2018", which argues that democracy has encountered its biggest crisis in 2017, as the respect for basic democratic rights and civil freedom principles has decreased once again. Seventy-one out of 195 countries respect political citizen rights less than before, while only thirty-five countries have made progress around freedom rights, and only forty-nine countries can be regarded as totally unfree, with fifty-eight counted as partly free.[3]

Again, the Bertelsmann Transformation Index 2018, which provides a ranking of countries according to civil democracy and social economy, has come to the conclusion that out of 129 countries assessed, only two had improved, while in thirteen countries the situation had deteriorated, and more than 3.3 billion people now live in autocratic regimes.[4]

Finally, the so-called Democracy-Index of the journal *The Economist*[5], which has measured the level of democratization in 169 countries since 2006, concluded that in 2017, only nineteen countries in the world fully

---

[1] Brot für die Welt (Christian Jakob, Maren Leifker, Christine Meissler), *Atlas der Zivilgesellschaft* (Berlin: Brot für die Welt, 2017), online: https://www.brot-fuer-die-welt.de/themen/atlas-der-zivilgesellschaft/ (last accessed September 2, 2018).
[2] *CIVICUS Monitor* (Johannesburg/New York/Geneva: CIVICUS, 2017), online: https://monitor.civicus.org/ (last accessed September 2, 2018).
[3] *Democracy in Crisis* (Washington, D.C./New York: Freedom House, 2018), online: https://freedomhouse.org/report/freedom-world/freedom-world-2018 (last accessed September 2, 2018).
[4] *Bertelsmann Transformation Index 2018* (Gütersloh: Bertelsmann Stiftung, 2018), online: https://www.bti-project.org/en/home/ (last accessed September 2, 2018).
[5] *The Economist Intelligence Unit's Democracy Index* (London: The Economist, 2018), online: https://infographics.economist.com/2018/DemocracyIndex/ (last accessed September 2, 2018).

realized and granted democratic principles. Thus, it describes the current situation as a "recession of democracy".

Reasons for this global crisis of democracy can be many and complex: increased trends to authoritarian regimes, hypertrophic nationalist ideologies, rigid concepts of exclusivism as protective means against globalization, and trends towards radicalization of political and religious language reinforce each other. From our partners in several contexts, we know that nationalist populism—while not being the only reason for the global crisis in democracy and the shrinking space of civil society—helps aggravate and accelerate political polarization, enmity and self-closure, which offers political justification for further restrictions.

"Nationalist populism" claims that the true and authentic will of the people is not represented by its properly elected political leaders and democratic institutions. It argues that such a nation needs special and truly patriotic or national "leaders", to express the authentic voice of the masses of the people. Legitimate criticism against those new and autocratic leaders is then portrayed as anti-national or as harming the national interest. In this same rhetoric, many of Bread for the World's partners in countries such as Kenya, India or Russia are defamed as "evil or uncivil society", "foreign agents", "fifth columns", "traitors" or "terrorists". Populism and defamation are important elements, which shrink the space of civil society and lead to repression. In some cases, media additionally enforces stigmatization through targeted campaigns and incitement to violence. Frequently, bloggers and journalists are severely threatened and hampered in their work, and therefore they cannot defend themselves against established media and their campaigns against civil society. All this significantly influences economic, social and cultural human rights and development as well. Defenders of these rights are often the ones most severely affected by persecution and intimidation.

Populism is gaining influence and power both in the United States of America and in European countries, where it is becoming an issue of deep concern. President Donald Trump has illustrated this form of ideological battle rhetoric in a frightening manner. Having just been elected with a small margin of votes (without a numerical majority of votes!), he claimed to be the only right and proper leader of the American nation which would be "transferring power from Washington, D.C. and giving it back to you, the American People"[6]—as if the American nation, one of the oldest democracies in the world, for decades did not live in a functioning democracy. Similarly, right-wing populist movements in Europe argue that the European political and democratic system is corrupt and that only a small elitist circle within the established parties is the secret sovereign in their countries (as stated, for example, in Article 8 of the party

---

[6] Donald Trump, *The Inaugural Address* (January 20, 2017), online: https://www.white-house.gov/briefings-statements/the-inaugural-address/ (last accessed September 2, 2018).

program of the German right-wing party *Alternative für Deutschland*). They claim that it is only the right-wing parties who rightfully represent the silent majority of the true people, which now needs to change the course of history. What we see at work here is a perverse combination of strategies which are inherently opposed and in conflict with one another. We see a propagandistic devaluation and decrying of existing democratic procedures used by those who, at the same time, are benefitting from them; in addition, we have these parties demonizing mainstream political leaders, while at the same time refusing to enter into serious political dialogue about current issues; and there is an excessive use of state funds and privileges for further spreading of right-wing ideologies and fake news, again, while at the same time slurring state authorities. These contradictory trends are tied in with strategies which gradually intend to undermine the confidence and active political participation of people in democratic processes. In the German context, this is not the first time in history that populism like this has shown its face. The churches in Germany are on high alert with regard to the unfolding political scenario.

Bread for the World and its founding figures were rooted in the understandings and theological presuppositions of the Confessing Church, which stood up against a fascist populist movement in Germany which later brought horrible suffering and destruction to several European countries and beyond. In the context of National Socialism, Dietrich Bonhoeffer developed a theological response against *nationalism, anti-Semitism, ethnocentrism and populism that is a valuable resource for today's challenges. Bonhoeffer* argued in favor of an attitude of Christian resilience over against the temptations of nationalism, exclusionism and adaptation to populist trends. He pointed to the inherently critical nature of Christian belief:

> "Christianity stands or falls with its revolutionary protest against violence, arbitrariness, and pride of power, and with its plea for the weak. Christians are doing too little to make these points clear [...] Christendom adjusts itself far too easily to the worship of power. Christians should give more offense, shock the world far more, than they are doing now."[7]

Developing meaningful responses to the challenges of right-wing populism and nationalist movements greatly profits from inter-contextual ecumenical exchange. The key question in this regard is: how can churches remain steadfast and strong in their witness and service to those in need of God's love and compassion beyond all cultural, national and ethnic boundaries?

---

[7] Dietrich Bonhoeffer, "Evening Sermon on 2 Corinthians 12:9 (London 1934)," in *Dietrich Bonhoeffer Werke* 13, Hans Goedeking, Martin Heimbucher and Hans-Walter Schleicher (eds) (Gütersloh: Chr. Kaiser Verlag, 1994), 411 (Bonhoeffer's English).

PUBLIC THEOLOGY IN CONTEXT—
RESISTING EXCLUSION

Public Theology in Hong Kong in Relation to the Religious-Political Reality in the People's Republic of China

Sung Kim

The involvement of Christian churches and theology in the public sphere of Hong Kong

Christians in Hong Kong are a minority. They hardly cover one of the seven million citizens.[1] Yet, Christianity is visible, in all its diversity. In terms of church-state-relationship, Hong Kong's Basic Law, not only guarantees religious freedom,[2] but encourages religious organizations to participate in shaping the public sphere, especially by contributing to social and educational efforts. Religious freedom is regarded as a common good for all Hong Kong citizens.[3]

---

[1] Official figures speak of less than 400,000 Catholics and less than 500,000 Protestants. https://www.gov.hk/en/about/abouthk/factsheets/docs/religion.pdf (accessed 20 April 2018).

[2] Article 32 of the Basic Law stipulates that "Hong Kong residents shall have freedom of religious belief and freedom to preach and to conduct and participate in religious activities in public".

[3] "Religious freedom is one of the fundamental rights enjoyed by Hong Kong residents." https://www.legco.gov.hk/research-publications/english/1718fs01-religious-facilities-in-hong-kong-20171208-e.pdf (accessed 20 April 2018).

The question is: How long?[4] Individuals and churches respond to the looming changes quite differently. The stances taken towards Beijing's obvious exercise of power cover the whole range of (non-violent) confrontation to (critical) cooperation. Christian ministers are divided on political matters as much as the rest of the population in Hong Kong. Not only in terms of how to react to Beijing's influence on Hong Kong, but also when it comes to addressing the current situation of religious freedom in mainland China.

Public theology as currently discussed in Hong Kong can only be understood, if put in relation to the religious-political reality in the People's Republic of China (PRC). For this goal, three dimensions of the discussion of religion and the public in the PRC need to be taken into account, which will raise some questions regarding public theology in Hong Kong.

Religion and the public in the PRC

In early 2018, it was officially announced that the State Administration for Religious Affairs (SARA) was dissolved by March. The relations between government and the religious bodies ever since are handled by the United Front Work Department (UFWD) that reports to the Communist Party directly. While it is too early to draw any conclusions from this, the change in this matter clearly indicates that the present government is willing to restructure the system also in terms of its relationship to the religious bodies. When it comes to the status of religious freedom in the PRC, there are three dimension to look at. The political order, the academic discourse, and the institutional situation of the churches.

Political order

The fundamental political order regarding the religious-political situation in the PRC can only be described by pointing out a fundamental tension inherent to it. On the one hand, the Constitution of the People's Republic of China explicitly guarantees religious freedom.[5] Of course, it is restricted;

---

[4] The political aspects have come to global recognition, mostly as a yearning for democracy. Hong Kong was "returned" to China in 1997. For a period of 50 years, it will stay independent in terms of administration, until 2047. Thus the term "Self Administrative Region" (SAR).

[5] Article 36 states that: "No state organ, public organization or individual may compel citizens to believe in, or not to believe in, any religion; nor may they discriminate against citizens who believe in, or do not believe in, any religion." http://en.people.cn/constitution/constitution.html (accessed 20 April 2018).

predominantly, by giving priority to matters of public order over religious freedom.[6] But still, it is regarded as something positive.

Whereas on the other hand, Document No. 19 expresses the viewpoint of the central committee of the Chinese Communist Party that it "insists that atheism is a basic doctrine of the Chinese Communist Party and that the whole Party and state are responsible for implementing the religious policy."[7] Until today, this tension between general positively connoted religious freedom and the Communist Party's duty to curb religious activities, especially because of the perception of religions as possible threats to public order, is "one of the liabilities of China's stride for modernization"[8].

Since religious freedom as guaranteed in the constitution is not connected to any right of assembly, many gatherings are held without official permission.[9] One interpretation on religious freedom in the PRC holds that it is only about private affairs, meaning: everybody can believe what he/she wants to believe, but only for him/herself.[10] It is evident that without the accompanying right of assembly, religious freedom has no space in the public sphere.

Therefore, one can say: The legal situation of the religious bodies in the PRC is one that allows them access to the public only if the government approves it. Whereas church-related social services are granted what looks like huge spaces to engage freely because their activities are regarded to be in alignment with the common good, congregations are more or less softly forced to confess their commitment to the country by becoming a member of the state-sanctioned "two institutions", the Three-Self Patriotic Movement (TSPM) and the Chinese Christian Church (CCC).

---

[6] "No one may make use of religion to engage in activities that disrupt public order, impair the health of citizens or interfere with the educational system of the state. Religious bodies and religious affairs are not subject to any foreign domination." (ibid.).

[7] Yang, Fenggang, *Religion in China: Survival and Revival under Communist Rule* (Oxford University Press 2011), 78. Document 19 itself says: "We Communists are atheists and must unremittingly propagate atheism."

[8] Yang, op. cit. (note 7), 84. The religions are not regarded as threats of the same kind, but distinguished as those that could spark ethnicity issues (Islam in Western China and Buddhism in Tibet) and those that have a tendency for "peaceful subversion" with ideas alien to China, Christianity. For the history of the regulation of the churches in China see Yang, op. cit (note 7), Chapter IV "Regulating Religion under Communism", 63-84.

[9] This is the reason why so many house churches exist and even announce their worship services on the internet. But, overall, they lack an official status.

[10] On the discussion of "public" and "theology" in China see Zhibin Xie, "Why Public and Theological? The Problem of Public Theology in the Chinese Context", *International Journal of Public Theology* 11 (2017), 381-404.

ACADEMIC DISCOURSE

Since the legal situation of the religions in the PRC is totally dependent on the interpretation of the freedom of religion by the government, it comes with a certain surprise that there is such a thing like Public Theology.[11]

This is possible, since there exists an academic discourse on religion and on Christianity and on its relationship to the public sphere. Although this discourse is perceived to deal with mostly cultural, and not political questions, the freedom to speak out is sometimes stunning.

A special interest has been given to scholars on Christian religion and their relationship towards churches. The term "cultural Christian" was adopted by some of them to express their focus on the intellectual aspect of Christian religion, somehow distancing themselves from an ecclesial approach to Christian theology.

Has this anything to do with the issues of the public sphere? Obviously, and not necessarily because academic positions have a more promising outlook than church positions in terms of economic or social standing. Scholarly debate can contribute to a discourse on the role of religions regarding the public sphere that can be understood by everybody regardless of their religious background.

To speak of religions and also of Christianity in terms of "culture" allows to discuss their function for the common good in a way that even diehard Marxists find necessary. At the same time, it is not due to the "inner truth" of the religions that they draw such attention, and also not due to their "historic relevance", at least in terms of Christianity. But it is because religions are a social reality and already publicly visible. Without the existing churches in China that are attractive to Chinese nationals, Christianity would perhaps draw as much public attention as Hinduism—close to none.

THE ROLE OF REGISTRATION FOR THE RECOGNITION OF THE CHURCHES

Officially recognized Protestant congregations belong to the "two institutions", the CCC and TSPM. The role of these institutions is debated among Protestants in a similar way to that of the equivalents on the Catholic side. The advantages of being registered consist in a more secure legal status that e. g. allows official visits by Hong Kong institutions and also to let

---

[11] Two of the main publications on "Public Theology" in the Chinese context are in English and by non-Chinese publishers. Yet, they contain a lot of names of scholars that live and teach in the PRC.

students participate in theological programs in Hong Kong. The question remains: How independent can a church be if it—by definition—needs to keep up the belief that what is good for the country, is also good for the church, and vice versa? On the other hand, one could ask what kinds of objectives congregations follow if their efforts if they do not result in the common good.

Obviously, these questions are asked all over the world. But in the PRC, they are inevitable, mainly because the definition of the country and its relationship to religious bodies are determined by the monopoly of the CCP. Remarkably, some congregations are seeking to register directly, without being embodied to the CCC and TSPM. Is that due to "dogmatic" reasons? Is the goal to achieve a legal status without what would be perceived as an organizational merger? We cannot tell yet. But it sounds as if the situation is changing also in this respect. There could be more than one way of legal and therefore public recognition for congregations.

PUBLIC THEOLOGY IN HONG KONG:
QUESTIONS IN RELATION TO THE POLITICAL DEBATE ON RELIGION IN PRC

In the political sphere, Beijing already exhibits measures in Hong Kong that cannot but be addressed as authoritarian when it comes to freedom of opinion and speech that are regarded as threats to the political order. It is no wonder that many citizens of Hong Kong are not only concerned but also try to figure out possible political scenarios for the future of their beloved SAR. Localism is voiced out as a major concept that allows different grades of independence.[12] In this context, even for those who are cautious about criticizing the given political order, it is a question that must be raised: How political must theology be in a minority situation when its participation in the public sphere is at stake?

Does it really suffice to point out the positive effects of Christian religion for the welfare of the society? How much control is to be exercised on freedom of assembly and presence in the public to avoid clashes of religious groups and guarantee negative religious freedom? When does official control become a factor that strangulates the vitality of religions?

These questions are not new at all. Yet, they come to new prominence because the PRC needs to counterbalance its ideas of a modern secularized

---

[12] Lap Yan Kung, "In Search of True-ness: Dialogue Between Political Localism and Theological Ecumenism in Post-Umbrella-Movement", *International Journal of Public Theology* 11 (2017), 431-454.

state with a rising number of adherents to religious groups that fill the spiritual void resulting from economic and social changes, and because Hong Kong is to become a part of that future.

In terms of Hong Kong itself, these questions are connected to a variant of the post-colonialism debate that puts everything from "the West" under suspicion of "foreign influence". In fact, all of the Christian churches in Hong Kong have not only been founded by—at least originally—overseas missionary activities but their majority is still closely connected to foreign churches. There is no explicit "patriotic movement" church in Hong Kong that is more indebted to the CCP than to other sister churches. In this respect, there is a striking conflict of systems between Hong Kong and the PRC. The churches within the PRC must comply with an understanding that sets the alignment with the political order higher than the solidarity with any other group within the political order, even if their rights be taken away.

It seems that the current discussion on non-registered churches in the PRC does not take fully into account the possible subversive character of this act of "public disobedience". Could it be that Hong Kong "localists" have much more in common with the "house churches" in the PRC than is commonly seen? At the same time, a cooperation with the non-registered churches results in official isolation. If one considers the fact that there are not many students of theology that are originally from Hong Kong and that the numbers of programs in Putonghua have surged in all institutions, one might also see the necessity of cooperation with the state-sanctioned religious institutions of the PRC. In this regard, the theological institutions that have their mission in educating Chinese ministers will most probably fully comply with the political order of the PRC—without raising too much criticism.

Moreover, it is true that Hong Kong faces several social problems that have nothing to do with the influence of the PRC: Excessive social inequality, the lack of positive perspectives for many young people, the marginalization of non-European immigrants etc. Is the liberal system the best way to address these challenges or does it only fuel competitive egoism?

It is hard to find one answer that fits all. On the other hand, one must admit that Hong Kong is a peaceful pluralistic society in which religious freedom is truly a common good.

And until now, there is a chance to speak out. Maybe it is good to change the perspective: Not only Hong Kong might be an irritation to the PRC that is actually a chance for it; a chance for integration in a way that allows plurality, but also the other way round. At least in terms of public theology.

The Church and Social Justice: The Peaceful Struggles of Minority Christians in Myanmar

Samuel Ngun Ling

Myanmar has existed as an independent kingdom for thousands of years. It has always been proud of the diversity of its culture, traditions and values. However, Myanmar came under British colonial rule in the nineteenth century. The history of Burma's independence is the history of the peoples' long-term struggle, resistance and rebellion against British political dominance and cultural imperialism. It was during the British colonial period that patriotism and nationalism intensified in the souls of Myanmar's people.

There are four things that make Myanmar a special land of interest in the eyes of outsiders today: (1) peoples' struggles for democracy; (2) religious and ethnic conflicts; (3) economic and environmental crises; and (4) the re-building of the nation through dialogue on peace and reconciliation. The term "peoples" in this paper refers to all nationalities and ethnic groups who are residing in the Republic Union of Myanmar.

The Union of Myanmar is made up of 135 ethnic groups of which there are eight major ethnic groups such as *Kachin, Kayah, Kayin, Chin, Bamar* (Burmans), *Mon, Rakhine* and *Shan*. According to a census conducted in 2014 by the Myanmar government, the minority ethnic population numbers more than fifteen or twenty million out of the total population of fifty-three million in Myanmar today. Buddhists form a majority of the population with 89.8 percent of the population, while the Christian minority stands at 6.3 percent, Muslims at 2.3 percent, Hindus 0.5 percent, animists 0.8 percent, others 0.2 percent and atheists 0.1 percent.[1]

---

[1] See www.radioaustralia.net,au/burmese and also See Ministry of Information, Union of Myanmar: Facts and Figures 2002 (March, 2002), 5.

STAGES IN MYANMAR'S POLITICAL HISTORY

Myanmar has come through several stages of crucial political transitions.

First stage: Myanmar had a monarchical rule from the early eleventh century to late nineteenth century, until 1885. The nation experienced three Anglo-Burmese wars during British colonial rule, in 1824, 1852 and 1885. The last Burmese monarch, King Thibaw, was dethroned in 1885 when the whole country became a colony of the British Indian Empire. Thus, Burma was administered as a province of the British Indian Empire until 1937. Burma began to receive Protestant missions, particularly American Baptists, beginning with the arrival of Adoniram Judson and his wife, Ann Judson, in 1813.

Second Stage: Myanmar experienced a long colonial rule under the British Indian Empire, which lasted for 124 years from 1824. The country regained independence from the British in 1948. During this colonial period, Burmese Buddhist nationalist movements developed, while Christianity and Christians came to be viewed as part of Western imperialist or expansionist three M scheme—Merchant, Military and Mission. Because of their long and militant stance as part of Western colonialism, Christian movements in Myanmar remain under a cloud of suspicion.

Third Stage: From 1948 to 1962, Burma experimented with a parliamentary democracy system under the first Prime Minister of Burma, U Nu. In August 1961, Buddhism became the state religion of Burma. This action prompted severe oppositions from religious and ethnic minorities, especially Christians and Muslims, leading to religious conflict. The combination of religious and ethnic conflicts led to the formation of Kachin Independence Army (KIA) and Karen National Union (KNU) insurgencies, largely Christian movements.

Fourth Stage: The purpose of the military coup of 1962, led by General Ne Win, who became military dictator, was to prevent further disintegration of the Union of Burma due to the divisions along religious lines with a Buddhist majority holding power over minority religions. It was at that time that the ethnic insurgencies that are still actively fighting the government today first today rose up. The military regime ruled the country for about three decades under the so-called "Burmese Way to Socialism" until 1988. During this long period of mismanagement and corruption by the military regime, socialism failed to bring prosperity and peace to the country, and Myanmar today remains one of the poorest countries in the world. The Socialist Constitution proposed in 1973 and confirmed in 1974 provided freedom of religion for all citizens. Since then, however, the interactions

specific contexts. To bring this thematic area to the conference and to open up for a dialogue between gender conscious theology and public theology is—together with global partners—the Church of Sweden's specific contribution to this conference. Institutions of theological education and research can be exemplary spaces for addressing sensitive issues in society and even related to family life. They are forums and have methodologies for opening up inclusionary spaces for meaningful exchange and critical thinking.

As representatives of the Church of Sweden at the conference, which took place at a critical time, we are convinced that this reflection will give us the possibility for a theological exchange that deepens our understanding of the churches' role in the public space. Our hope is that we will go forwards challenged and enriched by different perspectives and complex answers, even by new questions.

The following words of blessing by an unknown author sum up very well what public theology, and the public witness of the churches, is all about and could be a heading for the coming days: "May God bless you, granting you discomfort when confronted with easy answers, half-truth and superficial relationships, so that you may live out of the depth of your heart."

RESPONDING TO SEXISM

Resisting sexism theologically

Kirsi Stjerna

Perspectives and roots of persistence

Rising streams of populism, nationalism and extremism go hand in hand with racism, sexism and multiplied expressions of injustice—all of which hurt women in particular ways. Christian faith, including its Lutheran expressions, faces new, unimagined challenges today as compassionate wisdom and critical moral compasses are needed to re-build a world where equality and freedom are a reality—also for women.

This text reflects on persistence in the face of lingering misogyny, and considers sexism in its various expressions as sinful because it prevents women from experiencing the freedom Lutheran theology promises as a reality for every child of God. In addition to naming partners for the #MeToo movement from as far back as the sixteenth century, the text will also present an action plan for gender justice that draws on a draft statement from the Evangelical Lutheran Church in America (ELCA). In the end, Luther's theology is highlighted as a resource for Lutherans taking gender injustice into the public sphere where the gospel of freedom faces populist propaganda, in order to end violence against women.

She persisted!

When re-addressing Lutheran history and theological tradition from the perspective of women's experience of resistance, we could start by remembering the powerful persisting women from the sixteenth century.[1] The Lutheran tradition of persisting and resisting injustice has deep roots and deserves to be noted.

Lady Argula von Grumbach (1492-1563/68?) from Bavaria, Luther's friend, broke the boundaries set for women in her time by acting against the injustice she witnessed. At risk to her own wellbeing, she boldly rose to defend a young man persecuted for his faith, and to defend Luther and his theology as "Christian" theology. She was a lone woman challenging an all-male Roman Catholic university. She drew on Scripture for her authority—as did Luther. She spoke out from her experience as a woman, expressing her concern for justice, all the while defending her experience and perspective as a woman.

She defended her public theological discourse as "no woman's chit chat" and insisted that she was "speaking the truth" and that people should listen! Argula—"a wrinkly whore and desperado", as she was slandered by her male opponents—experienced persecution (physical, financial and emotional). Luther, with evident empathy, called her the valiant lonely hero of faith all Christians should emulate![2] Her widely circulated letters demonstrate her profound biblical understanding, combined with her conviction that a woman's experience counts, and that the gospel demands truth telling from all Christians, even at the risk of "losing a limb"[3].

Similarly, in the other corner of the emerging Protestant world, Argula's contemporary and fellow (proto) feminist Marie Dentiere (1495-1561), endured the fury of Calvin and others who found the vocal "diabolical" woman annoying when she was "meddling" with the Scriptures and preaching from street corners "unauthorized". In her "In Defense of Women", Dentiere argued that women should have equal rights to men in the church. Based on Scriptural evidence, women had not betrayed Jesus. Quite the contrary was the case. For instance, she noted, women had been the ones standing at the empty tomb following the resurrection. Dentiere's feisty writing meant memory of her was all but erased for a long time. However, her name was recently added to the Strasbourg Wall of the Reformers.[4]

---

[1] Kirsi Stjerna, "Reformation Revisited—Women's Voices in the Reformation" in *The Ecumenical Review* 69:2 (Summer 2017), 201-214; Kirsi Stjerna, "Mulheres e Reforma", in *Coisas do gênero: revista de estudos feministas em teologia e religião* vol. 3:2 (São Leopoldo: Faculdades EST, 2017), 36-48.

[2] See Luther on Argula, *WABr* IV:706, II:509; Kirsi Stjerna, *Women and the Reformation* (Malden, Mass: Blackwell, 2008), 79.

[3] See Peter Matheson, *Argula von Grumbach: A Woman's Voice in the Reformation* (Edinburgh: T&T Clark, 1995), and Stjerna, op. cit. (note 2), chapter 6.

[4] See Mary McKinley, *Epistle to Marguerite de Navarre* (Chicago: University of Chicago Press, 2004). Kirsi Stjerna, "Women and Theological Writing During the

Von Grumbach and Dentiere are just two of the female ancestors of the faith and Protestant theologians who persisted in articulating a theology for justice from the point of view of women and with a particular eye to human experience and Reformed theology. As early as the sixteenth century, they argued for women's right to theologize and interpret the Scriptures. We can only imagine their surprise if they knew about the struggles women still face today with the patriarchy's hold on all parts of church life and theology, and in the public sphere. In terms of our gender justice work today, it makes sense to know the female faith ancestors—many of whom were martyrs in one way or another. This is also important for getting the narrative right about the Reformation, and for assessing its impact on the lives of women as well as men.

Why is this aspect important for the churches fighting injustice and violent expressions of populism? Because, it makes sense to have a critical and compassionate—and inclusive—understanding of the roots and seeds we are dealing with. Which of those roots still hold us and which seeds are worth sowing? Related justice work involves explicitly naming women (many of whom remain nameless even today), who have operated, persistently, from the margins with a deep concern for justice. It is also spiritually and mentally important to know that we stand on the shoulders of our female faith ancestors whose presence we call upon when we continue in the footsteps of Christians proclaiming the gospel of freedom.

#MeToo—Lutherans too

The #MeToo movement[5] that made global waves in 2017 began as a support group for women of color who were survivors of sexual violence. It gained worldwide visibility as women in the entertainment industry in the United States of America began exposing the ugly truth to the whole world: even women in some of the most privileged locations, entertainers with opulent resources, have been subjected to sex crimes, blatant misogyny and illegal sexist behaviors. "Enough," said these women in the limelight, even protesting, using their privileged positions on the podium at the annual Academy Awards ceremony, the Oscars. This was a momentous moment: famous women—in

---

Reformation," Journal of Lutheran Ethics, 3 January 2012, http://elca.org/JLE/Articles/160?_ga=1.210577301.1686117201.1483478558.

[5] https://metoomvmt.org/ With Tarana Burke, the #MeToo movement started in 2006 to help women survivors of sexual violence, mostly persons of color initially. Since 1998, at least 17.7 million such crimes have been reported. The movement gained global visibility with the revelations about powerful predatory Hollywood men.

their way being imprisoned as movie stars, seemingly embodying perfection, while still needing to play hard ball in the business—were willing to share humiliating stories in order for the world to become a safe place for women. The world is still not a safe place for women.

This is a Reformation concern. The #MeToo movement could be considered a Reformation movement: people rising from surprising places to demand changes, to expose the truth, and to risk themselves for the sake of justice. The most powerful cries for "stop this" have so far not come from church leaders. It started with people who had experienced hurt in a misogynist, sexist culture, and who yearned for freedom from that, for themselves and for others. The #MeToo is a grassroots call to struggle, to name expressions of the sins of sexism/misogyny that fester under our very own eyes. These brave women have not been naming misogyny as a theological concern per se; that is the task of the church and its theologians.

Where does the Lutheran church in the United States stand on this issue? The ELCA has just, on the heels of the great Reformation anniversary year 2017, launched a draft statement on gender justice issues, titled *Faith, Sexism and Justice: A Lutheran Call to Justice*.[6]

Since the Churchwide Assembly voted to launch the study, it has taken ten years to get to this stage. Thirteen statements on other issues took priority. The Task Force on "Women and Justice: One in Christ" has drafted a holistic statement that reflects experiences women have had in church, society and the private sector. While critiquing Lutheran tradition for its past failures,[7] the draft statement envisions a way forward towards a more just world for women, with a call to concrete commitments from Lutheran churches: nine commitments for the societal changes and five for changes in the church.

After naming "Our Common Foundation", the document lists seven theses for the "Core Convictions", followed by five theses on "Analysis of Patriarchy and Sexism". Then the nine theses on "Resources for Resisting Patriarchy and Sexism" are followed by ten theses on "Response to God's Work: Call to Action and New Commitments in Society". After the last seven theses on "Response to God's Work: Call to Action and New Commitments Regarding the Church", the draft ends with a vision of "Hopes for Justice".

---

[6] http://download.elca.org/ELCA%20Resource%20Repository/Social_Statement_DRAFT_on_Women_and_Justice.pdf Feedback solicited until September 2018.

[7] The Fall 2018 issue of *Dialog: A Journal of Theology* is dedicated to the issues of women, body, and gender justice. Guest edited by Kris Kvam and Kirsi Stjerna, it includes responses to the ELCA's social statements from Marcia Blasi, Rhiannon Graybill, Jessica Crist, Man-Hei Yip, coordinated by Mary Streufert. Further, the issue of body and gender justice is addressed by Else Marie Wiberg Pedersen, Jennifer Hockenbery Dragseth, Marty Stortz, Scott McDougall, and Kirsi Stjerna.

The core convictions behind the draft document is the affirmation that "all people are created equal and are endowed with certain inalienable rights" and that "God creates humanity in diversity, encompassing a wide variety of experiences, identities, and expressions, including sex and gender".[8] Further, "This call to justice specifically means that we seek equity and justice for women and girls and others who experience oppression due to sexism and patriarchy"[9] .

The statement calls for a commitment:

" that diverse, gendered bodies be respected... First steps toward this goal are laws that do not deprive anyone of their human and civil rights"

"for the eradication of gender-based violence, including rape and sexual assault, by acknowledging both personal responsibility and the systemic aspects of such violence"

"for portrayals of people in entertainment, media, and advertising that do not objectify or stereotype"

"for medical research, health care delivery, and access to health care services, including reproductive health care"

"for economic policies, regulations, and practices that enhance equity and equality for women and girls"

"for services and legal reforms that attend to the particular needs of women, girls, and boys who are physically and economically vulnerable due to migration and immigration"

"for multi-faceted understandings of social and economic roles so that our human traits ... or callings ... are not prescribed by gender or sex"

"for resources for families and communities that empower parents ... to nurture, protect, and provide for their household in ways that do not reinforce gender-based stereotypes"

"for an increase in women's participation in local, state, and national politics."[10]

Furthermore, the document extends an invitation to do the following theological work:

(31) "Promote scriptural translation and interpretation that support gender justice, acknowledge the patriarchal context in which the Scriptures were written, and reject the misuse of Scripture to support sexist attitudes and patriarchal structures."

(32) "Promote theological reflection that is attentive to the gender-based needs of the neighbor."

---

[8] See *Faith, Sexism and, Justice: A Lutheran Call to Action*, ELCA, 2019, 2.

[9] Ibid, 3.

[10] Ibid, 7.

(33) "Use inclusive language for humankind and inclusive and expansive language for God. Encourage the use of language for God that expands rather than limits our understanding of God's goodness and mystery. In particular, we support developing liturgies, hymns, prayers, and educational materials that broaden our language beyond primarily male images. This practice follows the Scriptures' witness that God is wholly other and transcends human categories of sex and gender. Therefore, metaphors and images for God should be drawn from the lives of women and men, from nature, and from humanity in all its diversity to speak of the fullness and beauty of God."

(34) "Develop and support more extensive policies and practices within the ELCA that promote the authority and leadership of all women within this church in all its expressions."

(35) "Promote changes that are economically just, including equal pay..."

(36) "Seek and encourage faithful discernment and, where possible, joint action ... on issues of patriarchy and sexism."[11]

AT THE ROOT OF THE ISSUE: GOD-TALK

It is worth noting the attention given in the document to God-language and the theological reflection on central God-humanity questions. This attention is important because theology works with language and much of the church life and liturgy, hymns, prayers and imagination operate within language(s). With English and its gender-specific pronouns, the commitment to inclusivity goes to the deepest of theological concepts and perceptions.

Replacing "he/she" pronouns shuffles inherent power dynamics in theological discourse. It opens possibilities to view/hear/experience/conceptualize the divine and the meaning of Jesus in expansive ways. In the document, the doctrine of Trinity[12] and the maleness of Jesus are named as areas for critical reflection, with the premise that "metaphors and images for God should be drawn from the lives of women and men, from nature, and from humanity in all its diversity to speak of the fullness and beauty of God."[13]

Because of the well documented and deeply rooted androcentricity of Christian theological language, the question of inclusive language opens a

---

[11] Ibid., 7.

[12] Contemporary feminist theologians', such as Elizabeth Johnson's (She Who Is), explorations on God and God language rest on the pioneering work of women like Catherine Mowry LaCugna, and American theologians Rosemary Radford Ruther (Sexism and God Talk) and Sally McFague (Models of God).

[13] *Faith, Sexism, and Justice: A Lutheran Call to Action*, ELCA, 2019, 7.

Pandora's box. Behind the lingering efforts to ridicule discussions on the importance of inclusive language may well hide an implicit bias in favor of androcentric, male-experience-based and linguistically consolidated patriarchal views on the divine. This bias is, perhaps, exacerbated by the fact that Jesus, as far as we know, was a man, biologically speaking.[14] In her own way, the medieval mystic Julian of Norwich suggested gender-bending ways to look beyond Jesus' male biology to his mothering nature, taking freedoms from he/she pronouns when it comes to God. With all the evolutions in our languages and conceptions regarding gender, we could expect that our theological languages have fermented enough to stand with Julian of Norwich. One reason why we are still debating the matter may be that much of the doctrinal texts published by Christian theologians so far has been written by men, whereas women's efforts, especially those explicitly naming gender and feminist questions, have been dismissed as not doctrinally significant.

Regardless of where we stand on this matter personally or within our constituencies, ample evidence suggests that male-exclusive language and views on God influence how we see humanity, human relations and power structures. In a distorted space, where male experience dominates, violence against women appears permissible, and it would be irresponsible to claim that theology and theological language were irrelevant to that.

> In our efforts to ensure gender justice in this world and to suffocate misogynism/sexism, and its expressions in violence, Christian theologies need to name the holiness in the "being a woman", including in her body that shouts, "I am sacred", made in the image of God—who is neither male, nor female. Our God-language and theological expressions need to explicate this as a starting point towards gender justice, and for a theology that speaks to and with women's experience. This calls for a fundamental theological reform.

Partnering with Luther

The sixteenth century reformer Martin Luther can be an ally in our efforts to construct reformed theologies that support gender justice and equality. He said reformers must react when witnessing human pain because of a distorted or unsatisfactory explication of the gospel of freedom; a true reformer is a person who holds the church and its theology accountable when they fail to support people in their daily lives and instead limit their opportunities to live an authentically Christian life of freedom.

---

[14] See Julian of Norwich, *Showings, Classics of Western Spirituality* (Chicago: University of Chicago, 1997).

What would Luther, the reformer, say if he read the news from today? Would he be outraged by the silence from the church(es) in the face of the violent expressions of misogyny? Would he stand up to preach against the hyper-sexist/-sexual culture that is toxic for our children? Would he stop to consider how his "freedom theology" applies in women's lives? Would he proceed to write a new catechism, one on sex, for the sake of our children?

If Luther was listening to our news, he would surely observe the war against women's bodies and freedoms. Would he make an explicit connection between the impact of theologies on women and their bodies, and the (societal, political) freedoms versus violence vis-à-vis women's experience? Could we not imagine him exposing the connections between patriarchal theologies and gender injustices, and naming the matters on gender injustices as both political and theological urgencies—as sins—as should we?

It is illuminating to study Luther's deliberation on gender/sex and women's bodies, particularly at the end of his life, when he lectured on the Book of Genesis. All his "expertise" in gynecology and what he (thought) he knew about women is expressed in his interpretation of the fundamental creation and fall stories. In addition, with an astonishingly woman-friendly approach, he unfolds how God's salvation work for humanity was promised and carried to its fruition through the bodies of women, physically speaking.

LUTHER'S GENESIS COMMENTARY AS A RESOURCE

For his time, Luther pays unusual attention to the theological understanding of women and their bodies, and to relations between the genders. His interpretation of Genesis, chapters 1 to 3, offers insights on gender and sex that can benefit our deliberations.

Luther read Genesis 1:27 to prove that both male and female were created in the image of God. Luther appreciated the mystery of creation reflected in the texts, particularly Genesis 1: 26-2: and 2: 21-25 and used them to explain God's rationale for creating the two sexes, instead of just one. Disagreeing with some of his ancient and medieval predecessors, Luther underscored the spiritual equality of the woman created from the first human's rib, while noting other differences in their gendered being and vocations.[15]

There is a lot in Luther's sixteenth century theological-anthropological imagination that makes a twenty-first century feminist uneasy, such as: women being "nests" for their husbands; men leading and women serving;

---

[15] See Luther, in *The Annotated Luther*, vol. 6 of *The Annotated Luther*, vols 1-6, general editors Hans Hillerbrand, Kirsi Stjerna, Timothy Wengert (Minneapolis: Fortress Press, 2015-2017), 116.127-29.13-132.139-140.

gender-specific vocations in marriage and motherhood; women being created (primarily) for God's procreational purposes. At the same time, the fundamental points Luther makes about women's created and spiritual equality are worthy of attention, and to be recognized for their novelty in Luther's time.

In addition, Luther's interest in the bodies of Eve and Mary, both considered as the recipients and bearers of God's saving Word for humanity, is important to study further. Rich leads can be found in Luther's deliberation on the link between Eve, as the recipient of the first gospel—the promise of the seed that would crush the serpent—and Mary, as the bearer of the seed that would deliver humanity. Luther underscored how God's plan entailed that the savior be born from a woman's seed with no male intervention. Luther's attention to the woman's seed is noteworthy, given his context where scientific knowledge of "whose seed does what" was still very much evolving. Luther's point was this: Eve had heard and Mary delivered the promise God revealed to a woman: Whereas Eve heard that "In your seed shall all the gentiles be blessed" (Gen 22:18),[16] "[Mary] found the promise fulfilled in herself".[17]

These are just a few indications of how Luther's voice remains relevant as Lutheran theology focuses on gender justice. There is much more to say about Luther and women, and gender equality. The time has come for a new focus in Luther's theology, where women's bodies are considered holy, equal, and part of God's plans, not only for procreation, but, more importantly, for redemption, and as the foundation on which the church is built.

CONCLUSIONS

Lutherans have a reputation to uphold as a reforming body of believers whose theology provides a rationale for justice and freedom, inclusivity and equality.

Not just Luther, but our sixteenth century faith mothers, set a model for what it means to be a reformer in one's own place, and they had specific expectations regarding freedom in the lives of women. It is now time for us to meet those expectations, for the sake of our daughters, and our sons.

---

[16] That Jesus Christ Was Born a Jew, in *WA* 11:324-336; LW 45:199-299; in *The Annotated Luther*, vol. 5, 410. The text continues the themes from the 1521 Magnificat (*WA* 7:544-604; *The Annotated Luther*, vol. 4), underscoring Mary's special role in salvation history, and as the proof for God's promise.

[17] "For the text [Gen 3:15] clearly states that he will be the seed of woman." (*The Annotated Luther*, vol. 5, 407-408).

Instead of continuing to argue about the traditional theological hang-ups that have preoccupied Lutherans for centuries, we could follow Luther's steps in naming the forces behind human suffering today, and then gather our theological arguments to reform. In this, we could take freedom as our focal point.

Freedom, a core human value, lends a crucial perspective for unfolding Luther's fundamental theological insight on "freed-by-grace" and its different ramifications in the real world.

Today, the challenges are many. In Luther's world, the spiritual abuse he identified was the selling of indulgences. In our world, the abuse of human bodies in "human trafficking"[18] should motivate us to reforming actions.

This modern-day slavery is not only a societal issue but a theological urgency. Out of about four million people trafficked around the world each year, some two million of them are children, involving girls between ages five and fifteen; eighty percent of the victims are women. Much joint effort is required to reform our culture and mindset(s) that, based on the evidence, are open to sex trafficking and abuse of human bodies. In addition to strong advocacy for the victims, substantial critique and reforming theological work is needed on prevalent notions on sex, gender, sexuality and power.[19] Human trafficking is a tragic and glaring example of suffering where the churches cannot stay silent. That would not be the way of Luther or the Reformation mothers, who in their own time articulated and risked for the theology of and for freedom.

---

[18] Commercial sexual exploitation involves "the recruitment, harboring, transportation provision or obtaining of a person for the purposes of a commercial sex act". See *Victims for Trafficking and Violence Protection Act of 2000.* "Human Trafficking", Polaris Project, http://www.polarisproject.org/human-trafficking/.

[19] See Kirsi Stjerna, "A Lutheran Feminist Critique of American Child Protection Laws", in: Ron W. Duty and Marie A. Failinger (eds), *On Secular Governance: Lutheran Perspectives on Contemporary Legal Issues* (Grand Rapids, MI: Eerdmans 2016), 141-159.

Pentecostal Female Politicians, Populism and Reproduction of Wifely Submission in the Public Spheres. Religio-Cultural Discourse in Zambia's Political Spheres

Mutale M. Kaunda and Chammah J. Kaunda

Introduction

This chapter maintains that Zambian Pentecostal women politicians utilize the religious discourse of wifely submission in order to exercise religio-political power and to negotiate male-dominated politics in Zambia. This reinforces populism. Employing African feminist nego-missiologization theory (explained below), this chapter argues that Pentecostal female politicians, though successful in gaining power, have failed to resist patriarchal power. In this, Zambia mirrors a challenge present in other global contexts. Women break through the patriarchal ceiling into positions of power, but then fail to challenge patriarchal attitudes, and instead conform to them and at worst, perpetuate them.

This chapter focuses on two notable Pentecostal women politicians in Zambia–Rev. Godfridah Sumaili and Dr Liya Mutale. Zambian President Edgar Lungu nominated Sumaili on 15 September 2016 as the first minister of national guidance and religious affairs. She is a pastor at a neo-Pentecostal Church called Bread of Life Church International (BLCI), under one of the most popular preachers, Bishop Joe Imakando. BLCI is the largest single congregation in Zambia, with more than 12,000 members.

During the 2016 presidential campaign, Mutale, a medical doctor and ordained Pentecostal clergyperson, was instrumental in forming a campaign wing called Christians for Edgar Lungu, which became defunct after Lungu won the election. This Pentecostal network mobilized people of faith into a populist movement, promoting a Pentecostal nationalist agenda based on conservative resistance to abortion, homosexuality and the "decline" of traditional family values. This form of populism not only emphasized organizational, economic and political issues but also addressed many conservative religious subjects. Mutale was rewarded with the position of permanent secretary—Ministry of Tourism and Art.

This chapter draws on data[1] collected in Zambia between 2016 and 2017. The study engaged 250 Pentecostal men and women through open-ended interviews as well as questionnaires in order to understand Pentecostal views regarding the declaration of Zambia as a Christian nation. Issued by President Frederick Chiluba in 1991, the declaration was enshrined in the preamble of the national constitution in 1996 and reaffirmed by President Lungu in 2015. The question is, in what ways are Pentecostal women politicians in Zambia deploying religious discourse to either reinforce or utilize populism and patriarchy?

ZAMBIAN PENTECOSTALISM AND GENDER

In Zambia, Pentecostalism has been instrumental in advocating for women's empowerment in the public sphere. Scholars have applauded Pentecostalism, arguing that it empowers women to reject their marginalization in the patriarchal society, and legitimizes ambitious women's achievement of economic, social, and political independence.[2] Recent research demonstrates that Pentecostalism offers a gender paradox, as it promotes gender equality, while simultaneously reinforcing male preeminence as divine order.[3] Pentecostals are less likely to engage in transforming structures of unequal gender relations[4]. Jennifer Cole observes that Pentecostalism defined the public role of

---

[1] The research was funded by the Nagel Institute for the Study of World Christianity, Calvin College, Grand Rapids, MI, which was funded by the John Templeton Foundation, West Conshohocken, PA.

[2] Charlotte Spinks, "Panacea or Painkiller? The Impact of Pentecostal Christianity on Women in Africa," *Critical Half* 1:1 (2015), 21–25.

[3] Adriaan van Klinken, "God's World Is Not an Animal Farm—Or Is It? The Catachrestic Translation of Gender Equality in African Pentecostalism," *Religion and Gender* 3:2 (2013): 240–58, at 250.

[4] Adriaan S. van Klinken, *Transforming Masculinities in African Christianity: Gender Controversies in Times of AIDS* (Farnham, UK: Ashgate, 2013); Chammah J. Kaunda, "Ndembu Cultural Liminality, Terrains of Gender Contestation: Reconceptualising

women less by transforming patriarchal structures "than by offering women an alternative source of authority, as well as an alternative set of practices, from which to forge social personhood and subjective sense of self"[5] within already defined structures. In other words, women are expected to seek their legitimation by inserting themselves within already defined social structures of gender and power. There is a clear tension between wifely/womanly submission to male authority in the home, and women's involvement in public spheres. Gender justice is seen to be based on submitting to male authority, especially at home, in maintaining the "divine order" imperative.[6] However, Mutale and Sumaili have been using the same notion of submission in a subtle way in order to execute power in the public sphere. Zambian women use submission subtly, even in marriages. Karla Poewe[7] noted that women in Zambia have a way of engaging a man to make him think he has made the decision when in essence women made the decision. Jane Soothill concludes that Pentecostal gender discourses do not "challenge the structures that reinforce and perpetuate gender inequalities"[8] at home or in public spaces. It positions women as gaining access to public spaces based on male merit. Yet, clearly Mutale rose to her position by navigating the Zambian political sphere herself, mobilizing the Pentecostals for Lungu.

POPULIST PENTECOSTALISM AND POPULIST POLITICS IN ZAMBIA

Pentecostalism has become a political force in Zambia[9]. The Pentecostals have positioned themselves as the chief guardians of the constitutional declaration that Zambia is a Christian nation. The declaration functions as a national foundation for Pentecostalism and populist politics in contemporary Zambian society. Pentecostals often appeal to the declaration

---

Zambian Pentecostalism as Liminal Space," *HTS Teologiese Studies* 73:3 (2017), https://doi.org/10.4102/hts.v73i3.3718.

[5] Cole, "The Love of Jesus Never Disappoints: Reconstituting Female Personhood in Urban Madagascar," *Journal of Religion in Africa* 42 (2012), 384–407, at 388.

[6] Jane E. Soothill, "The Problem with Women's Empowerment: Female Religiosity in Ghana's Charismatic Churches," *Studies in World Christianity* 16:1 (2010), 82–99, at 84.

[7] Karla Poewe, *Matrilineal Ideology: Male-Female Dynamics in Luapula, Zambia* (New York: Academic Press, 1981).

[8] Jane E. Soothill, *Gender, Social Change and Spiritual Power: Charismatic Christianity in Ghana* (Leiden and Boston: Brill, 2007), 63.

[9] Chammah J Kaunda, "'From Fools for Christ to Fools for Politicians': A Critique of Zambian Pentecostal Theopolitical Imagination," *International Bulletin of Mission Research* 41/4 (2017): 296–311.

to argue that a Christian president should rule Zambia. Most politicians, therefore, have utilized the declaration as a campaign strategy to appeal to Pentecostal longings for a Christian president.[10] This desire to have a Christian head of state worked to Mutale's advantage as she crossed borders between religious and political spheres. Because of current efforts of Pentecostalism to advance women's empowerment in the public sphere, Lungu chose to appoint a woman clergyperson as head of MNGRA. While he was interim president after President Michael Sata's death in office in 2016, Lungu positioned himself as a born-again Christian. During his campaign, pictures of Lungu in church or with clergy were constantly posted on social media, depicting him reading the Bible or kneeling in prayer.[11] The pictures and his public appearances in prayer meetings and services seem to have popularized him as the right candidate for Zambia's presidency, and Mutale formed a Pentecostal campaign for him. Utilizing her leadership role in the Pentecostal church, she mobilized numbers of Pentecostal Christians who rallied behind her and voted Lungu into power.

Zambian Pentecostalism has a strong populist inclination toward politics. Scholars have argued that populist politics have found a fertile ground within Pentecostalism, which is seen as a populist religion.[12] Cas Mudde and Cristobal Kaltwasser observe that, "conceptually, populism has no specific relationship to gender; in fact, gender differences, like all other differences within 'the people', are considered secondary [...] Yet populist actors do not operate in a cultural or ideological vacuum."[13] The societies within which populism operates are subject to gender dynamics. Hence, there is a need for feminist scrutiny of how populism operates and whose interests are promoted. Furthermore, when populism engages with religion, women often tend to be at the forefront because they form majority in religious groups. Scholars have noted how Zambian Pentecostalism is populated by women who are involved in the redeeming work of God in the world within their societies.[14]

---

[10] Chammah J Kaunda, "Christianising Edgar Chagwa Lungu: The Christian Nation, Social Media Presidential Photography and 2016 Election Campaign," *Stellenbosch Theological Journal* 4/1, (2018): 215–245.

[11] Ibid.

[12] Donald E. Miller & Tetsunao Yamamori, *Global Pentecostalism: The New Face of Christian Social Engagement* (Berkeley: University of California Press, 2007).

[13] Cas Mudde and Cristobal R. Kaltwasser, "Vox populi or vox masculini? Populism and Gender in Northern Europe and South America," *Patterns of Prejudice* 49:1-2 (2015): 16–36, https://doi.org/10.1080/0031322X. 2015.1014197.

[14] Chammah J. Kaunda, "Neo-Prophetism, Gender and 'Anointed Condoms': Towards a Missio Spiritus of Just- Sex in the African Context of HIV and AIDS," *Alternation* 23:2 (2016), 64–88.

African Feminist Nego-missiologization

Superficially, it would seem that Zambian Pentecostal gender discourse pushes women to promote men in political campaigns. However, a closer look would suggest that Zambian women are ingeniously getting into these political spaces themselves by utilizing their religious power. Female Pentecostal politicians are navigating the constitutional declaration by translating ecclesiastical authority into political acceptance. In the Zambian context, religio-cultural texts play major roles in reinforcing a populist stance that relegates women to the margins. Yet both Mutale and Sumaili used the same discourse that privileges male authority to break the glass ceiling for women in politics. African feminist nego-missiologization perceives culture as a vital component, because, too often, religion utilizes cultural resources to reinforce oppression against women.[15] It appears that Mutale and Sumaili used the same culture to become prominent politicians in Zambia. Nego-missiologization theory builds on Obioma Nnaemeka's concept of Nego-Feminism that she developed within "the foundation of shared values in many African cultures."[16] Nego-missiologization regards African feminist religio-cultural traditions as deeply entrenched within "the principles of negotiation, give and take, compromise, and balance."[17] Nego-missiologization understands incarnation as a divine paradigm for "give and take/exchange" and "cope with successfully/go around."[18] Jesus challenged social power relations through negotiated dialogue. The process of negotiated dialogue implies struggling against patriarchy and becoming aware when, where, and how to resist patriarchy. African feminist nego-missiologization "is an act that evokes the dynamism and shifts of a process as opposed to the stability and reification of a construct, a framework."[19] It understands the mission of God as a process of entering into a compromised and sinful world without compromising divine holiness (Hebrews 4:15). To what extent are Zambian female Pentecostal politicians able to negotiate unequal power relations without compromising the values of African feminist nego-missiological imaginations?

---

[15] Musimbi Kanyoro, *Introducing Feminist Cultural Hermeneutics: An African Perspective* (Sheffield: Sheffield Academic Press, 2002); Isabel Apawo Phiri and Sarojini Nadar, "What's in a Name? Forging a Theoretical Framework for African Women's Theologies," *Journal of Constructive Theology* 12:2 (2007), 5–23.

[16] Obioma Nnaemeka, "Nego-Feminism: Theorizing, Practicing, and Pruning Africa's Way," *Signs*, 29.2 (Winter 2004): 357-385, quote at 377-378.

[17] Nnaemeka, op. cit. (note 14), 378.

[18] Ibid.

[19] Ibid.

Zambian Female Pentecostal Politicians and Populism

As already stressed, while Pentecostalism in Zambia promotes women's involvement in the affairs of the nation, it also reinforces conservative gender roles. This view of the woman as a submissive partner in marriage has influenced how Pentecostal female politicians have conceptualized politics. Female politicians have equated the nation of Zambia to a home where the president is the father of the nation. From the perspective of African nego-missiologization, the home discourse is a dangerous ideology for African women and girls which must be resisted.[20] However, there is legitimacy in how Mutale and Sumaili have negotiated the public sphere that would otherwise not be keen on welcoming women.

It appears that these two women understand women's exclusion from both the public and private spheres and seek to stand in solidarity with their fellow women at the grassroots. They have, thus, sought to "house-nize" (make it into the house) the nation by granting Lungu the title "father of the nation", which must be understood as a negotiation tool. However, their notions of political morality are constructed from a conservative theology of wifely submission.[21] Mutale and Sumaili demand and practice submission to the president in order to access political power. Nonetheless, they use gained legitimacy in subtle ways, 'treading softly' around patriarchy before challenging it, transposing wifely submission into national politics. Mutale believes that submission to the president is a moral contribution that Pentecostals can make to politics:

> We come in with values of loyalty, we come in with submission, we come in with honoring authority. You know, I mean you can't go out there and insult the president. No, that's wrong. The Bible tells me that I should submit, honor authority. I should pray for my leaders. So, all those values that I bring with me from my spiritual life, I think they add value to the political arena.[22]

Holding high office grants Mutale a position from which she can boost the sociopolitical and economic emancipation of women in Zambia. However,

---

[20] Isabel Phiri and Sarojini Nadar, "'Going through the Fire with Eyes Wide Open': African Women's Perspective on Indigenous Knowledge, Patriarchy and Sexuality," *Journal for the Study of Religion* 22:2 (2009), 2– 22.

[21] This affirms that "populists strive for a society and a state that is firmly grounded in a shared moral system that encompasses private as well as political and economic institutions" (Christl Kessler and Jürgen Rutland, "Responses to Rapid Social Change: Populist Religion in the Philippines," *Pacific Affairs* 79:1 (2006), 73-96: 73).

[22] Dr Liya Mutale, interview with the author, Lusaka, 30 May 2016.

it is also a dangerous position. Unless she treads softly, she is likely to lose power. As representatives of Zambian women, Sumaili and Mutale have a responsibility for furthering gender and social justice. However, they only do that through negotiated dialogue with the authorities. Their preoccupation with submission as a negotiating tool can be turned against them. For example, Sumaili classifies her Pentecostal ministry in populist language and argues that just as a home has values, so should a nation.[23] Sumaili argues,

> Actually, the Lord Jesus has given us that structure. The man, you're the head of the family . . . and love your wife. Wife submit to your husband. Children obey your parents. Parents do not be harsh to your children. These are the biblical guidelines. The way in a nation ... a Christian nation means there has to be discipline . . . if you love your child, discipline your child.[24]

Sumaili appeals to the ordinary people of Zambia to regard president Lungu as the desired leader of the nation of Zambia and frames his authority in terms of the home. It is a man who first criticized Sumaili's "house-nization" of Zambia. Elias Munshya argues, "Zambia is not a home with a father and mother ruling over children in a household. The biblical model of a home cannot be extrapolated to the Zambian state. Zambia is a republic with a constitution that assigns roles to each branch of government."[25]

Mutale and Sumaili have demonstrated that while they are public figures, they also appreciate their positions as women, mothers and cultural custodians. African feminists grapple to find ways women can speak for those who cannot speak about their marginalization and struggles. In their way, Mutale and Sumaili succeed in this. They draw on the life-giving aspects of African religio-culture while rejecting the life-denying aspects, just as African feminists demand.

Mutale and Sumaili use Pentecostal belief and cultural practices to justify their moral understanding of politics. How they utilize culture and religion

---

[23] Joseph Mwenda and Stella Goma, "Sumaili Explains Her Plan for Religious Ministry" (9 April 2017), https://diggers.news/local/2017/04/09/sumaili-explains-her-plan-for-religious-ministry/.

[24] ZambiaBlogTalkRadio, "Rev. Godfridah Sumaili, Minister of National Guidance & Religious Affairs," http://www.blogtalkradio.com/zambiablogtalkradio/2017/05/20/rev-godfridah-sumaili-minister-of-national-guidance-religious-affairs (last accessed September 2, 2018).

[25] Elias Munshya, "When the State Becomes a False Prophet: How Rev. Sumaili's Views Threaten Zambia's Constitutionalism," Elias Munshya Blog (22 May 2017), https://eliasmunshya.org/2017/05/22/when-the-state-becomes-a-false-prophet-how-rev-sumailis-views-threaten-zambias-constitutionalism.

identifies them as empowered subservient women. These two women seem to be sitting in hot seats. They have no theological background to enable them to understand how to engage in politics theologically. Their lack of political theology means that they must rely on personal experience as a theological framework. This leads one to surmise that that African Pentecostal women politicians have made no clear contribution to transforming the political and gender structures upon which African governments are established.

CONCLUSION

The alliance of religio-political power that projects Lungu as the father and president of the nation as advanced by Pentecostal female politicians promotes the process of "house-nization" of Zambia. This process is based on the Pentecostal notion of wifely submission, which has invaded the political sphere, reinforcing gender dynamics patterned after the traditional husband-wife relationship. Mutale's and Sumaili's discourse of wifely submission is grounded on the African patriarchal model of distribution of power as expressed in the Pentecostal-traditional home paradigm. Their religio-political discourse of wifely submission promotes domestic forms of respect toward the president of the nation. Lungu's presidency is conceptualized in a traditional African and Pentecostal form of governance in which the citizens are treated as children. In this paradigm, the children (citizens) are not to question the leadership of their (father/pastor) president.

PUBLIC THEOLOGY, POPULISM AND SEXISM: THE HIDDEN CRISIS IN PUBLIC THEOLOGY[1]

Esther McIntosh

INTRODUCTION

Why do I claim that there is a crisis in public theology, and in what sense is it hidden? After all, public theology has been enjoying something of a revival in recent years, spearheaded by the Global Network of Public Theology (GNPT) and the associated *International Journal of Public Theology* (*IJPT*); in addition, an array of new centers for public theology has sprung up in various locations around the globe. However, those centers are predominantly named after and led by men, mostly white men; there is also a clear gender imbalance in the works referred to and published under the heading "public theology." This might not seem like a crisis, especially not a hidden one, if there are not many women working in this field and fewer still using the title "public theology". However, we need to dig a little deeper and ask why female theologians are not referred to or do not refer to themselves as public theologians, and, relatedly, we need to ask why male public theologians appear to be unconcerned by the lack of women's voices in this field. A male-dominated public theology structurally fails

[1] Presented at the "Churches as Agents for Justice and Against Populism: Public Theology in Global Intercontextual Dialogue" conference, 2-4 May 2018, Dietrich-Bonhoeffer-Haus, Berlin, Germany. I am grateful to Linda Thomas for critical comments on the issues of race and gender.

to engage with important public issues that are especially urgent in light of populist encroachments of democracy, minority rights, and equality.

THE EVIDENCE

I first encountered the GNPT at its initial triennial consultation in Princeton in 2007. At the time, I was working on a critique of the concept of sacrifice, specifically the way it serves to provide theological legitimization for domestic violence against women. In the previous year, the Church of England (CoE) had released a document entitled *Responding to Domestic Abuse*[2] in which it recognizes its own failures in allowing a masculinist interpretation of the divine to be used as justification for male domination, especially when this is accompanied by teaching on self-sacrifice that weighs more heavily on women than men. While these were welcome acknowledgements from the CoE, I do not believe that the document adequately counters the damage done by its teaching on these issues, since it continues to promote both male God-language and self-sacrifice.[3] During the consultation in Princeton, I was asked whether my work could really be considered to be public theology. I was taken aback by this question; after all, the GNPT refers to itself as "an academic research partnership that promotes theological contributions on public issues, especially those issues affecting the poor, [and] the marginalized,"[4] and the *International Journal of Public Theology (IJPT)*, which publishes papers from GNPT consultations, refers to "the growing need for theology to interact with public issues of contemporary society."[5] To my mind, domestic violence, and its apparent theological rationalization, is clearly both a theological and a public issue; moreover, since Christianity is a patriarchal religion and we live in patriarchal societies, violence against women is an issue affecting the marginalized.

I will return to intimate partner violence later, but first, in case my experience at the 2007 gathering might be dismissed as one anecdotal instance of the side-lining of women's concerns in public theology, let me

---

[2] The Archbishops Council, *Responding to Domestic Abuse: Guidelines for Those with Pastoral Responsibilities* (London: Church House Publishing, 2006).

[3] See Esther McIntosh, "The Concept of Sacrifice: A Reconsideration of the Feminist Critique," in *International Journal of Public Theology*, 1:2 (2007), 210-229.

[4] See "The Global Network for Public Theology," University of Chester, https://www.chester.ac.uk/node/15313 [last accessed 9 May 2018].

[5] See "International Journal of Public Theology," Brill, https://brill.com/view/journals/ijpt/ijpt-overview.xml [last accessed 9 May 2018].

elaborate on two further encounters. Several years after the consultation in Princeton in 2015, I was presenting a paper at the annual meeting of the American Academy of Religion (AAR) in Atlanta, Georgia, where I noticed a session, chaired by Dwight Hopkins, in which each of the papers employed the terminology "public theology" in their titles and/or abstracts. As I listened to the three papers in the session, delivered by young white academics, two male and one female, I became increasingly aware of the lack of diversity in the references they employed. Each paper cited between twenty and thirty scholars and all but one of the citations belonged to a white male academic. I asked the speakers whether they were aware of this monopoly and they responded with surprise: on the one hand, they had not noticed the lack of diversity in their sources, and, on the other hand, now that it had been pointed out, two of the speakers (one male) still did not think it was a problem, so long as they had presented a coherent argument.[6] As an analytic scholar, I am, of course, in favor of coherent arguments, but I do not regard this as a sufficient condition for contemporary scholarship. After decades of black theology and feminist theology, to continue to rely almost exclusively on the works of white men is to ignore the challenges that marginalized groups have levelled at mainstream theology and, hence, is to continue to perpetuate their marginalization. In effect, to carry on a theological conversation without including previously excluded groups in that conversation, is decidedly one-sided; it is talking to less than half of the interested population. Thus, even a coherent argument is only a partial argument if it sustains the status quo and considers only the dominant perspective. Furthermore, articles and publications in which authors demonstrate their awareness of the problem of gender-exclusive language by referring to "she" rather than "he" in their own fictional examples, while failing to read or cite any female scholars, reveal a profound lack of awareness of the deeper problem of public and academic recognition.

Jumping forward one year to the GNPT triennial in South Africa in 2016, it became apparent that all the keynote speakers were male (and mostly white); ironically, I was presenting a paper at this consultation on the missing voices that needed to be heard for "race, gender and sexual justice in public theology."[7] The organizers of the conference, having read and accepted my abstract, acknowledged my point and explained that they

---

[6] The other male speaker thanked me for pointing this out and agreed that it was an issue he needed to address. (Several members of the audience—female, male, ethnic minority and white—also expressed their gratitude.)

[7] For a fuller discussion of this topic, see Esther McIntosh, "'I Met God, She's Black': Racial, Gender and Sexual Equalities in Public Theology," in S. Kim and K. Day, eds, *A Companion to Public Theology* (Leiden: Brill, 2017), 298-324.

had invited two women, who were unable to attend. I have heard this explanation at many a conference: "We asked a woman, but she wasn't able to come," as if there are only one or two female theologians in the entire world. When I presented my paper, there was a room full of women in attendance (and a few men too). Most of the women in that room were giving short papers on weighty topics, such as the churches' involvement, both positive and negative, with survivors of rape during the conflict in Rwanda; any one of those women could have been invited to present a keynote address at that consultation, but they were overlooked. Several deep-seated biases are buried in the claim that "we invited a woman and she couldn't come." First, as with the aforementioned reference to papers that change "he" to "she" in illustrations but do not cite women, the inviting of only one woman shows a certain recognition of the need to consider gender balance and, yet, the inviting of *only one* woman betrays the shallowness of that recognition: conference organizers fail to take gender balance seriously when they are content to give up on their efforts after a single invitation. Second, the fact that none of the women present were considered as keynote speakers betrays an unconscious or implicit bias regarding *who* and *what* we take to be the significant voices and issues in the field (again, this bias is replicated in papers that cite only the usual white male suspects).

THE HIDDENNESS

This brings me to the hiddenness of the crisis, after which I will explain why I think this is a crisis and what steps I think public theology could and should be taking to address it. Following my experience at the GNPT consultation in Princeton, I proposed guest editing an issue of the *IJPT* exploring the nature of public theology from a feminist perspective. In the issue, Heather Walton explores her "distaste for most of what appears under the heading 'public theology.'"[8] Through her engagement with the work of Duncan Forrester and the Centre for Theology and Public Issues (CTPI) at the University of Edinburgh, she identifies a persistent reliance on a Habermasian notion of the public sphere as the site of communicative reason that reinforces the distinction between public and private; a distinction which feminists strongly dispute, because it assumes that bodily and domestic matters fall outside of the scope of reasoned discussion. On the contrary, as Carol Hanisch famously states: "the personal [or private]

---

[8] Heather Walton, "You Have to Say You Cannot Speak: Feminist Reflections Upon Public Theology," in *International Journal of Public Theology*, 4:1 (2010), 21-36 at 22.

is political."[9] If public theology aims to challenge politicians and church leaders to change public policy for the better, as it claims, it must take seriously the discrimination against women that takes place in church, academy, society *and* the home, in what are otherwise considered to be the public *and* the private or personal spheres. Consequently, drawing on the work of Denise Ackermann and Rebecca Chopp, Walton asserts that "public theology must include within its registers much more than rational discourse, if it is to approach the unbearable mystery of human suffering."[10]

Women's experiences and women's voices have not been heard by the rational discourse that is characteristic of the Habermasian public sphere and now also of public theology; furthermore, I believe that public theology has done little to comprehend or transform this omission. Public theologians have been largely silent on the matter of female ordination in the Anglican and Roman Catholic churches in the United Kingdom (UK) and the underrepresentation of female clergy in other denominations. Despite approving the ordination of women in 1992, the CoE did not approve female bishops until 2014, and even then, it retained its policy of allowing parishes to refuse to accept a female priest or bishop. Public theologians should be speaking out against this continued discrimination against women, and yet, when we turn our attention to what appears to be the received canon of public theologians, we find that the representation is overwhelmingly male and apparently uninterested in what are deemed to be "women's issues." How has public theology arrived at this juncture?

Influenced by Reinhold Niebuhr's and Robert Bellah's analyses of American religiosity, Martin Marty coined the term "public theology" in 1974 in his description of American civil religion, that is, the interaction of Protestantism with political motifs in American society.[11] David Tracy further developed the notion of public theology in his 1981 text, *The Analogical Imagination*, in which he refers to church, academy and society as the three publics with which theologians should engage.[12] Since the inception of the GNPT and its affiliated journal, *IJPT*, Marty and Tracy have been frequently cited. Similarly, regular reference is made to the South African scholars, John de Gruchy and Dirkie Smit, whose work has

---

[9] Carol Hanisch, "The Personal is Political," in Shulamith Firestone and Ann Koedt, eds, *Notes from the Second Year: Women's Liberation* (New York: Radical Feminism, 1970), 76-78.

[10] Ibid., 34.

[11] Martin Marty, "Two Kinds of Two Kinds of Civil Religion," in *American Civil Religion* (1974), 139-157 and "Reinhold Niebuhr: Public Theology and the American Experience," in *Journal of Religion*, 54:4 (1974), 332-359.

[12] David Tracy, *The Analogical Imagination: Christian Theology and the Culture of Pluralism* (New York: Crossroad, 1981).

been promoted through the Beyers Naudé Centre for Public Theology, at the University of Stellenbosch in South Africa; the Beyers Naudé Centre was launched in 2002 with a focus on human rights and justice.[13] A few years later, in 2008, not long after the first consultation of the GNPT, the Dietrich Bonhoeffer Research Centre for Public Theology was inaugurated at Bamberg University in Germany with the intention of following Bonhoeffer's "critical and constructive theological stand in the face of public discourses and disruptions."[14]

I have no intention of disputing the importance of the work of these scholars, nor of dismissing the laudable approaches of the centers named after such hugely significant historical figures. Nevertheless, I am deeply troubled by a public theology that stops short of looking beyond these figures and their male identity. Women and other marginalized groups are not granted equal access with men in the three publics Tracy identifies. If public theologians genuinely seek to reflect on public issues of contemporary importance, they must critically reflect on their own positions of privilege and power. In the advancement of rights and justice, public theologians refer to "speaking truth to power" in the wake of rising homelessness and food banks in the UK, for example, (or in the face of rising incarceration and racial profiling decried by the Black Lives Matter movement in the United States of America, or the urgency of environmental degradation in Oceania); seeking to effect changes in public policy on these matters is crucial, but "speaking truth to power" should not assume that justice can be achieved through gender-neutrality. The Black Lives Matter movement was started by women—Alicia Garza, Patrisse Cullors and Opal Tometi—because the black liberation movement was dominated by black, heterosexual, cis-gender men; the fight against police brutality and racism in the US involves multiple layers of suffering experienced by black women and LGBT+ communities, as well as by black men. Likewise, fighting for the impoverished in the face of a government intent on pursuing an austerity agenda that penalizes the least well off in the UK must include a critique of the disproportionate effect that such cuts have on impoverished women, especially those in abusive relationships who are economically tied to their abusers, because of benefits cuts and the closure of women's refuges. Similarly, those promoting greener policies and land redistribution in Oceania need to be cognizant of practices that have a negative impact on women's

---

[13] See "History, Vision and Aims of the Beyers Naudé Centre," Stellenbosch University, https://www.sun.ac.za/english/faculty/theology/bnc/about-us/vision-aims-history [last accessed 9 May 2018].

[14] See "Dietrich Bonhoeffer Research Center for Public Theology," University of Bamberg, https://www.uni-bamberg.de/en/fs-oet/ [last accessed 9 May 2018].

livelihoods and wellbeing, especially if women lack rights to land and are subjected to gender-based violence (GBV). When citing the same handful of men is seen as sufficient, women's participation is neither promoted nor taken seriously, with the effect that the faith-based abuse endured by women and LGBT+ persons, for instance, is left out of this narrowly conceived arena of public discourse. Herein lays the hiddenness of what I am calling the crisis in public theology: it is hidden because the dominant public theologians have not noticed that which they have omitted.

In my opinion, intimate partner violence is a public issue, and one on which theologians should speak. On 21 March 2018, Restored, an international Christian organization working towards ending violence against women, put out a media release entitled "In Churches Too: Domestic Abuse Happens to Churchgoers."[15] The media release was referring to a study among churches in Cumbria in England, which found that "One in four (n=109) of the sample had experienced at least one abusive behavior in their current relationship"[16] and yet the majority of respondents "were much more aware of domestic abuse outside the church than within it."[17] Equally worryingly, the researchers, Kristin Aune and Rebecca Barnes, report that only "two in seven churchgoers thought their church was equipped to deal with disclosures of domestic abuse."[18] In fact, in keeping with my earlier critique of the theological concept of sacrifice, this new research confirms "examples of dangerous practice and disclosures of domestic abuse being minimized or silenced;"[19] in particular, the expectation that wives should submit to their husbands contributes to the non-disclosure of intimate partner violence and the victimization of women.[20] Cases of male victims of abuse were also reported, but the overwhelming conclusion of the findings with respect to gender differentiation is that "women experience

---

[15] See Carolina Kuzaks-Cardenas, "Press Release: In Churches Too – Domestic Abuse Happens to Churchgoers," in *Restored*, 21 March 2018, https://www.restoredrelationships.org/news/2018/03/21/press-release-churches-too-domestic-abuse-happens-churgoers/ [last accessed 6 April 2018]. N.B. 230 churches were invited to advertise the research, 129 agreed (those who refused were evangelical), 438 responses were received from a range of denominations.

[16] Full report: Kristin Aune and Rebecca Barnes, "In Churches Too: Church Responses to Domestic Abuse – A Case Study of Cumbria" (March 2018), https://restored.contentfiles.net/media/resources/files/churches_web.pdf 5 and 31.

[17] Ibid., 6 and 23.

[18] Ibid.

[19] Ibid., 7 and 51.

[20] Ibid., 56.

abuse that is more frequent, more severe and has more serious impacts."[21] Trans persons are even at more at risk from abuse than cis-women; in both cases, though, the perpetrators of violence are overwhelmingly cis-gender males, which lends further support to the claim that a heteronormative, patricentric Christianity encourages, rather than challenges, toxic masculinity (and femininity).

Thus, if public theologians do not address the social construction of maleness (and femaleness) and the related prevalence of intimate partner violence both within and outside of the church, they are complicit in maintaining the silence of victims and survivors; they are complicit in sustaining the invisibility of perpetrators, and they are complicit in perpetuating the damage done to women and LGBT+ persons under the auspices of a heterosexist theology.

The Missing Women

Admittedly, there may be male theologians who are wary of wading into a gendered debate and risking the wrath of feminists who do not want men to speak on their behalf; this is an understandable anxiety, but it is not a cogent argument for failing to read and converse with female theologians and their critique of gender inequality. Similarly unconvincing is the presumption that there are no female public theologians with whom to deliberate. While very few female academics are referred to as public theologians—the only female scholarly work regularly referred to as public theology is Linell Cady's examination of the role of religion in American public life[22]—there are substantial numbers of women speaking and writing about public issues from a theological perspective. In the UK, the first person to come to mind here is Elaine Graham, who argues that public theology needs to incorporate the performative theological expression that takes place outside of church and academy, in, for example, "creative writing, drama or music."[23] Moreover, as I mentioned earlier, it is short-sighted to limit the scope of public theology to those who use that terminology explicitly, limiting the field in this way seems to mean that public theology avoids the demanding and disruptive task of self-critique.

---

[21] Ibid., 6 and 40. That is, 57.4% of women experienced abuse, compared to 16.7% of men; 90.8% of perpetrators were men (40).

[22] Linell E. Cady, *Religion, Theology and American Public Life* (New York: SUNY Press, 1993).

[23] Elaine Graham "Power, Knowledge and Authority in Public Theology," in *International Journal of Public Theology*, 1:1 (2007), 42-62 at 61.

For decades, Elisabeth Schüssler Fiorenza has been disputing androcentric interpretations of biblical texts and highlighting the extent to which such interpretations oppress women.[24] Likewise, Rosemary Radford Ruether has campaigned relentlessly for female ordination in the Roman Catholic Church, whilst critiquing the exclusionary nature of male God-language and its negative impact on notions of female redemption.[25] In addition, womanist scholars, such as Jacquelyn Grant and Delores Williams, have promoted a black, imminent, liberationist image of Christ, and identified with Hagar as a figure of black female oppression;[26] Mercy Oduyoye has developed an African theology that is inclusive of women, Musa Dube offers us a feminist, post-colonial reading of the Bible and a theological response to the HIV epidemic;[27] while Kwok Pui-Lan gives us a post-colonial critique from the perspective of Asian women's Christianity.[28] Nevertheless, public theologians rarely cite these authors, nor do they participate in the promotion of gender inclusive God-language and liturgies. Furthermore, these scholars are merely the tip of the iceberg; female theologians are numerous, but theology courses in academic institutions either continue with male-dominated reading lists, or they offer courses in feminist, womanist or trans theology as options that students are not required to take. If public theologians care about equality, they should be advocating diverse reading lists and inclusive course structures. Just as black university students are questioning the whiteness of degree curricula,[29] public theologians should

---

[24] From Elisabeth Schüssler Fiorenza, *In Memory of Her: A Feminist Theological Reconstruction of Christian Origins* (London: SCM Press, 1983) to Changing Horizons: Explorations in Feminist Interpretation (Minneapolis: Fortress Press, 2013).

[25] From Rosemary Radford Ruether, *Sexism and God-Talk* (Boston: Beacon Press, 1983) to *Women and Redemption: A Theological History*, 2nd edn (Minneapolis: Fortress Press, 2012).

[26] Jacquelyn Grant, *White Women's Christ and Black Women's Jesus* (Atlanta: Scholars Press, 1989) to *Perspectives on Womanist Theology* (Atlanta: ITC Press, 1995); Delores Williams, *Sisters in the Wilderness* (Maryknoll: Orbis, 1993); for womanist ethics, see Katie Cannon and Emilie Townes.

[27] From Mercy Oduyoye, *Daughters of Anowa: African Women and Patriarchy* (Maryknoll: Orbis, 1999) to *Beads and Strands: Reflections of an African Woman on Christianity in Africa* (Maryknoll: Orbis, 2001); and from Musa Dube, *Postcolonial Feminist Interpretation of the Bible* (Atlanta: Chalice Press, 2000) to *The HIV and AIDS Bible* (Scranton: University of Scranton Press, 2008).

[28] From Kwok Pui-Lan, *Introducing Asian Feminist Theology* (Sheffield: Sheffield Academic Press, 2000) to *Postcolonial Imagination and Feminist Theology* (Louisville: Westminster John Knox Press, 2005).

[29] Mariya Hussain, "Why is My Curriculum White?," in *National Union of Students*, 11 March 2015, https://www.nus.org.uk/en/news/why-is-my-curriculum-white/ [last accessed 8 April 2018].

be leading the way in addressing the under-representation of women and the over-representation of white men in their theological reading, their teaching and their speaking invitations.

THE CRISIS

You might, at this point, still be wondering why I have called this a crisis: if successful public theologians are ignorant of and content with the gender imbalance in their midst, then this will not be experienced as a crisis by them. Male academics are under no formal obligation to share with marginalized groups the power and authority that they give to each other (although I believe that there is a moral obligation here). Conferences could continue to have male-only panels and journals could continue to publish editions with all-male authors. In fact, the recent developments in analytic theology seem to be proceeding from an assumption that black and feminist theology have been done, and so the task of the theologian is to return to what is seen as theology proper; namely, a theology that pretends black and feminist theology does not exist or is no longer needed. The 2011 text, *Analytic Theology,* edited by Oliver Crisp and Michael Rea, states that: "theology as a discipline has been beguiled and taken captive by 'continental' approaches, and that the effects on the discipline have been largely deleterious;" of the fourteen chapters in the book, two have female authors, and references throughout the text are overwhelmingly to male scholarship.[30] In 2013, the *Journal of Analytic Theology* was founded with an all-male line up of editors; while from 2015-2018, the John Templeton Foundation has provided millions of dollars to fund analytic theology projects at Fuller Theological Seminary and the University of Innsbruck, each project having been proposed and formed with all-male teams. It is telling that of the four women included in the list of thirteen Faculty at the Logos Institute for Analytic and Exegetical Theology at the University of St. Andrews, two are honorary and the other two are administrative assistants. (The whiteness of analytic theology is also disturbing.) These organizations are well regarded, but their accomplishments mark a crisis for public theology, because their silence on matters of gender is deafening, especially at a time when misogyny is high on the political agenda.

Indeed, during the 2016 populist presidential election campaign in the United States, in the wake of Donald Trump's misogynistic and racist remarks, the Twitter hashtag #whitechurchquiet lamented the lack of

---

[30] Oliver D. Crisp and Michael C. Rea, eds, *Analytic Theology: New Essays in the Philosophy of Theology* (Oxford: OUP, 2011), 1.

rebuke coming from mainstream evangelicals. In the same year, the UK voted to leave the European Union (EU) on the basis of a populist Brexit campaign that drew erroneous connections between austerity and immigration (now exposed by the Windrush scandal).[31] According to Lord Ashcroft, nearly sixty percent of Christians voted leave.[32] Part of the explanation for this preference is to be found in the demographics: over ninety per cent of British Christians are white and twenty per cent are elderly (aged over sixty-five); in addition to this, though, fringe evangelical Christian groups asserted support for the leave campaign on biblical grounds. Ellel Ministries, a non-denominational Christian healing and training ministry, founded by Peter Horrobin in the Lancashire village, Ellel, in 1986, and which has now spread to twenty countries worldwide (including South Africa, India, Colombia, Singapore and Rwanda), argued in its blog, on 24 March 2016, that the UK should leave the EU "for deeply spiritual reasons."[33] Horrobin's opinion was later supported by Jerry Johnson, president of the long-standing evangelical association of Christian communications, National Religious Broadcasters, who praised the outcome of the vote to leave on the grounds that the EU is a secular and sinful organization; whereas, Brexit, he alleges, is an opportunity for the UK to "revive" its Christian heritage and for "God to bring a spiritual awakening to Great Britain."[34] Mainstream Christian leaders of the Anglican church, the archbishops of Canterbury and York, and the bishops of Durham and Guilford, amongst others, were dismayed by the result; they openly, if not assertively, supported the remain campaign, along with Cardinal Vincent Nichols, head of the Roman Catholic Church of England and Wales. In response to the unexpected result, the archbishops called for "unity."[35] Absent from most of the political and theological

---

[31] Greenberg Center for Geoeconomic Studies, "What Brexit Reveals About Rising Populism," *Council on Foreign Relations*, 29 June 2016, https://www.cfr.org/interview/what-brexit-reveals-about-rising-populism [last accessed 24 April 2018]. Populist in the sense that it saw the EU as the elites and sought to mobilize animosity of the "common" people against the EU.

[32] Harry Farley, "Christians and Brexit: Did God Command the UK to Leave the EU?," *Christian Today*, 28 June 2016, https://www.christiantoday.com/article/christians.and.brexit.did.god.command.the.uk.to.leave.the.eu/89427.htm [last accessed 24 April 2018].

[33] Peter Horobin's Blog, Ellel Ministries International, 24 March 2016, http://blog.ellel.org/2016/03/24/in-or-out/ [last accessed 24 April 2018].

[34] Mark Woods, "US Evangelicals Hail British Vote to Leave EU," *Christian Today*, 27 June 2016, https://www.christiantoday.com/article/us.evangelicals.hail.british.vote.to.leave.eu/89323.htm [last accessed 24 April 2018].

[35] Harry Farley, "Unity vs Defiance: Church Leaders Respond to Brexit," 24 June 2016, https://www.christiantoday.com/article/unity.vs.defiance.church.leaders.respond.to.brexit/89186.htm [last accessed 24 April 2018].

discourse during the Brexit campaign, however, was any sustained analysis of the gendered implications of the vote. A headline in the *Guardian* newspaper read "Brexit is a feminist issue," but, as Helen Lewis notes in the piece, the debate between the leavers and remainers was dominated by white male elites.[36] Furthermore, when the Brexit negotiating teams sat down together, the British side was accused of having "more beards than women."[37] Given that laws protecting women from discrimination in the workplace have come from the EU, there is no guarantee that the present British government will maintain those protections; on the contrary, the current female Prime Minister, Theresa May, is presiding over austerity measures in which "86% of the burden of austerity since 2010 has fallen on women."[38] Where are the public theologians who should be speaking out on these issues? Are their tongues tied by theologies of gender inequality that they have yet to overturn?

Subsequently, as the Harvey Weinstein scandal gathered pace, and women from across the globe used the hashtag #MeToo (borrowed from an earlier campaign for sexual assault survivors, begun by African-American Tarana Burke in 2007) to reveal the ubiquitous occurrence of sexual harassment and assault in the workplace, Christian women began to share their stories of being abused by clergy and fellow Christians using the #ChurchToo, initiated by Hannah Paasch and Emily Joy. Through social media, abused women are shining a light on a twisted theology that tells rape victims to repent and absolves the male abusers of their crimes.[39] Hence, women rebuked and silenced in churches by a patriarchal culture and an androcentric theology that belittles their suffering and demeans their talents are finding expression online. As Gina Messina-Dysert, Monica Coleman, Mary Hunt and other feminist theologians attest, digital media has opened

---

[36] Helen Lewis, "Brexit is a Feminist Issue," *The Guardian*, 20 March 2016, https://www.theguardian.com/politics/2016/mar/20/women-europe-referendum-debate-brexit [last accessed 24 April 2018].

[37] Siona Jenkins, "Is Brexit Bad for Women?," *Financial Times*, 7 July 2017, https://www.ft.com/content/a1ec120c-6307-11e7-91a7-502f7ee26895 [last accessed 24 April 2018]. Also, all white (and the EU side is only slightly better).

[38] Heather Stewart, "Women Bearing 86% of Austerity Burden, Commons Figures Reveal," *The Guardian*, 9 March 2017, https://www.theguardian.com/world/2017/mar/09/women-bearing-86-of-austerity-burden-labour-research-reveals [last accessed 24 April 2018].

[39] Casey Quackenbush, "The Religious Community is Speaking Out Against Sexual Violence with #ChurchToo," *Time*, 22 November 2017, http://time.com/5034546/me-too-church-too-sexual-abuse/ [last accessed 8 April 2018] and https://www.huffingtonpost.co.uk/entry/sexual-abuse-churchtoo_us_5a205b30e4b03350e0b53131 [last accessed 8 April 2018].

up a space in which women can share their personal stories and receive support rather than disbelief or blame.[40] Through online social networks women are accessing new opportunities to be participants and activists, contesting discriminatory interpretations of their faith in an arena where they do not need to conform to male authority, to a particular standard of religious education or to a theological language from which they have been excluded. In other words, if women are not listened to and championed by public theology, they will seek sustenance elsewhere.

Two especially pertinent contexts for the immediate future are sexual abuse and reproductive rights. In March and April 2018, the Independent Inquiry into Child Sex Abuse (IICSA) in the UK was hearing of the CoE's staggering inadequacy in disciplining abusers and supporting survivors, prompting Linda Woodhead to conclude that "a ruthlessly honest theological audit is going to have to be part of the solution," because "a faulty doctrine of forgiveness was used by abusers to salve their consciences, by church officials to move on without dealing with the problem, and by parishioners and clergy to marginalize 'unchristian' victims and whistleblowers."[41] On 25 May 2018, Ireland held a referendum on abortion in which Christianity was again in the spotlight. Tina Beattie is just one of the female Roman Catholic theologians who have grappled with that church's male hierarchy's resistance to change on reproductive rights; she charts a more nuanced path between the binary opposition of female choice and Vatican condemnation. She asserts that abortion is "an issue for politics and public health" and, hence, that:

> Public theology therefore has a constructive and critical role to play in the increasingly polarized and sometimes violent confrontation between opposing positions with regard to abortion, since it brings Christian reflection to bear on a matter of far-reaching concern for women themselves, but also for our shared communal values and our understanding of the meaning and dignity of human life.[42]

Thus, I assert that public theology is in the grip of a hidden crisis: it has yet to become conscious of its male dominance, but if it fails to awaken to the

---

[40] Gina Messina-Dysert and Rosemary Radford Ruether, eds, *Feminism and Religion in the Twenty-First Century: Technology, Dialogue and Expanding Borders* (New York and Abingdon: Routledge, 2015).

[41] Linda Woodhead, "Forget Culture. It's a New Theology We Need," in *Church Times*, 6 April 2018, https://www.churchtimes.co.uk/articles/2018/6-april/comment/opinion/iicsa-forget-culture-new-theology-we-need [last accessed 8 April 2018].

[42] Tina Beattie, "Catholicism, Choice and Consciousness: A Feminist Theological Perspective on Abortion," in *International Journal of Public Theology*, 4:1 (2010), 51-75 at 52-3.

inequality in its midst, it will not be able to pursue credible dialogue with women on these contemporary matters of public disquiet. Such a failure will leave public theology on the wrong side of history.

WHO BENEFITS? EXPLORING A GENDERED THEOLOGICAL SPACE

Gunilla Hallonsten

There is a growing lack of trust, and a major worry about the future in Swedish society today, even among the youth.[1] Indeed, there is also a struggle to define the future! Who benefits in times of populism? Could a post-colonial discourse and method of intersectionality help define the future? What is the role of the academy and the church amid such angst?

THE STRUGGLE TO DEFINE THE FUTURE

Nationalistic populist movements in Sweden are founded on ideologies that declare that the people and the nation are one, that they are defined by culture or race, and that the democratically elected government is not legitimate. The populist discourse also includes anti-Semitism, racism and sexism, and it affirms violence in rhetoric and praxis.[2]

One aspect of these nationalistic populist ideologies that needs attention is their sexist nature and how this is affecting women's human rights, their Sexual and Reproductive Health and Rights (SRHR) and the roles women play in church and society. These nationalistic populist movements are strong opponents of feminism because they perceive feminism

---

[1] Barnombudsmannens årsrapport 2018, *Utanförskap, våld och kärlek till orten. Barns röster om att växa upp i utsatta kommuner och förorter* (Stockholm: Barnombudsmannen, 2018).
[2] Christer Mattsson, *Rapport 7 Nordiska motståndsrörelsens ideologi, propaganda och livsåskådning*, (Göteborg: Göteborgs universitet, Segerstedtinstitutet, 2018).

as splitting the nation.[3] Women's sexuality is ideologically closely related to the nation, and reproduction is a woman's first duty and service to the nation, these movements contend.[4]

Political priorities regarding family politics derive from a nationalistic populist view of what the family is, which is to say they strengthen traditional gender roles, and the nuclear family made up of a heterosexual couple, where the woman is expected to stay at home and the man is the breadwinner. (Of course, any family politics that make women financially dependent on men will make it difficult for women to leave relationships where they are exposed to domestic violence.)[5]

Populist nationalistic movements connect their appeal to "traditional family values" with hostile rhetoric towards immigrants, particularly towards Muslim immigrants. When these populist movements talk about strengthening the family as an institution in society, some families are excluded. They want to drastically reduce the influx of immigrants' relatives residing in Sweden.[6]

Today, the nationalistic populist movements in Sweden, and elsewhere in Europe, also discriminate against the lesbian, gay, bisexual, trans- and queer people (LGBTQ) community, threaten them, and systemically attempt to deny their human rights. They are, among other things, denied the right to marriage, insemination and adoption. Populist parties do not accept that families might live by norms other than those of the traditional nuclear family, and propose that people who insist on doing so not be granted the same rights and opportunities to create families.[7]

SHRINKING OR RESTRICTED DEMOCRATIC SPACE

The LGBTIQ community, and those who support women's rights or challenge traditional gender roles, are harassed, humiliated and ridiculed. In addition, they are regarded as threats to national unity and identity.[8]

This can be discussed within the framework of a shrinking democratic space for civil society organizations, particularly those focusing on gender justice. Women's rights movements are more at risk to threats and are

---

[3] RFSU, Swedish Association for Sexuality Education, *En nation, en form av familj och en form av sexualitet* (Stockholm: RFSU, 2017).

[4] Christer Mattsson, op. cit (note 2).

[5] RFSU, Swedish Association for Sexuality Education, *En nation, en form av familj och en form av sexualitet* (Stockholm: RFSU, 2017).

[6] Ibid.

[7] Ibid.

[8] Ibid.

restricted from acting due to a democratic deficit in society and governments neglecting to keep to their international human rights obligations to protect and respect human dignity and rights.[9]

THEOLOGY AS TAKEN-FOR-GRANTED

According to the sociologist Pierre Bourdieu's theory on symbolic power and male dominance, the legitimization of power relations functions as the connection between classes and groups. [10] The ideological assumption provides a strategy that supports domination, and reinforces the legitimacy of the dominating group or class, both within and beyond the dominating group. Bourdieu speaks about the active role of the "taken-for-granted".[11]

The process of international policy making does not explicitly take theological aspects into account. However, in policy making lie imbedded and implicit values and attitudes on human dignity and human rights, which derive from social and political as well as theological and cultural interpretations. The theological perceptions are implicit in the discourses of SRHR and gender equality, as taken-for-granted.

Grace Jantzen suggested Western culture is rooted in death and gendered violence and termed it "moral imaginary", equating it with Bourdieu's concept of the cultural unconscious.[12] For Jantzen, the moral imaginary constitutes "that which is taken-for-granted, the space—literal and figurative—from which moral thinking is done."[13]

Theology that is taken for granted is based on a patriarchal structure that legitimizes the same structure. In many parts of the world, the privilege or power of definition on SRHR and gender equality lies with faith community leaders.[14] Therefore, they hold the power to create change on SRHR, especially on the local level. The chance to achieve social transfor-

---

[9] ACT Alliance and CIDSE: *Space for Civil Society. How to protect and expand an enabling environment*, (Denmark: ACT Alliance and CIDSE, 2014).

[10] David Swartz, *Culture & power: the sociology of Pierre Bourdieu*, (Chicago: University of Chicago Press, 1997).

[11] Pierre Bourdieu, *Language and symbolic power*, (Cambridge: Harvard University Press, 1991).

[12] Elaine Graham, "Redeeming the Present," in *Grace Jantzen Redeeming the Present*, ed. Elaine Graham (Surrey: Ashgate, 2009).

[13] Grace Jantzen, "Flourishing. Towards an Ethic of Natality," *Feminist Theory* 2, no. 2 (August 2001): 221.

[14] Gunilla Hallonsten, *Not the Whole Story. The Impact of the Church, Traditional Religion and Society on the Individual and Collective Perceptions of HIV in Swaziland*, (Lund: Lund University, Lund Studies in Sociology of Religion 10, 2012).

mation through policy making on SRHR and gender equality–locally and globally–will, therefore, increase by developing a post-colonial methodology where it can become transparent regarding who, when and where the theological interpretations are produced.[15]

POST-COLONIAL FEMINIST AND SOCIOLOGICAL THEORY OF INTERSECTIONALITY

Post-colonial strategies on intersectionality offer an approach within feminist sociology which makes it possible to think and reflect on gender within a multi-dimensional understanding of power.[16] The strategies are theoretical tools that can be used to analyze complex power constructions which may be relevant to gender, sexuality, class and ethnicity. At the same time, it is essential that these concepts and how they function in society are articulated, and that their meanings are placed in their historical contexts.

Feminist post-colonialism has contributed to making visible the relation between male dominance and the exclusion of ethnic nationalistic projects.[17] Gayatri Spivak extends the feminist notion of "the woman" both ethically and politically, asking the questions "not merely who am I? But who is the other woman? How am I naming her? How does she name me?"[18]

A METHODOLOGICAL STRATEGY, CRITERIA FOR INTERSECTIONALITY

The following criteria can be perceived as a transformative production of knowledge within a continuity of re-assessment, re-interpretation and re-formulation. This set of four criteria for intersectionality, developed by Paula de los Reyes and Diana Mulinari[19], may contribute to the exploration of gendered theological spaces.

---

[15] Gunilla Hallonsten, "Religious Doctrines and the Body: Clashing Notions of Sexual and Reproductive Rights," in *Faith in Civil Society: Religious Actors as Drivers of Change*, eds. Heidi Moksnes and Mia Melin (Uppsala: Uppsala University, 2013), 93-102.

[16] Kwok Pui-lan, *Postcolonial Imagination & Feminist Theology* (London: SCM Press, 2005)

[17] Chandra Talpade Mohanty, *Feminism without Borders: Decolonizing Theory, Practicing Solidarity* (Durham: Duke University Press, 2003).

[18] Gayatri Chakravorty Spivak, *In Other Worlds: Essays in Cultural Politics* (London: Routledge, 1988).

[19] Paulina de los Reyes and Diana Mulinari, *Intersektionalitet: kritiska reflektioner över (o)jämlikhetens landskap* (Malmö: Liber, 2007).

CRITERION I – TO QUESTION STEREOTYPIC AND FRAGMENTED REPRESENTATIONS

Categorization makes up an important strategy for exercising power and creates fragmented representations while simultaneously suppressing the historical motives or reasons for inequality and its social construction.

How is cultural identity constructed over time? How can pluralistic counter-narratives be combined with visions of identities? The post-colonial context suggests that an African woman immigrating to Sweden cannot be "authentically" African and at the same time she cannot be "Western" enough. She will therefore always place herself somewhere in between those descriptions. Pui-lan describes the in-between space as a "space that opens up new possibilities for negotiating identity, exploring cultural hybridity and articulating different cultural practices and priorities."[20] Social categorization and its fragmented representations exclude the complex identities of women as well as commonly shared experiences, needs and desires. Such categorization, then can help thereby clarify how differences are constituted, and how dialogues and strategies that exceed established boundaries or limits can be formulated.

CRITERION 2 – TO LINK TOGETHER AND ARTICULATE

Intersectionality comes with an epistemological critique of a positivist view on knowledge, knowledge production and world view. Categorization is a central tool for the naturalization of dominance in the construction of unequal relations on various levels, be it between individuals, peoples, countries or regions. It forms a natural point of departure for interpretations of action, approaches to context and within a scientific construction where differences are taken for granted and thereby are not expected to change or end.

"To relate and to articulate is therefore also to create coherence and context and new arenas for dialogue and collective action"[21], based on an understanding of inequality and submission, exclusion and injustice as socially constructed phenomena.

---

[20] Kwok Pui-lan, *Introducing Asian Feminist Theology* (Sheffield: Sheffield Academic Press Ltd., 2000), 19.

[21] Paulina de los Reyes and Diana Mulinari, *Intersektionalitet: kritiska reflektioner över (o)jämlikhetens landskap* (Malmö: Liber, 2007), 128 (translation: Gunilla Hallonsten).

CRITERION 3 – TO BRING FORWARD INSTITUTIONAL CONTEXTS

Intersectionality is primarily about power structures and construction of power, which includes the linking of societal structures, institutions and agents.

Not seeing the specific situation in the vulnerability and exclusion of the individual in these structures, leads to a praxis of discrimination that makes invisible people's historically different experiences of oppression and opposes the formulation of collective strategies against power[22].

This point of departure, or criterion, emphasizes an institutional perspective as a way to clarify power structures which contribute to vulnerability and exclusion of individuals, and to counter or oppose stigmatization of individuals, families and groups. When the focus lies on specific individuals and groups, they become accountable and empowered as rights-holders.

CRITERION 4 – TO CHALLENGE HEGEMONY THROUGH THINKING ALTERITY

Post-colonialism and feminism stress the necessity to bring forward alternative voices and to formulate counter-narratives that can transform the established order. This pre-supposes an awareness of the importance of history and an active engagement in the discourses of alternative narratives that aim to challenge the hegemony around power, gender, knowledge and experience.

Althaus-Reid discuss the hegemonic understanding of theology as follows:

> Theology as ideology, that is, a totalitarian construction of what is considered as 'The One and Only Theology' which does not admit discussion or challenges from different perspectives, especially in the area of sexual identity and its close relationship with political and racial issues.[23]

Thinking about alterity can help establish visibility for the other, and expose experiences of discrimination and oppression in a way that makes clear the construction of social identities. There will be a need for strategies that promote participation in the public dialogue, and in order to make this possible within the academy and the church, a critical approach has taken around knowledge production about femininity, equality and gender relations, as well as the opposition to racist perceptions and ethnic discrimination.

---

[22] Ibid.

[23] Marcella Althaus-Reid, *The Queer God* (New York: Routledge, 2003), 172.

234

Exploring a gendered theological space in times of populism

Exploring a gendered theological space can mean, among many things, entering a familiar space through the ABCDE[24] of the church's engagement in the public space by: Assessing public issues in participatory ways; Building relationships of trust; Challenging injustice; Discovering signs of hope; and Empowering people in need. In line with this, there are a few insights from the anti-racist organization Expo in Sweden: produce counter-narratives with positive messages; be locally rooted/anchored; and provide an entrance to a wider engagement for people.[25]

The post-colonial feminist approach that I have outlined earlier in the text follows these general approaches to the public space, but it is especially suitable for the analysis and critique of sexism in the public space—and it is meant to inspire theological responses.[26] How can this be conceptualized? Does the church dare to achieve something through re-assessment, re-interpretation and re-formulation by risking critique?

It is also possible to combine the explored and unexplored terrains and methodologies. The methodology will then be inductive, can be culturally specific, based on intersectionality, as well as inter/cross-cultural. The defined theological issues will, therefore, be derived from experiences of oppressions and struggles.[27]

Grace Jantzen frequently asks the question "who benefits?"[28] Jantzen argues in a way that "a new moral imaginary is informed by its efficacy in serving 'the practice of justice'."[29] In line with this question, she writes:

The struggle against suffering and injustice and towards flourishing takes precedence, beyond comparison, to the resolution of intellectual problems; and although it is important that the struggle is an intelligent

---

[24] The Lutheran World Federation, *The Church in the Public Space. A Study Document of the Lutheran World Federation*, ed. Department for Theology and Public Witness (Geneva: LWF, 2016).

[25] Expo lecture, (Strängnäs, 2018).

[26] Kwok Pui-lan, *Postcolonial Imagination & Feminist Theology* (London: SCM Press, 2005).

[27] Musa Dube, "Postcoloniality, Feminist Spaces and Religion," in *Postcolonialism, Feminism, and Religious Discourse*, eds. L. Donaldson and K. Pui-lan, (New York: Routledge, 2002), 100-122.

[28] Grace Jantzen, *Becoming Divine: Towards a Feminist Philosophy of Religion* (Manchester: Manchester University Press, 1998), 68.

[29] Elaine Graham, "Redeeming the Present," in *Grace Jantzen Redeeming the Present*, ed. Elaine Graham (Surrey: Ashgate, 2009), 1-19.

one, there is no excuse for theory ever becoming a distraction from the struggle for justice itself.[30]

What should be the agenda of theology and of the churches in this regard? One answer could be the exploration of critique and that of questions from the intersections of oppression, which will raise new questions and new hermeneutics for interpretation of theological encounters with people's daily lives.

Finally, consider the words of Emilia Fogelklou, Sweden's first woman theologian, who issues this challenge:

> There are more paths to God than you in your pride and vanity believed. Such a common and simple relationship: That we all are different should be the foundation for all our conversations. I now know that everyone's dream is the fulfilled life, which we in reality live! The truth is within us all. There is a universe that you now know nothing of![31]

---

[30] Grace Jantzen, *Becoming Divine: Towards a Feminist Philosophy of Religion* (Manchester: Manchester University Press, 1998), 264.
[31] Emilia Fogelklou, *Minnesbilder och ärenden* (Stockholm: Bonniers, 1963) (translation: Gunilla Hallonsten).

"Beautiful, modest, and housewife": Women, politics and religion in Brazil

Marcia Blasi

Daily reality

> 5 am! The dogs in the neighborhood were barking a lot. I woke up. Remained in bed. I reached for my cell phone. A click on Facebook. First post, a sad call, the headline of a local newspaper. "Woman is executed with 5 shots in the head in the Itamaraty neighborhood." I looked at the city: Artur Nogueira. I thought to myself, "I'm not going to start my day reading such sad news." Not even five minutes later, the cell phone rang. A leader of the Lutheran Congregation of Artur Nogueira calls me. I answer, and in tears she tries to inform me about the news that says that "our" Ana Paula was murdered.[1]

The words of Evandro Meurer, Pastor of the Evangelical Church of the Lutheran Confession in Brazil, are terrifying. Violence against women has escalated. It has gone beyond being an idea, a topic of study, and an issue we need to raise awareness about. Violence against women is present in our families, communities, churches, in the whole society. In fact, it has been like that since long but we did not want to see it.

In 2002, the Lutheran World Federation presented the document "Churches say 'No' to Violence against Women: an action plan for churches"[2].

---

[1] Words of Pastor Evandro Meurer, published in the *O Caminho* newspaper, April 2018.
[2] Lutheran World Federation. *Churches Say 'No' to Violence Against Women*, Geneva 2002 https://www.lutheranworld.org/sites/default/files/Churches%20Say%20No%20 to%20Violence%20against%20Women.pdf [accessed 1 December 2018].

The translated document was shared with ministers and women's organizations in the Evangelical Church of the Lutheran Confession in Brazil. Unfortunately, few people studied it in congregations or even read it themselves. The idea that such "things" do not happen "among us" was very strong and continues, despite the evidence to the contrary. Words and experiences such as those of Pastor Meurer challenge the whole church to take the reality of violence against women very seriously. According to the World Health Organization, Brazil ranks as the fifth country in the world for femicides. Partners, husbands, ex-husbands, or boyfriends kill women daily. The approval of the Femicide Law[3] has not diminished the killings, even though it is a very important achievement of the feminist movements.

On 14 March 2018, Marielle Franco, a human rights activist and a councilwoman was executed in the city of Rio de Janeiro. Marielle was an outspoken leader against the military occupation of the favelas in Rio, and denounced the violence of police against the population.[4]

Some people argue that these are isolated and unfortunate events of daily violence in Brazil. This is wrong. They are not. They are neither isolated facts, nor just unfortunate events. Ana Paula and Marielle represent all the women who suffer the consequences of sexism and bad politics.

TWO MODELS FOR WOMEN

During the campaign for presidential election, a little girl asked candidate Dilma Roussef: "Can women be president?" Her answered was, "Yes, we can", and she did. In 2011 she became the first woman president of Brazil. Even before the beginning of her mandate she faced comments about her hair, her clothes, her lipstick, or even the lack of it. Her wit, her strong words, her courage, her being, all of that was portrayed as negative. Had she been a man, those attributes would have been a positive sign of leadership.

On 1 April 2016, President Dilma Roussef was facing the worst moment of her time in the government. A well-known magazine offered to the "concerned" Brazilian population a picture of the president. The article was

---

[3] The Law N° 13.104, of 9 March, 2015, defines femicide as the killing of a woman because of her gender. http://www.planalto.gov.br/ccivil_03/_Ato2015-2018/2015/Lei/L13104.htm [accessed 1 December 2018].

[4] Brad Brooks. "Unfazed by Brazil's army, Rio drug gangs willing to wait out occupation" https://www.reuters.com/article/us-brazil-rio-violence-insight/unfazed-by-brazils-army-rio-drug-gangs-willing-to-wait-out-occupation-idUSKBN1HV1TM, [accessed 1 December 2018].

entitled: "A president beside herself". The cover image showed a screaming "mad" woman. The article continued:

> If the moral, politic and economic crises were not enough, Dilma Rousseff also lost the emotional conditions to lead the government."(...) "The outbursts, the intemperate pursuits and the denial of reality reveal a president completely out of line and incapable of managing the Country.[5]

The article came as a bomb in the media discussions. "Her angry face, her hand pointing during speeches, her strong words, all of that was just a sign of her unstable condition", commented the male newsreader of the largest television channel.

The article finished with a reference to *"Maria I, a louca"* (Maria I, the crazy woman), first woman to become queen of Portugal, and thus Brazil's first queen since Brazil was a colony of Portugal. Maria I made several improvements during her reign, suffered strong opposition and became portrayed in history as crazy and incapable of making reasonable decisions, becoming "dangerous" the more she was put under pressure. Even though not making a direct connection to President Dilma, the article implied that there were similarities among their stories.

> Misogyny is the hate speech specialized in constructing a visual and verbal image of women as beings belonging to the field of the negative ... Misogyny is present when women are associated with madness, hysteria, or nature—as if there were a predisposition that gave them a natural, original unreliability.[6]

Eighteen days later, another magazine presented a woman's picture on the cover. The words read: "Marcela Temer, the great bet of the government". Marcela Temer, the wife of Brazilian Vice-President, Michel Temer, eager to become president with Dilma's impeachment, became the model of the perfect wife: beautiful, modest, and housewife.[7]

The article was in fact a well-written piece of propaganda against President Dilma, without even mentioning her. It was a call to all women to go back to their "natural" role and place in society—the home, and of course, to focus on their femininity. As philosopher Marcia Tiburi states,

---

[5] Sérgio Pardellas and Débora Bergamasco. "Uma presidente fora de si". *Isto é.* https://istoe.com.br/450027_UMA+PRESIDENTE+FORA+DE+SI/. (1 April 2016)

[6] Marcia Tiburi, *Feminismo em comum: para todas, todes e todos* (Rio de Janeiro: Rosa dos Tempos, 2018), 39.

[7] Juliana Linhares, "Marcela Temer: bela, recatada e do lar", *Veja.* http://veja.abril.com.br/brasil/marcela-temer-bela-recatada-e-do-lar/ . (18 April 2016)

"To sweeten the people marked as women, the 'feminine' was invented"[8]. Some quotes from the article represent exactly this idea: "Lucky woman", "He was her first boyfriend", "She still wants a little girl", "Marcela is a vice-first lady-housewife", "She has everything to be our next Grace Kelly", "She likes dresses down to her knee and in soft colors". The article finishes with the following words: "Michel Temer is a lucky man". Well, is this not a dream of all men in a patriarchal society?

Instead of the woman who challenged patriarchal culture in every word she spoke, in every act she took, in every color she dressed, now there was the option for Marcela Temer to make things right again: sweet, homey, feminine—beautiful, modest and housewife.

The magazines presented Brazilian society with two models of women. On one side, the crazy angry bitch; and on the other, the sweet modest housewife. This is not merely incidental. Putting women down and "killing their spirits" is what sexism is very good at. Violence then is not abnormal, violence is normal and increases every time a woman steps out of "her place" and patriarchal powers feel threatened. It was so with Marielle, Ana Paula and Dilma, and even with Marcela.

Unfortunately, fundamentalist religious leaders did not speak out against the violent attacks of President Dilma. On the contrary, many congressmen and congresswomen who voted for her impeachment did it in the name of God. The alliance of right-wing politics and religion has proven to be a great threat to democracy, human rights, and a particular threat to gender justice.[9]

POPULISM OR FASCISM?

Populism has different meanings in different contexts. In Latin America, populist governments are defined as being led by a strong charismatic leader, with great support from the people, nationalist and anti-imperialist discourse and policies, among others. It was in the time of populist governments that most changes happened in the lives of oppressed and mar-

---

[8] Tiburi, op. cit. (note 6), 50.

[9] Besides these magazine articles presented here, cartoons and stickers were used in sexist and homophobic ways. "In addition to stating that it was/is a coup, it is stated that 'the coup is misogynist'. This means that the conditions necessary for the process that involved President Dilma Rousseff to be effective depend heavily on sexist and heterosexist values and practices triggered in a variety of ways and at different times—before, during and after August 2016.", André Musskopf, "O sexo, o gênero e a sexualidade da política e da religião: Uma análise de representações culturais e releituras teológicas possíveis" (to be published).

ginalized groups of the society, such as: the right to vote, sexual health, reproductive rights, laws to prevent violence against women and LGBTI community, public policies, racial quotas in the education system.

The experience now in Latin America, and very strongly in Brazil, is not of populism, but of fascism. Discourses of hate, intolerance, misogyny, elitism, polarization are our daily reality. One of the most important headlines in media and politics nowadays is a fundamentalist discourse that spreads the idea that crazy feminists are at work aiming to destroy families and traditions through the establishment of something they nickname "gender ideology". The presidential candidate who incorporates all that is considered by many to be the "Trump of the tropics": "Jair Bolsonaro has openly cheered dictatorship and publicly insulted women. He has deployed Trump-like tactics in his race for the presidency"[10]. Bolsonaro's campaign has nothing to do with ending hunger, social justice, education and health for everyone, but on the contrary, brings out the most sexist, racist and homophobic feelings in his followers.

Is there hope?

Patriarchy and its by-product, sexism, are sins. Mix them with fascist politicians and get the endorsement of religion, you will have a recipe for a death sentence of women. The two models of women represented in the media and politics are also part of the Christian tradition. Women have been described as being like Eve (sinner, rebellious) or Mary (sweet, humble, quiet) as if they were opposite models. Feminist theologians question those interpretations and lift up the marvelous creation of God in all its diversity and creativity.

Even though the Lutheran tradition has for over 500 hundred years proclaimed that humans beings are saved and justified by God's grace and not by merits, women continue to be entangled in webs of shame and guilt, most often imposed on them by church leaders and traditions. It is time to stop pretending sexism does not exist in church and society. It is time to name evil by its name. In order to do that, women's stories have to be heard and believed. Gender justice needs to be part of the church's theological content and way of being, from hermeneutics, to methodology, all the way to practice. Churches are called to stand up and speak out; to

---

[10] Tom Phillips, "Trump of the tropics: the 'dangerous' candidate leading Brazil's presidential race". *The Guardian*. https://www.theguardian.com/world/2018/apr/19/jair-bolsonaro-brazil-presidential-candidate-trump-parallels, [accessed 1 December 2018].

provide safe and just space for women, to be a place where hope can be experienced. Hope is not naïve, it is an act of defiance, it is a dream we work to live, one day, by God's grace.

It is time for churches to proclaim even more bravely the revolutionary belief that we are liberated by God's grace and, therefore, we are called to work to change systems that prevent all people from experiencing such liberation. Calling evil by its name is a good start. "Justification by faith is acceptance, but it is also confession, confrontation, proclamation, celebration and commitment."[11]

---

[11] Wanda Deifelt. "The relevance of the doctrine of justification", in: Wolfgang Greive (ed.), *Justification in the World's Context*. LWF Documentation 47 (Geneva: The Lutheran World Federation, 2000), 41.

Populism and Truth

What is Truth? A reflection on populism through the lens of John 18:28-38

Chad Rimmer

"Post-truth" was the Oxford dictionary's word of the year for 2016 because of the way that exclusionary populist strategies were normalized in contemporary international social and political discourse. It seems as if the goal of honest deliberation has been supplanted by unreflective mobilization, and to that end it is acceptable to neglect factual, critical analysis as a basis for open public discourse about the common good.

The psychological difficulty of processing twenty-four-hour news, coupled with the unfiltered, uncritical nature of social media, contributes to the post-truth nature of our context. In the book, *How to save politics in a post-truth era*,[1] Ilan Baron suggests that what we need is a different kind of knowledge—*I would say a different kind of wisdom*—that helps people see through appeals to emotion and nationalist mythologies, in order to discern goodness or justice when they see or hear it. We ask how can we, as churches, contribute to deliberations about what is good or just if there is no longer a normative consensus about the Truth?

Of course, this problem is not new. In John 18, Pilate interrogates the high priests and Jesus in order to decide what constitutes justice in the case of the man from Galilee. Frustrated by a lack of evidence, he finally asks one of the most profoundly theological questions in the whole of the biblical corpus, "What is truth?"

---

[1] Ilan Zvi Baron, *How to save politics in a post-truth era: Thinking through difficult times* (Manchester: Manchester University Press, 2018), 154.

Before thinking about the theological significance of this question, let us look at the social-historical context of this passage. Based on the references to the destruction of the temple, and the frequent use of certain phrases, we estimate that this gospel was most likely written at the start of the second century of the Common Era, certainly after the destruction of the temple by Titus in 70 CE. This event was the climax of the populist revolt that struggled against the economic and military occupation of the Roman Empire since the disintegration of Hasmonian and Herodian dynasties. The division of Herod's kingdom between his sons, and Archelaus' inability to govern the population, were the reasons that Roman prefects were established in Jerusalem. Pontius Pilate was the fifth prefect.

The Johannine account of the prosecution of Jesus reveals the complex relationship between the Roman government and the temple leadership, as well as the dynamic between religious and Roman law in the public space. Under Roman law, Judean leaders maintained the right to capital punishment, even though the coincidental timing of the Passover celebrations led the High Priest to pass this particular judgement regarding Jesus on to Pilate. Realizing the political implications of this responsibility, Pilate sought to clarify the basis on which the High Priest declared a capital offence. Pilate asks, "What accusation do you bring against this man?" In reply, the representative did not offer proof of criminal activity. Rather, he deployed circular logic that merely defended the traditional power of the High Priest to make a public charge, saying, "If this man were not a criminal, we would not have handed him over to you."

Interestingly, this is the same tactic deployed by the court of the High Priest when Jesus defended himself in the previous verses. Annas questioned Jesus about the nature of his teachings. Jesus insisted on inclusive transparency, saying that none of his teachings were done in secret, and therefore the court was free to question his disciples or those present in the synagogues when he taught. The court police struck Jesus for daring to expose the exclusionary nature of the deliberation, saying only, "Is that the way you speak to the High Priest." Jesus responded, "If I have spoken wrongly, testify to the wrong. But if I have spoken rightly, why do you strike me?" Jesus points to the need for justice to be deliberated on the basis of truth, not out of emotional deference to a leader based on national, ethnic or religious appeals.

This legal proceeding reveals several exclusionary populist dynamics. It is worth noting that Caiaphas, who served as the High Priest that year, is identified as the one who suggested "it was better that one person die for the people" (John 18:14). The religious leaders had a strong desire to appease the populist movements of the day, collectively referred to as Zealots, including Barabbas and some among Jesus' disciples, which culminated in the Bar Kochba Revolt of the second century. In order to appease or leverage the general anxiety of "the people", the High Priest excludes Jesus' truth from deliberation. In times of broad social, political or economic anxiety, populist leaders will often narrow the definition of "the people" in order to appease those who belong to the dominant culture and exclude the legitimate concerns of "others" from being addressed in traditional mechanisms for deliberating on matters of justice. But Isaiah (59:14) declares that "when truth falls away from the public square, righteousness stands far off, and justice is turned back". And, in light of this tactic to blur deliberations, Pilate asks, "What is truth?"

If we trace the *Koiné* Greek word for Truth, *Aletheia,* through Scripture, the Psalms (85:10) affirm that Truth is not only about facts, but it refers to the divine nature. Mercy righteousness, peace and truth are divine characteristics. Ephesians (4:21, 24) relates truth to the likeness of God that was in Jesus. And in the prologue to this gospel, the author writes that grace and truth came through Jesus. In other words, while the leaders struggled to discern the facts in that politically charged situation, Jesus was the fullness of Truth, revealed in the midst of that deliberation, and yet, somehow excluded from contributing to the discourse. Pilate asked, "What is truth?" of the very body in which Truth was reconciled creation. Here, Truth is not only recognized in a word spoken, but in the non-violent, creative and redeeming Word of God, embodied love that reconciles all creation into one (political) body.

In his commentary on this gospel, Robert Kysar writes that ""Truth", as Jesus uses it in this Gospel "means the whole of the revelation...it is the content of the revelation (i.e. God's character as redemptive love) which is both the sanctifying power and the purpose for the consecration (commissioning) of the believers." Kysar shows why this is important for the church's agency. The Church, the body of Christ, is a political body, "a people" in the world. When the truth and truth-telling bodies are marginalized or disappeared[2] from deliberations in the public sphere, the church can stand in physical solidarity with those who are excluded. In our assembly, we can publicly amplify their experience, and embody the indisputable fact of their being, and therefore their right to participate in public deliberation regardless of national, ethnic, gender or religious based affinity to the dominant culture. Wherever the Church publicly manifests itself as a people, willing to reconcile the politically, ethnically, sexually, economically and socially excluded into one political body of Christ in the

---

[2] As demonstrated powerfully in William Cavanaugh, *Torture and Eucharist: Theology, Politics and the Body of Christ* (New York: Wiley, 2007).

world, we can offer a vision of wisdom and a model of the fullness of Truth in the public discourse.

In the Gospel of John's passion narrative, Jesus exemplifies this kind of political agency. When truth and justice were not realized in the public square, Jesus embodied them from the cross. Crucifixion represents the nihilistic power of the state to deny political participation. Capital punishment ultimately cuts off the possibility of a body to be represented in public and has the psychological and real effect of disintegrating "the people" and, therefore, limiting inclusion. But, at that precise moment, when Jesus and his followers faced the nation's will-to-power, he demonstrated the political agency that comes from faith.

The ultimate divine will-to-life motivates faith that operates beyond even the limits of death. Therefore, faith provides an agency that goes even beyond rights-based discourse, which finds the limit of our ability to arbitrate justice at the point of death. Not even death could disintegrate and exclude that which constitutes the body of Christ. Even as he suffers the ultimate disintegration and exclusion from the public sphere, Jesus looks down at his mother and the beloved disciple standing in the shadow of the cross and redraws the lines of belonging. And, even after Jesus' presence on earth, the body of Christ, continues to manifest itself as a reconciling communion of bodies, regardless of race, ethnicity or gender. Where dominant powers that seek to disintegrate, disappear or disenfranchise bodies as a means to exclude them, faith motivates us to re-draw the circle to include their being and their voice to embody the fullness of truth. In the face of exclusionary populism, such is the political agency of a community of faith.

Thinking of Miroslav Volf's writings on the redemptive nature of embrace in the face of exclusion[3], when the church embraces the excluded, we witness to Truth in a fuller sense of the word. In the shadow of our post-truth age, the Church is called to represent those bodies through public advocacy and in our social communities and liturgical communion—the abused, gendered, differently-abled, female, and children's bodies marginalized by populist discourse. Gathering in public worship or embodying inclusive community is an inherently political act. In each act of faithful assembly, the church becomes a living, undeniable, diverse body in the world. When our charismatic leaders begin to deliberate about justice, and ask Pilate's question, "What is truth?", we can stand in the public space like Jesus, and reflect the image and likeness of God that is embodied in the reconciled body of Christ.

---

[3] Miroslav Volf, *Exclusion and Embrace: A Theological Exploration of Identity, Otherness, and Reconciliation* (Nashville: Abingdon Press, 2010).

The chances and limits of a multi-religious society. Reflections on rationality and truth

Olga Navrátilová

Plural society and secular state

To what extent is it possible for various religions to peacefully co-exist in a single state? This question has recently re-emerged, even in liberal, secular, democratic states. Most Christian churches have accepted the idea of religious tolerance together with the idea of the secular state. These closely interconnected ideas enable the peaceful coexistence of various religions in a single state. Christian churches gradually acknowledged not only religious tolerance, but also the secular state, though sometimes reluctantly and after a struggle to determine the borders between churches and the modern state. The churches have had to abandon their exclusive claim to provide the moral and legal norms which govern the life of individuals and society. The secular state has helped bring those churches, which originally had not demonstrated openness to liberal political values, to recognise the necessity of accepting and respecting otherness. Respect for the religious freedom of individuals has gradually been recognized by many churches and is now part of their Christian commitment and advocacy.

I lay aside the question concerning what extent the genesis of the secular state may be seen as a product of the integral development in Christianity itself; and to what extent the secular state has arisen from opposition to the political claims of Christian churches and from the attempt to liberate the society and public life from the traditional forms of Christianity. Both can be true.

The idea of the modern secular state is derived in political thinking from at least two sources. (1) On the one hand, its genesis was enabled by the development of modern political philosophies, which founded their theories about the origins and the legitimation of state power in a universal human nature. We can understand the nature of political society only if we understand human nature properly, as the political union of men and women in a commonwealth necessarily follows from the universal human condition. The emancipation of philosophy from theology becomes evident also in the field of political philosophy: the only authority in creating, recognizing or acknowledging social norms and institutions is the faculty of reason, which is accessible to all rational human beings. The authority of reason becomes superior to any religious authority, be it the authority of the hierarchical church or Scripture. (2) On the other hand, a crucial element of the secular state is respect for the freedom of conscience of an individual, motivated either religiously or philosophically. Each person endowed by reason is able to lead his or her life according to what he or she recognizes as truthful and binding.

However, a universal claim of reason in discerning the essence of human nature and the norms of social life, and the respect for the conscience of an individual, can be at odds with each other. Rational insight into the nature of things brings with it a claim to general validity which should be acknowledged by any rational being, and that is why the norms based on such an insight have an obligatory character. On the other hand, the idea of conscience claims that the highest authority belongs to individual understanding of what is right or wrong, yet its motivation for accepting certain attitudes may be of various natures and may take their origin from diverse cultural and religious backgrounds. Individual views on what is right and binding may differ and this may lead to conflicts. Universality of reason guarantees unity; individuality of conscience may divide.

For the thinkers of the Enlightenment, though, there is no, or very little conflict, between the two. They pre-suppose that if every person uses her or his reason properly, the discordance will lessen or even disappear. That is why public education came to be seen as necessary in the Enlightenment, education by which means everyone is led to the use of reason and is liberated from any external authority. Together with modern political theories, the concept of natural religion is also further developed, discerning the common rational basis of all monotheistic religions from the particular content, which has arisen more or less contingently, and which is the source of dissimilarity between the individual forms of religion. Religiously motivated conflict among humans, as well as among particular denominations, originates in the fact that contingent and historically conditioned contents are mistaken for what is the substance of religion.

This presupposition of the Enlightenment has been, nevertheless, challenged. The critique of modernity has brought about also the critique of the universalistic claim that there is only one form of rationality. There is no rationality common to all people, just as there is no common language. Rationality is limited and culturally bound. The claim to universality is in fact a disguised claim to power and control. The whole project of the Enlightenment, when properly perceived and understood, does not permit any real cultural or religious diversity, but enforces uniformity. Secularism, if placed above the individual forms of religions, proves to be an ideology.

The model of "overlapping consensus" of John Rawls

It seems that if the consensus about basic values, which are expressed in shared social and legal norms in a plural society, is to be possible, it is necessary to seek the source of unity somewhere other than in the concept of universal secular rationality.

A well-known proposal on how to think of both the unity and plurality of society is the concept of "overlapping consensus" of the political philosopher John Rawls.[1] Rawls does not want to proceed in his reflections on the nature of the liberal state from insights into the essence of human nature, but intends to establish the rules of common life in a political society through pragmatic considerations. The pragmatic approach of John Rawls separates practical reasonability, which enables justice in social relations to be realized, from theoretical reason, which intends to discover and comprehend the rational structures of reality.

The concept of overlapping consensus enables agreement about liberal political values, even though the justification of these values may come in different "comprehensive doctrines". Christians may thus find rationale for respecting fellow human beings in their likeness to God, whereas the followers of Kant's ethics will find such justification in the universal validity of the moral law. The common political values, which Rawls identifies with the formal rules of justice, originate in the necessity of overcoming conflicts and establishing a stable political society. The formal and non-comprehensive character of these values makes them suitable for being adopted by various religions or world views.

Rawls differentiates between *"modus vivendi"* and "overlapping consensus".[2] Modus vivendi is a mere balance of power between conflicting parties and

---

[1] Cf. John Rawls, *Justice as Fairness: A Restatement* (Cambridge, MA: Harvard University Press, 2001), 184–198.
[2] Ibid., 192.

ceases at the moment when one party gains superiority over the other. This was the situation in Europe after the confessional wars in the seventeenth century, when neither Protestants nor Roman Catholics were able to acquire conclusive victory. Only later, when tolerance, although at first enforced by necessity, proved to be a more powerful means to attaining peace and social unity than was the quest for uniformity, was *modus vivendi* transformed into a real overlapping consensus and mutual recognition became a positive political value in itself. Whereas *modus vivendi* arises from mere exterior necessity, overlapping consensus is characterized by interior acceptance. Respect then attains moral features and becomes a moral obligation.[3]

The question of whether political liberalism, with its respect for the diversity of comprehensive doctrines, is possible is thus answered by Rawls with the observation that it must be possible since it has become real in liberal political societies. The experience of respectful co-existence, advantageous for all and ensuring stability, plays a crucial role and, according to Rawls' perhaps optimistic view, the political liberal values once adopted are not easily overridden.[4] Embracing these political values then leads to the transformation of comprehensive doctrines, in those respects in which they are not compatible with them, rather than giving up these values for the sake of comprehensive doctrines. This is possible because, according to Rawls, humans are endowed with practical reasonability, which enables them to transcend their interests and point of view and to set, together with others, common rules of a just social life.[5]

PLURALITY AND THE QUESTION OF TRUTH

Rawls' concept of overlapping consensus offers a pragmatic solution to the question concerning the conditions under which unity in plural society is possible. The pragmatic approach deliberately renounces the question of truth. Nevertheless, even if the critique of the universal rationalistic claims of Enlightenment is kept in mind, we may ask whether such a resignation on the theoretical reason and its quest for truth is appropriate or even possible. The potential conflicts, which are always latently present in plural society, originate from the fact that what a particular religion or world view recognizes as truth must be, from their point of view, understood as normative for all (at least in some respects). The rules of social life are never merely formal and the political values, although distinguishable, can hardly be completely

---

[3] Ibid., 195.
[4] Ibid., 189, 193.
[5] Ibid., 191, 195–198.

separated from moral or religious ones. The pragmatic approach adopts a point of view, so to speak, from outside; it is a deliberately chosen agnosticism that can never be fully accepted by particular religions or world views, even though they may appreciate its usefulness in social life. It is, therefore, important to explore the problem of the possibility of unity in plural society from the inside, and relate it to the question of truth.

The fact that religions and world views are essentially interwoven with the question of truth does not only contain the potential for conflicts between the different beliefs and opinions, but it also enables agreement resulting from the character of what we experience as truth. Truth is usually understood as potentially accessible to all human beings. We gain experience with truth in the moment when reality opens itself to us as meaningful and when we find ourselves to be bound by this revealed meaning. Truth attracts us, and, at the same time, lays claims on us. There is no private truth, as that would be a contradiction; rather, the universal feature of truth presupposes that this experience is and can be shared and communicated. There are various ways in which one can be led to experience the same opening of reality and share the same point of view, be it different forms of persuading, growing into common tradition, and/or the awakening of the imagination or emotions as happens in art or liturgy. These forms are indispensable, yet, at the same time, they may be misused and transformed into a very subtle form of violence, used e.g., in propaganda.

From the time of ancient Greek philosophy, particularly Socrates and Plato, nevertheless, the notion of truth is, at least in the Western tradition, associated with rational argumentation and discussion, with the quest for rational insight, which lies open to anyone who learns how to employ his or her reason. This presupposed shared rationality is the essential condition for any serious dialogue in which the partners acknowledge each other as free persons, and where they all accept truth as the general norm. To renounce this notion of rationality means to give up the possibility of having a dialogue. This is the case also in political discourse: even though other methods of persuasion are usually employed, and prove successful, methods which aim at other components of human personality than reason, freely led discussion remains in liberal political societies at least an ideal. The co-existence of different religions, world views and cultures in one state is possible when and only when this essential condition is accepted.

TRUTH AND DIALOGUE

The experience of truth as meaningfulness, which is at least in some respect accessible by the means of reason, is, however, enlarged by other experience: We experience truth as something that transcends our individual point of view. Truth is revealed to us often first in the form of a question, as something that we have to search for. Our experience with truth is the experience of openness as well as the experience of disguise, meaningfulness as well as the lack of meaning. Acceptance of this ambiguous character of truth opens the space for plurality. This understanding of truth also has its roots in the Greek philosophical tradition, which seeks truth by through dialogue. We reach truth only together with others and through others; there is no private truth, which one could keep only for oneself. This is a common experience of philosophy and of religion, as long as religion takes seriously the idea that God is revealed to the world as immanent as well as transcendent. This experience with the transcendent side of truth is a necessary condition for the genuine respect of others in a plural society.

It could be argued that this understanding of truth is closely connected to the Western cultural tradition. Even the Rawlsian model presupposes, though, that the unity of a plural political society is possible only if the citizens of different beliefs and cultural backgrounds accept basic liberal values, which are the result of Western cultural development. The same presupposition has to be made here. The accent on shared rationality, which was brought forth by the Enlightenment, and which is connected with the emphasis on the freedom of men and women in their quest for truth, is crucial and cannot be abandoned. Without this notion of rationality focused on truth, the peaceful co-existence of different religions and world views in one society is in liberal states barely imaginable.

Siblings Choose How to Relate. Reconnecting Abrahamic Faiths in Times of Rising Polarization

Michael Nausner

In this short chapter I want to propose the double strategy of self-criticism and defense of others in interreligious encounters as a bold and constructive attitude in times of rising polarization. I do so by first providing a glimpse into the discourse on religion in the Swedish public context. Secondly, in conversation with Jonathan Sacks and Navid Kermani, I sketch a way of peaceful co-existence between Abrahamic faiths in the context of the Noah covenant.

Resistance to Religious Discourse in the Public

In Sweden, religious discourse frequently is depicted in polarizing ways. Mattias Martinson's study on secularism, populism and xenophobia critically examines the public discourse on the role of religion in Swedish society.[1] Alongside many others, he diagnoses a change in the discourse on religion after the terror attacks in the United States of America in September 2001. So called "religious violence" has since been dominating reports on religion in Western media, and a tendency to "fear religion's irrational power" can be observed again.[2] Critics of religion have received growing attention, and often the critique generalizes and is quite ill-informed.[3] As a result, there is a general dismissal of religion

---

[1] Mattias Martinson, *Sekularism, populism, xenofobi. En essä om religionsdebatten* (Malmö: Eskaton, 2017).
[2] Ibid., 9.
[3] Ibid., 17.

and its ability to offer valid orientation in people's lives. Instead, critics of religion ascribe normative meaning to "scientific reason", most often without any awareness that "reason" also comes in many cultural forms[4] and that a blind trust in reason can also lead to some form of "pseudo-theology". Such dogmatic trust in scientific reason often ends up in the polarizing conviction that a belief in reason automatically means resistance to any kind of belief in God.[5] Martinson criticizes such polarizing attitudes, and he observes that behind such critiques there is a kind of "secularist urge to purify"[6], and a normative intention behind such need of purification.

This becomes obvious when a leading representative of secular humanism in Sweden, Christer Sturmark, claims that "secular humanism is ... the typical Swedish worldview."[7] It is one thing to identify secular humanism as a typical Swedish worldview, but it becomes problematic to claim that secular humanism needs to be the norm for public discourse. At times one really does get the impression that a certain drive toward "secular purity" is advocated here, and an unwillingness to see religion as anything but ir-rational. Martinson identifies a similar drive toward purity among Sweden Democrats, a political right-wing party in Sweden that is on the rise. Sweden Democrats do not want to eliminate the church, but they want to purify it so that it remains Swedish or becomes more culturally Swedish again. The presupposition here is that the Church of Sweden has a purely Swedish identity that is sullied by foreign influences, and that its former purity needs to be regained. Such a presupposition is blind to the church's living reality, "which is a changing and culturally living entity".[8] Notwithstand-ing the necessarily culturally hybrid and mixed identity of the Church of Sweden, Sweden Democrats want to preserve its "Swedish-ness", which is an equally unidentifiable phenomenon as "Deutsche Leitkultur" in Germany.[9] "Deutsche Leitkultur" (guiding ideal of German culture) is claimed by some politicians and citizens as a necessary measure for what should be norma-

---

[4] Cf. Rainer Forst's critical analysis of different understandings of reason, in: Rainer Forst, *Normativität und Macht. Zur Analyse sozialer Rechtfertigungsordnungen* (Frankfurt: Suhrkamp, 2015), 11ff.

[5] Martinson, op. cit. (note 1), 21.–It is not so surprising that this juxtaposition sometimes ends up in xenophobia which necessarily builds on sharp boundaries, p. 30 and 33.–See also Martinson's observation that the "impure" oftentimes is identified with other, inhumane cultures, p. 64.

[6] Ibid., 41.

[7] Ibid., 45.

[8] Ibid., 55.

[9] For a critical perspective on the term when it was coined around the turn of the cen-tury see: Torsten Krauel, "Was ist deutsche Leitkultur?", in: *Die Welt* online 20 October 2000: https://www.welt.de/print-welt/article539521/Was-ist-deutsche-Leitkultur.html

tive in Germany. However, it is less an attempt to grasp German identity in all its complexity, and more a strategy for exclusion of cultural and religious expressions which are considered non-German, above all Islam. But to claim a seemingly pure cultural/ethnic norm does not so much clarify one's own identity as it clarifies whom one is *against*. When it comes to the attempt to claim *non-religious* norms for societal coexistence, the discursive hostility to religion seems to be stronger in Sweden than in Germany.

Martinson identifies Sturmark's rather trivial understanding of faith as an attitude that believes in something without reason as an example for a polarizing view of religion.[10] At the same time it is also part of a quite well established tradition of critique of religion in Sweden. Martinson identifies in this tradition a certain "phobia of religion".[11] Many critics of the church and of religion in general advocate a kind of non-religious normativity that is based on a quite shallow understanding of Christianity and religion in general. Despite the wide-spread talk of *post-secularism*—a time of increased significance of religion in the public square—it seems that it still is quite common in certain circles to judge religious thinking and praxis as irrelevant.

But religious discourse itself is not immune either to the polarizing and populist tendencies found in secular discourse. At times, secular and religious versions of populist arguments merge and advocate for the kind of exclusionary policies that can be seen emerging in many European contexts. Under the pretense of protecting one's own identity, these discourses construct polarities between religions, ethnicities and cultures to exclude "the others". They tend to be resistant to argumentation that is not in line with their own thinking. At times, one can identify a resistance not only against arguments, but also against facts. There have been many discussions in the media about "fake news", "alternative facts", and "post-truth". Post-truth does not mean that the age of the search for truth is over. Rather, it means that the meaning of truth has shifted in public discourse. The philosopher Lee McIntyre defines post-truth succinctly as the "contention that feelings are more accurate than facts, for the purpose of the political subordination of reality".[12]

Here, the church as part of a worldwide community needs to be attentive, since this kind of feelings-based discourse often ends up in an exclusionary politics that targets minorities in different cultures: Muslims in the United States of America and elsewhere, Kurds in Syria, immigrants in Europe, to just name a few examples.

---

[10] Martinson, op. cit. (note 1), 66.
[11] Ibid., 94.
[12] Lee McIntyre, *Post-Truth* (Boston, MA: MIT Press, 2018), 174.

Reconnecting the Abrahamic Faiths
in the Face of Rising Polarization

A reconciling voice is needed, not least in interreligious relations, since it is a field in which polarization, protectionism and populism constitute an increasing problem. In the media, religions are far too often rendered as mutually exclusive from one another. In real life, however, religions never meet each other as homogeneous opposing entities, but rather in the form of encounters between believers. And believers can always choose how to relate. I limit myself here to relations among three of the so-called Abrahamic religions. As a Christian theologian, I want to offer some brief reflections on the thoughts of both a Jewish thinker and a Muslim thinker: the English Rabbi Jonathan Sacks and the German-Iranian writer Navid Kermani. They both strike me as thinkers who, amid polarizing and populist discourses on the assumed hostility of religions, talk about inter-religious affairs in a constructive and reconciling tone, and I believe that we need more religious voices from across the spectrum who inspire. It is a way of effectively countering stifling and destructive polarization.

Jonathan Sacks is such a voice. In his book *Not in God's Name. Confronting Religious Violence*[13], he contests the increasingly common view that religion is the root cause of much violence. This is in tune with the document *The Church in the Public Space*, which strongly opposes violence in the name of religion.[14] Instead, Sacks understands the relation between the three Abrahamic religions as a relation between siblings, and, of course, there is also rivalry between siblings. Sibling rivalry is part of the Jewish-Christian-Muslim narrative tradition, Sacks suggests, and it needs to be looked at if we want to understand and heal the hate that leads to violence in the name of God.[15]

He then offers an intriguing reading of Genesis, which to him is the book of sibling rivalry par excellence. Time and again, he shows that the classic rivalries between Isaac and Ismael, between Jacob and Esau, and between Joseph and his brothers, need not be read in purely antagonistic terms, which is how much of the Christian tradition has read it. Instead, in these stories, complexities emerge upon closer reading. These complexities make it impossible to understand them as narratives about right and wrong, good and bad, inside and outside. Perhaps most importantly, for the relation between Christians and Jews on the one side, and Muslims on the other, Sacks presents the story

---

[13] Jonathan Sacks, *Not in God's Name. Confronting Religious Violence* (New York: Schocken Books, 2017).

[14] *The Church in the Public Space. A Study Document of The Lutheran World Federation* (Geneva: LWF, 2016), 35.

[15] Cf. Sacks, op. cit. (note 13), 92.

of Isaac and Ismael as a story of reconciliation, in which God has not forsaken Ismael,[16] and Ismael and Isaac show up together at the funeral of Abraham,[17] which in the Christian tradition rarely, if ever, is noted, let alone interpreted as a symbol of reconciliation. In all of the key stories, Sacks detects God's inclusive love that has the last word: That Jacob is chosen, does not mean that Esau is forsaken,[18] and commenting on the story of Joseph and his brothers, Sacks emphasizes that God does not prove God's love by hating others.[19] The most important conclusion in Sacks' book builds on this non-exclusive reading of the stories of sibling rivalry in Genesis. Those are stories, Sacks maintains, which show that we all have a place in God's universe of justice and love.[20]

For Sacks, this conviction is rooted in the inclusivity of the Noah covenant, which is valid for all of humanity and which is not in opposition to God's covenant with Israel at Sinai. Without going into the complexities of the relation between the covenant of Noah, the covenant of Sinai, the covenant in Jesus Christ, and then the covenant of Mohammed, from a Christian perspective, I would like to conclude that there are important lessons to be learned here about seeing believers from the other Abrahamic faiths, not as competitors, but as siblings waiting to be reconciled. They are part of the same faith family, and the tools for reconciliation it can be found right in our common narrative tradition.

This is in tune with some of the key affirmations in the document *The Church in the Public Space,* which reminds us that God loves the *world* (not a specific community of faith) and never ceases to engage with it,[21] which is why the church never is called to dominate the public space,[22] but rather to share it with people of other faiths and convictions.[23] And I specifically want to highlight some additional affirmations in the same document, which seem to me to be in tune with Sacks' trajectory. We need a non-absolutistic understanding of Christian community in order to create the kind of "participatory public space" the document talks about, a space that fosters dialogue and cooperation.[24] Such dialogue is not in opposition to Christian witness, but it "deepens mutual understanding" and "constitutes a strong public witness".[25]

---

[16] Cf. ibid., 111.
[17] Cf. ibid., 118.
[18] Cf. ibid., 142.
[19] Cf. ibid., 173.
[20] Cf. ibid., 218.
[21] Cf. *The Church in the Public Space,* 8.
[22] Cf. ibid., 22f.36.
[23] Cf. ibid., 22.
[24] Cf. ibid., 25.
[25] Ibid., 29.

The Muslim writer Navid Kermani has a bit to say about such "mutual understanding". In his non-polarizing view of religions, he is a soul friend of his Jewish colleague Jonathan Sacks. In a speech delivered in 2015, Kermani, in a critical prophetic tone, talks as a Muslim about a Christian monastery in Syria that had as its mission *to love Muslims*. Inspired by the leader of that monastery, Father Jacques Mourad, he offered a very simple two-fold rule for the encounter between Muslims and Christians. "Father Jacques defended the community he does not belong to, and criticized his own."[26] A rule of conduct in the encounter with people from other faiths is first, defend the representatives from other faiths against misrepresentation. Do not easily believe in the generalizing judgements of believers whose belief you do not share. Give them the benefit of the doubt, and above all, refrain from final judgement without having personally met a person of different faith or conviction. The second rule is, if you love your faith community, criticize it, in the same way as Mourad criticized his Christian brothers and sisters for forgetting them in their struggle for peaceful coexistence in Syria. During his speech, Kermani added: "The love of one's own—one's own culture, one's own country and also one's own person—manifests itself in self-criticism."[27]

I conclude that there are constructive ways to resist a polarizing view of the relation between religions. Sacks and Kermani are leading the way, and as representatives from two other great Abrahamic religions, they can inspire Christian leaders, intellectuals and practitioners to refrain from polarizing or antagonistic talk about their religious siblings. And maybe the way into the future is less a way of *rational argument* for or against and more a way of attentive praxis in terms of dwelling at the boundaries between the religions and *witnessing* about the way of Christ, who had no problems with respectful interaction with his religious siblings. This is shown in his encounters with the Samaritan woman, the Syrophoenician woman and the Roman captain. Yes, the Abrahamic siblings can choose how to relate, and I consider it a Christian vocation in times of rising antagonism to relate in a mutually respectful and non-exclusionary way.

---

[26] Navid Kermani, "Beyond the Borders – Jacques Mourad and Love in Syria", Speech given at Paulskirche in Frankfurt, 18 October 2015, 3-4. Cf. http://www.friedenspreis-des-deutschen-buchhandels.de/445651/?mid=1042759B (last accessed on 6 August 2018)

[27] Ibid., 4.

A Post-Soviet Eclipse of Religious Consciousness in Estonia

Joona Toivanen

Introduction

This paper is divided into three parts. First, I want to present a short historical overview of the influence of atheism in Estonia. Second, I give a brief overview of the religious discourse in Estonia. Finally, I make a few concluding remarks concerning the issue of populism in Estonia and its cultural consequences. The topic has been discussed by various authors in Estonia, but I will rely mainly on Atko Remmel, who has written extensively on the subject.

A discourse of religious consciousness in a post-Soviet country

The discourse of religious consciousness in Estonia today is influenced by three strands of atheism.[1] First of all, there was a vulgar or social atheism that was integral to the communistic ideology. Secondly, there was its developed form, so-called "Scientific Atheism" and thirdly, after the re-independence, American "New Atheism". The first wave of atheism had its roots in the emergence of a mechanistic world view during the early modern period. To put it briefly, the Cartesian method was adopted as metaphysics

---

[1] Atko Remmel, *Ateistlikud traditsioonid Eestis.* (Ajalooline Ajakiri, 2012, 3/4 (141/142)), 309–336.

and thinkers began to view the world increasingly as a machine haunted by subjective consciousness within and by God from the outside. As God had no real role in this new metaphysics, God was quickly discarded as an unnecessary hypothesis, and only the human consciousness remained. The world was thus divided into mind and matter, and as evolutionary and biological sciences advanced, many desired to reduce human consciousness to material causes. Even today, human consciousness is viewed by some thinkers as another cog in the mindless machine of the mechanistic world. This sort of world needs no gods, souls or spirits, yet people still have a desire to believe in purpose, meaning and most of all, love.

In nineteenth-century Estonia, it was popular to criticize the church, as Christianity was often seen as a religion of the oppressing noblemen. It must be noted that this is only partly true, for the narrative was, in part, a fabrication used by Soviet propaganda to justify class conflict and the workers' revolution. Religious and national awareness were shaken by creating a narrative of Estonian peasants suffering under various oppressors and being forced to receive an alien faith, i.e. Christianity. A myth of the "true" Estonian was constructed: he was believed to be an animist, a child of nature, unblemished by greed, hypocrisy and the violence of stereotypical crusaders, witch hunters, monks and clergy.

Later in the twentieth century, Lenin wanted to increase Marxist awareness through education, which included ideological materialism, and thus, also atheism. He propagated the development of the so-called "scientific atheism", which was—rather not surprisingly—not at all scientific. Nevertheless, scientific-sounding articles defending atheism were written, false dichotomies such as the "unresolvable conflict between faith and science" or "rational knowledge versus irrational faith" were presented as problems. Atheism was presented as the rational solution. Interestingly, in the end, both faith and science were said to be constructs of society and "tools of capitalistic oppression".[2] The indoctrination of the people was achieved in the same way any sort of ideological education works today: atheism was incorporated into formal education, particularly at higher levels of academic learning. This meant that all university students had to complete a course of scientific atheism in order to get through their formal education. Curiously, even though scientific atheism was not intellectually persuasive, the indoctrination process which included ridicule, demagogy, bullying and manipulation, managed to give negative connotations to religious thinking.

In addition, because of the history of atheism and the lack of any significant evangelical or fundamentalist Christian discourse in Estonia, the literature of the so-called New Atheists did not really contribute any new ideas.

---

[2] Ibid.

The religious discourse in Estonia today

The generations brought up in the Soviet cultural milieu retain that narrative as part of their identity. They, in turn, have taught certain attitudes and values to their children. As religion has not played a significant role in people's lives, questions of faith or existential issues are seldom posed. I have often found that people suffer from a lack of religious vocabulary and rudimentary knowledge about religions and religious thought. People are often unable to express their religious feelings or pose existential questions because they lack the knowledge and are, therefore, incapable of asking them. I recall the professor of religious education in Tartu University remarking in one seminar, that, in her experience, people in academic circles can be extremely intelligent in their own field of expertise but be unbelievably immature or even fundamentalist when it comes to religious thinking and religious hermeneutics. Many people have adopted a vague animism and experiment with different religious movements and superstitions in the "religious marketplace".

During the Soviet era, the only people left in the churches were poor, ill-educated and certainly not members of the Communist party. This created a stereotype of the believer that has remained until today: Religious people are weak, poor, uneducated and strange. There is no real virtue in being a Christian. This calls to mind the criticism of virtues by Friedrich Nietzsche in his book *The Gay Science* or *The Joyful Wisdom*. According to Nietzsche, classical virtues such as diligence, obedience, chastity, piety and justice are mostly harmful to those who possess them. He writes "When you have a virtue—a real, complete virtue (and not just a small drive towards some virtue)—you are its victim!"[3]

Many people want to have their wedding in a church, but do not want to be part of the Christian community because they subconsciously fear ridicule and resentment from family and co-workers. A peculiar though diminishing example of this phenomenon is the non-religious funeral, where people still want to hear the Lord's prayer. Because of this kind of thinking, less than thirty percent of the population of Estonia claim to belong to a Christian denomination. Around twelve percent of the population belong to the Lutheran church. Some thirteen percent belong to the Orthodox church.

In a way, people in Estonian society stand outside the church and occasionally see and hear what is happening within. The atheism of the past has kept people out of the churches and the strong capitalism and

---

[3] Friedrich Nietzsche, *The Gay Science* (Cambridge: Cambridge University Press, 2008), 43f.

materialism of today carry on this same agenda. Peculiarly, this has led to some conflicting views: in a quickly changing materialist and capitalist society, people often long for nostalgic stability and moral guidance from an "old fashioned" institution such as the church. At the same time, there is a conflicting urge to somehow bring the church up to date with certain developments in society. For many people, the church exists solely as something that brings back childhood memories and positive feelings.[4]

The influence that Christianity has had in the country is often filtered from discourse on Estonia's history or national identity. For example, I work as a pastor in St. Mary's parish in Tartu, a congregation that played a significant role in the national awakening of the Estonian people and its Song Festival tradition. Our pastor, Rev. Adalbert Willigerode, was one of the leaders of the first Song festival in 1869, and the grand rehearsal was held in our church. The church building was destroyed in the Second World War. During the Soviet period, the building was appropriated by the government and reconstructed as a sports hall during the 1960s. The church building was given back to the parish in 2008 and now the parish wants to rebuild it. That building has tremendous cultural value for the people of Estonia, but despite the efforts of the local congregation, the government has not been interested in contributing financially to the project.

This last point connects with the role of the church in the public space and the challenge of populism. On a practical level, it is difficult to prove to society that church has something to offer to the public discourse. On the one hand, the voice of the church, including the clergy, is ignored when it comes to social or political issues. It is often ignored and seldom highlighted by the media. On the other hand, some populist right-wing movements look to the Lutheran church to legitimatize their policies. This has created a new problem as the church is being used from the outside to gain power for their political agendas.

CONCLUDING REMARKS

How is my topic related to the issue of the growth of populism? I will say this: the atheistic discourse as a cultural meta-identity resembles the cultural crisis envisaged by Nietzsche in the *The Joyful Science*, where he speaks about the allegory of the death of God. For him, the death of God is a cultural phenomenon, which has been encoded within the development of Western intellectual culture, as I explained in beginning of my

---

[4] *Usust, elust ja usuelust*. http://www.saarpoll.ee/UserFiles/File/Elus,%20usust%20 ja%20usuelust_2015_ESITLUS_FINAL.pdf

presentation. This does not mean that people in the West today are not religious nor that the *conditio humana* or "ontological inner dissonance of human *dasein*" would now magically be resolved by science once and for all. People still suffer and hurt, but they are looking for saviors and solutions in an increasingly fragmented society from socio-political communities formed around sexuality, gender, race, language or other particular interests. People do this because they feel that they are not heard or loved. Individuals and groups increasingly blame the prevailing power structures for their personal failures to be happy and find purpose in a world where God is dead. Because God is dead, the only way to quench the thirst for purpose, justice and love is to complain publicly and let everyone around know how offended one is. Life is seen as a perpetual struggle of individual will over another.

I want to emphasize that the death of God in this instance is an allegory that means the disappearance of purpose, values, ontological wonder and the experience of belonging to the world, or, more simply put, the experience of being loved. Nietzsche explains this further as follows: "After Buddha was dead, they still showed his shadow in a cave for centuries—a tremendous, gruesome shadow. God is dead; but given the way people are, there may still for millennia be caves in which they show his shadow.—And we—we must still defeat his shadow as well!"[5] The so-called populists, i.e. the individuals and political parties that use Christianity to legitimize their political goals, are worshipping the shadow of God. They cling to the fragments of faith and Christian morals without seeing nor seeking the true God. They have no desire to do this, because they lack understanding of the highest good.

I will end with a quote from St. Bonaventure:

> "Since happiness is nothing other than the enjoyment of the highest good and since the highest good is above, no one can be made happy unless he rise above himself, not by an ascent of the body, but of the heart. But we cannot rise above ourselves unless a higher power lift us up."[6]

---

[5] Nietzsche, op. cit. (note 3), 108.

[6] St Bonaventure, *The Soul's Journey Into God* (Mahwah, NJ: Paulist Press, 1978), 59.

CHRISTIAN NUDGES: OUT OF—OR INTO THE DIGITAL FILTER BUBBLE? THEOLOGICAL REFLECTIONS ON SOCIAL MEDIA COMMUNICATION

Florian Höhne

Scrolling through my Facebook timeline, I bumped into an advertisement by a Christian magazine that some of my Facebook friends had liked. The ad presents three photos representing different topics: Islam, the persecution of Christians and pro-life. "What a biased choice," I thought. "How populistic!" Isn't that a case of Christianity being populistic or—maybe worse—populism wearing the garments of Christianity? Do these advertisements point to the existence of a Christian filter bubble, where our values are reinforced? Have these Christians lost touch with global realities? Can they honestly claim these three topics are the most relevant today, as opposed to the vast social injustice on this globe?

Asking these questions in a well heated office with a freshly brewed cup of coffee makes a less curious and more disturbing question arise: is it my filter bubble of an academic theologian that makes me think like that?[1]

These questions, the self-critical one and the not so self-critical one, arise in the context of social media communications. The ad has made it

---

[1] For a nuanced and critical perspective on the relation of populism and religion see f.e. Walter Lesch (ed.), *Christentum und Populismus: Klare Fronten?* (Freiburg im Breisgau: Herder, 2017). Lesch also points to such a lack of self-criticism (Walter Lesch, "Religion und Populismus: Blinde Flecken der Wahrnehmung," in op. cit., 12-25: 12).

into my Facebook filter bubble, which triggered my emotional reaction. Do social media pander to populism and sentimental reactions?

In this paper, I aim to focus on one dynamic (out of many) in the interplay of social media, academic theology, religious practice and populism. To shed light on it, I will refer to Priester's understanding of populism as latent mentality and show how social media's filter bubbles make its manifestation more likely. I will explain how two opposing notions of religion make the practice they inform both prone to, and resilient against, the retreat into filter bubbles.

POPULISM

Populism is easy to exemplify but hard to define. While some have argued that populism is an ideology, strategy or discourse, Karin Priester critiques these approaches, calling populism a mentality instead.[2] She names four characteristics of populism.

- Populism refers to a "latent" mentality critical of the elites. This mentality is to be found primarily in the middle and lower class while often instrumentalized by quite privileged populists.[3]

- This mentality is characterized by the dichotomy between the "good" common people and the "depraved" elite.[4]

- This is combined with references to organic community as opposed to anonymous society.[5]

- Populism is a reaction to social transformation and understands itself as a reaction to a crisis which it paints most colorfully.[6]

Given these characteristics, Christianity and Christian theologies are indeed not void of populistic tendencies. In the example I started with, the news agency's choice of topics envisions a crisis of persecution of Christians, an

---

[2] For this aspect as well as different qualifications of populism (f.e. as ideology, strategy, or discourse (190ff)), and the following see: Karin Priester, "Definitionen und Typologien des Populismus," in: *Soziale Welt* 62 (2011), 185–198.

[3] Ibid., 188, 191.

[4] Ibid., 191.

[5] Ibid., 196.

[6] Ibid., 191.

onslaught on the right to live. It often refers to the close-knit communities of Christians, and divides the world into simple and faithful Christians and the deprived elites in theological faculties or church administrations. This could be called populism insofar as it draws on the populistic mentality critical to elites in such a dichotomizing way.

If populism is a latent mentality[7], the question at hand is what role is social media playing in manifesting it.

Filter Bubbles

Theological discourse has already noted that digital transformation enhances populism. Filter bubbles show one way populism is fostered. Eli Pariser has explained how Google, Facebook, Yahoo and You Tube personalize the information diet they offer each user:[8] What I get to see is not what everybody gets to see, but what dynamic algorithms have chosen just for me, based on my previous preferences.[9] According to Pariser, this creates filter bubbles, individual information universes tailored to each user's needs, invisible to the user.[10] I get to see what I already agree with, get to learn about "facts" that confirm how I have seen the world already, and get to meet people who think like, and are like, me.[11] Whether this leads to a fragmentation of society is a contested thesis.[12] Sociological studies of different milieus raise the question of how new these bubbles and their communication barriers really are.[13]

Independent of this debate in the macro-perspective, we know that filter bubbles foster communications in which populistic mentalities reinforce themselves. The perception of a crisis becomes more real because the filter bubble gives more information confirming such a crisis. The resentment

---

[7] Ibid., 196.

[8] See Eli Pariser, Filter Bubble: *Wie wir im Internet entmündigt werden* (München: Hanser, 2012), 16, 22. The page-numbers in the following paragraphs refer to this text.

[9] Ibid., 17.

[10] Ibid., 17f.

[11] Ibid., 20-24.

[12] See Jan-Hinrik Schmidt, *Das neue Netz. Merkmale, Praktiken und Folgen des Web 2.0* (Konstanz: UVK, 2011), 99f; Christoph Neuberger, "Internet, Journalismus und Öffentlichkeit," in: Christoph Neuberger, Christian Nuernbergk and Melanie Rischke (eds.), *Journalismus im Internet: Profession - Partizipation - Technisierung* (Wiesbaden: VS Verlag für Sozialwissenschaften, 2009), 19–105, 44.

[13] See particularly Pierre Bourdieu, *Die feinen Unterschiede. Kritik der gesellschaftlichen Urteilskraft* (Frankfurt am Main: Suhrkamp, 2016).

against elites is fostered by virtually bringing together people who think alike in the bubble, reinforcing a sense of organic community.

I would like to dare a comprehensive but cautious thesis: digital filter bubbles make latent populistic mentalities more likely to become manifest in a form of online populism that employs filter bubbles.

MODELS OF RELIGION

Theology's susceptibility to and resilience[14] against filter bubble inspired populism are examined in the theological theories of religion in George A. Lindbeck's famous typology. How does the notion of religion that a given theology works with make the religious practice this very theology informs—including the practice of the reflecting theologian herself—prone to filter bubble populism? Lindbeck has identified three types of theories of religion, while proposing a fourth alternative.[15] Two of these types are of interest here.

"Experiential-expressive" approaches postulate a "basic religious experience" that is common to all humans [16] and thought of as being pre-reflective and internal to the self.[17] This experience is described differently.[18] For Schleiermacher, it is the "feeling of absolute dependence"[19] or for Rudolf Otto the "*mysterium fascinans et tremendum*" [20]—the experience of the holy. Religious doctrines are expressions of this experience and translate it into "noninformative and nondiscursive symbols of inner feeling".[21]

Lindbeck suggests working with a cultural-linguistic notion of religion: "religions are seen as comprehensive interpretive schemes, usually embodied in myths or narratives and heavily ritualized, which structure human

---

[14] While I focus on the meta level here, Torsten Meireis has already shed light on doctrinal and institutional resources and challenges of theology in the attempt to further democracy: Torsten Meireis, "Public Theology in a Post-democratic Age? Perspectives from a European Context," in Torsten Meireis, Rolf Schieder (eds.), *Religion and Democracy. Studies in Public Theology* (Baden-Baden: Nomos, 2017), 19–35, 25–31.

[15] See George A. Lindbeck, *The Nature of Doctrine. Religion and Theology in a Postliberal Age* (Louisville, KY: Westminster John Knox Press, 1984).

[16] Ibid., 21.

[17] Ibid., 16, 21.

[18] Ibid., 21.

[19] Ibid., 21.

[20] Ibid., 31.

[21] Ibid., 16, 21.

experience and understanding of self and world".[22] Religion works like language.[23] This already hints at where Lindbeck sees one decisive difference to the experiential-expressive model. While the latter presupposes a basic experience that seeks to be expressed in different ways (in which it is never grasped fully), cultural-linguistic approaches emphasize how the experience is "in a sense constituted" by external linguistic systems.[24] "One learns how to feel, act, and think in conformity with a religious tradition".[25]

While this difference names two sides of one dialectic[26], it has practical consequences insofar as it distinguishes notions of religion used by theology to normatively inform its own subject. Take, for example, Christian education. Experiential-expressivist theologians will work hermeneutically, cultural-linguistic theologians will work performatively. The former will search for experiences to relate Christian interpretations to. The decisive factor is what makes sense for the individual, what allows the individual to make sense of her feelings. The latter will work with exemplifications: "Ritual, prayer, and example are normally much more important."[27] The narrative is decisive. It does not need to be understandable to the individual at first, just as when one is learning a foreign language that it is not initially understandable. However, in the process of learning, it will enable the individual to have new experiences.

Both experiential-expressive and cultural-linguistic approaches inform religious practices—not least those of theologians themselves. The question is how prone to or resilient against such filter bubble inspired populism are theologians?

Religion and Filter Bubble Populism

Both approaches make religious practice prone to and resilient against populism. To conceptualize religion as an expression of common religious experiences of individuals creates resilience. It establishes the individual and her irreducibly individual experience as the basic criterion of critique. What does not make sense for the individual, is not to be believed. This is erosive to all dogmatic ideologies, including those meant to trigger populism.

---

[22] Ibid., 32.
[23] Ibid., 18.
[24] Ibid., 34, 39.
[25] Ibid., 35.
[26] Ibid., 33.
[27] Ibid., 35.

On the other hand, experiential-expressive approaches tend to make the social emergence of the subject and its deepest experiences invisible. What we feel is already a product of the culture we live in. This is what Byung-Chul Han's Foucault-based analysis of the "Psycho-politics" points to.[28] The subject[29], the self[30], and human emotions[31] are formed in power structures. Hence, the invisible filter bubble transforms my deepest experience, which includes the erosion of the basic criterion of critique. Experiential-expressivist approaches will tend to ignore this, which makes them underestimate the necessity of politics and social ethics to establish structures that support critical individuals.

The claimed commonality of the basic religious experience can function as a nudge to get one out of the filter bubble. If others have the same basic experience, and if different symbols for it can help to deepen one's relation to it, practices need to be fostered in which people come to learn about other symbols, different cultures of interpretations.[32] Thus, the theory supports the idea of one getting outside the narrow bubble of her own personal experience.

On the other hand, the determination of the basic religious experience is necessarily open, because—as Rieger points out—it either is a symbolization of an actual basic experience—meaning it necessarily falls short of expressing the underlying experience completely—or it is transcendental reconstruction—and therefore refers not to a positive experience but to a transcendental condition for positive experience that can itself not be experienced.[33] Thus, the translation of the basic religious intuition into concrete instances of positive religion is necessarily open and hence not sufficiently secured against being filled with nationalistic sentiments. Then, the commonality of the experience quickly turns into an exclusive and excluding sentiment.

To sum up, experiential-expressivist approaches rightly emphasize that individuals can both critique and nudge others from their bubbles. However, these approaches underestimate how much the individual is embedded in social power structures and overestimate its resilience against the seduc-

---

[28] See Han, Byung-Chul, *Psychopolitik. Neoliberalismus und die neuen Machttechniken* (Frankfurt am Main: Fischer, 2014).

[29] Ibid., 9.

[30] Ibid., 42.

[31] Ibid., 67.

[32] See Lindbeck, *Nature*, 23.

[33] See Hans-Martin Rieger, *Theologie als Funktion der Kirche. Eine systematisch-theologische Untersuchung zum Verhältnis von Theologie und Kirche in der Moderne* (Berlin: de Gruyter, 2007), 293.

tive powers of social media. However, that can arguably be mitigated by integrating it into a social ethic sensitive to power structures.

Cultural-linguistic notions, first and foremost, provide an interpretative framework that can help theologians and religious practitioners to understand how filter bubble populism works within particular traditions. Understanding religions and traditions analogous to language highlights their incommensurability with each other and the absence of an epistemological neutral ground. To put it in the language of metaphor: If I speak and understand only German and you only Chinese, we not only will not be able to understand each other, we won't be able to make this lack of understanding explicit to each other. Nevertheless, either of us could win the other's attention by the way we behave. Therewith, the cultural-linguistic approach provides a framework that makes sense of the conflict between manifest populisms and points to a way of dealing with populism: to live a (distracting) example.

The same feature of this notion becomes a factor of susceptibility, where normatively applied to one's own religious tradition. As such, it makes the existing commensurabilities between different traditions invisible and creates the tendency to see only a dichotomy between one's own community and the opposing world. While this can lead to an inspiring critique of the majority culture, it displays clear elements of a populistic mentality: a self-understanding of the underdog, the persecuted Christian, and a dichotomy of church and world. As such, a cultural linguistic self-understanding of religion is prone to idealizing an analogue Christian filter bubble.

This leads to a second ambivalence: cultural linguistic approaches will work with a strong sense of community—the community is needed as a place where the language is learned. On the one hand, this is prone to populism insofar as it idealizes organic communities as opposed to the plural nature of society. On the other hand, it creates structures for a counter-culture in which an alternative lifestyle and mentality can be lived—even an inclusive alternative to any filter bubble inspired populism.

"... AND THE TRUTH WILL SET YOU FREE". PROPAGANDA, WITNESSING AND THE CHALLENGE OF CHRISTIAN POLITICAL ENGAGEMENT

Elisabetta Ribet

OUR STARTING POINT

The proliferation of different forms of fundamentalism and radicalism in all aspects of human life is a worrying characteristic of our times. Two of the contexts where this dynamic is most evident are the political and the theological-religious.

In my home country, Italy, people deal with structural problems, such as a weak welfare system, an educational system with many challenges, a massive exodus of the young and mid-young generations due to difficulties finding a job. From a geographical point of view, our country functions as a "bridge" for refugees and migrants seeking a safer place to live. In this context, Italy held its national election in March 2018. It took several weeks for the government to be formed. A strongly populist leadership is presently facing issues such as a growing racist violence, the growing toleration of discrimination and stereotypical anti-European attitudes. It is evident that those who are paying the heaviest bill are the minorities or the socially weakest: refugees and migrants; women; lesbian, gay bisexual, transgender and queer (LGBTQ) persons; youth; and non-Roman Catholic religious communities.

For these reasons, the task of theology today is of fundamental importance. Christianity should function as a part of society providing strong analysis, critique and detection of key words and ideas with a spirit of freedom and responsibility. From this point of view, I propose that we focus on three elements representing crucial overarching points between the fields of politics and theology-religion. First, the issue of "truth"; second, the message and the way it is proclaimed; third, the challenges and the mission of the church and of believers in the political context.

TRUTH—REALITY

The Christian understanding of history and of eschatology constantly faces the dialectic between necessity and freedom, "must" and "can", "is" and "might be". In this context, as the French jurist, theologian and sociologist Jacques Ellul used to affirm, the gap between reality and truth measures the space given to hope, as it is exactly in the distance between them that one can test the closeness to the *kerygma* and to the accomplishment of the promise. In other word, the closer we are to truth and reality, the closer we are to the accomplishment of the promise "I shall be with you"; "the Kingdom of God is near".

Moreover, the dialectic between truth and reality is not a prerogative of the Christian language. It is strongly present also in the political sphere, and, of course, it is an important issue for populism. Jan-Werner Müller[1] remarks that, as populists affirm, "we are the people", the meaning of this statement is (at least) double. First, this means that those who are not part of the populist movement *are not* "the people". This is the basic element that underlies the anti-pluralist attitude of certain forms of populism. Second, the populist leadership tends to present itself as the executioner of a "people's will" to which a deep moral value is given, a moral value which is antithetical to any other one—and, in fact, it is often presented as *the only* honest and pure one. The populist understanding of reality is, therefore, exclusive and tends to be dogmatic. The populist movement is presented as the only way to really care for and understand "the silent majority", the only way to make truth and reality come together.

This leads us to say that the problem of what truth is, particularly as we attempt to discern the difference between "belief" and "knowledge". When what we *believe* slips into being what we *know*, truth is at stake. Here, we touch the root of faith, of science, and of political convictions. Here lies the key of any transformation of ideas into dogmas, the origin of all radicaliza-

---

[1] Jan-Werner Müller, *What is Populism?* (Philadelphia: University of Pennsylvania Press, 2016).

tion. This is the starting point of a meditation on the evangelical statement: "You will know the truth, and the truth will make you free" (John 8:32).

PROPAGANDA AS A DYNAMIC OF THE TECHNOLOGICAL SOCIETY

The main question revolves around the issues of approaching and transmitting truth—or truths. The message that is told and reported has multiple ways of being communicated and many recipients. Are we witnessing, informing or propagandizing? And what sort of perception do we have of the "people", the "community" who are supposed to receive our message?

According to Jacques Ellul, on the sociological level, propaganda belongs to the main modes of communication in the technological society. In *The Technological Society*, Ellul is talks about "the ensemble, 'the totality of methods rationally arrived at and having absolute efficiency ... in every field of human activity'."[2] In such a system, technology has replaced nature, and has become the background, the location of modern life. Thus, technology has also acquired the role of the "sacred", which used to be attributed to nature.

The French scholar has deepened the analysis of the propagandist action. I want to share with you some notes taken from an article published in 1952[3]. First, propaganda acts upon the masses while focusing on the individual; second, propaganda is not interested in truth, but it aims at the efficiency of its own work of persuasion with the final goal being to obtain choices and actions—and particularly, adds Müller, with the ultimate goal of activating a passive delegation of any choice or any action of the populist leadership. The reason is, definitely, that propaganda, as Ellul used to say, wants to avoid ideas[4].

"Stabilizing and unifying," the phenomenon that Ellul calls "social propaganda" is an integrative propaganda of conformity "made inside the group (not from the top)." It "springs up spontaneously; it is essentially

---

[2] Jacques Ellul, *The Technological Society*. Trans. John Wilkinson (New York, NY: Vintage, 1964); *The Technological System*. Trans. J. Neugroschel (New York, NY: Continuum, 1980); *The Technological Bluff*. (Grand Rapids, MI: Eerdmans, 1990). Quoted by Richard L Kirkpatrick, "Social Propaganda and Trademarks." *Ellul Forum* 60 (2017), 12–18.

[3] "La propagande agit sur la masse en atteignant l'individu dans la masse": Jacques Ellul, "Propagande et vérité chrétienne", *Bulletin du Centre protestant d'études*, 4/2 (1952), 1–10.

[4] "La propagande a un but bien déterminé qui est d'éviter justement les idées" (Ibid., 2).

diffuse; ...it is based on a general climate, an atmosphere that influences people imperceptibly without having the appearance of propaganda; it gets to man through his customs, through his most unconscious habits. It creates new habits in him; it is a sort of persuasion from within. As a result, man adopts new criteria of judgment and choice, adopts them spontaneously, as if he had chosen them himself. But all these criteria are in conformity with the environment and are essentially of a collective nature. Sociological propaganda produces a progressive adaptation to a certain order of things, a certain concept of human relations, which unconsciously molds individuals and makes them conform to society"[5]. In a few words, propaganda works as a strong normalization, standardization tool. And it is dangerously ambivalent, as it works on both sides: the individual loses him/herself inside the mass, and, at the same time, he/she feels special and unique, as soon as a populist, generalized message is offered to him/her.

We can find a further confirmation of these dynamics in the fact that populist movements have a strongly ambivalent relationship towards mass media and the worldwide web. We could summarize it with a formula: discredit, in order to replace. Not only, then, "we are *the* people", but also "we have *the real* information". Furthermore, Müller remarks that populism takes over a strategy of "mass clientelism"[6], aiming to discredit oppositions[7] and practicing a "discriminant legalism": "Everything for my friends; for my enemies, the law"[8]. On the basis of this strategy, there is a simple and charming message: "they"—the political élite, do not understand the true problems and pains of "the people". "We" do.

On the theological level, as we move to the sphere of faith, it seems significantly important to point out that Ellul claims that a fundamental task of believers and churches is to ask two questions related to meaning and to the sacred. Two questions that, when confronted with populist dynamics, gain a significance that is not only systematic and theological, but also political. Asking questions concerning the meaning and the sanctity of choices, principles, personalities, means to act against paternalistic populistic dynamics.

---

[5] Jacques Ellul, *Propaganda: The Formation of Men's Attitudes*. Trans. Konrad Kellen and Jean Lerner (New York, NY: Vintage Books, 1965), 64. See Ellul, "The Obstacles to Communication Arising from Propaganda Habits", *The Student World* 52/4 (1959), 401-410.

[6] Müller, op. cit. (note 1), 44.

[7] Ibid., 45.

[8] Ibid., 46.

THE WITNESS AND THE PROPAGANDIST

There is a basic distinction, necessary and fundamental, between "witness" and "propagandist", and Jacques Ellul points to it out through four characteristics. On one side, propaganda aims to "massification", to normalize individuals; on the other, God builds personal, unique relationships with the person. Secondly, while propaganda exploits the leftover reflex, faith calls people to a reflexive and critical attitude. Third, this happens because propaganda works on automatism while faith aims to free the individual. Fourth, propaganda tends to lead the human being, to control him/her, while God's grace "let the Totally Other enter his life, something coming from outside to modify the fundamental structures"[9].

In this context, the witness and the propagandist assume three different attitudes[10]. First of all, the witness "is engaged in the same adventure" as the person he/she is talking to, while "propagandist never has to believe in what he/she says". Secondly, the witness is a witness *of faith*, of the risen Christ, of the transcendent, while the propagandist *is* the message that he/she is bringing: no more propagandist, no more message. On the contrary, when a witness disappears, the *kerygma* lives on. The main consequence is that the witness can live in communion with the other persons, and the propagandist cannot.

Once more, then, as a church of witnessing people comes into relationship with the society it lives in, it must ask questions about meaning and the sacred in life.

As a result, as it confronts a populist dynamic, the church can ask the following question—while bringing its own witness: what do we mean when we talk about *citizenship*, and *plurality*? In order to witness to a Christian idea of citizenship, we are called to present an idea of a welcoming, reconciling community, in which we engage in constant reflection on the biblical understanding of *demos*, people, and of *oklos*, mass. Through this, the church, as well as the single believer, can open a discussion on what the concept of "people" means, and in what way a "people" can or has to be somehow "sacred", "sanctified" or "sacralized". The same can be applied to the concept of plurality. The biblical text is itself a pluralist writing, a polyphonic revelation. Starting from this, too, both individuals and churches can propose a rich and enriching challenge concerning differences and the multiple ways to invite differences in a dialogue, and even towards a communion.

---

[9] Ellul, op. cit. (note 3), 5-7.
[10] Ibid., 7-9.

"...AND THE TRUTH WILL SET YOU FREE"

As a word of conclusion, we can claim that only if we are aware that we have been set free, that we are being loved and welcomed, can we be present in the world as welcoming people engaged in relationships. Through this, as believers as well as Christian churches, we shall be able to offer a message free from "propagandism", which can penetrate reality, a provocative hope in the face of closemindedness and the violence of populist movements.

APPENDICES

Churches as Agents for Justice and Against Populism. Summary of Major Findings

When truth falls away from the public square, righteousness stands far off, and justice is turned back.
    Isaiah 59:14

Do not be overcome by evil, but overcome evil with good.
    Romans 12:21

I therefore, the prisoner in the Lord, beg you to lead a life worthy of the calling to which you have been called, with all humility and gentleness, with patience, bearing with one another in love, making every effort to maintain the unity of the Spirit in the bond of peace.
    Ephesians 4:1-3

Introduction

From 2 until 4 May 2018 over 65 participants from 25 countries around the globe gathered at the Dietrich-Bonhoeffer-Haus in Berlin to confer on the theme "Churches as Agents for Justice and Against Populism". The conference opened with words of welcome from the organizers of the event: Evangelische Akademie zu Berlin, the Lutheran World Federation, Brot für die Welt and the Church of Sweden. The opening addresses identified recent trends that suggest a crisis in democracies around the globe. Data shows that the space for meaningful participation of all in political processes and for jointly deliberating on matters of public concern is shrinking. Operational space for civil society actors is narrowing, including for churches and faith based actors, as they encounter difficulties to contribute to critical social and political discourse. Through interdisciplinary dialogue between theologians, ethicists, church leaders and social and political scientists, the conference sought to reinforce and reform the public role of theology, and strengthen the churches' agency to create inclusive, just and safe participatory spaces within society.

This summary offers a précis of some of our major findings.

Understanding "Populism" and Exclusionary Politics

A variety of political, cultural and economic forces are root causes for the phenomena of shrinking democratic space in different contexts. At the outset, the conference discussed that the term "populism" is used to describe a broad range of alleged anti-elitist, anti-establishment reactionary and exclusionary movements. Such movements arise from very different historical and cultural contexts, and therefore deploy diverse conceptual differences, goals and methods that must be understood in their complexity. Exclusionary populism can be understood as a symptom of the crisis of democracy and unjust economic systems, as well as a factor contributing to the crisis. In Europe and in the US especially, though not exclusively, ethnonationalist populist movements are a threat to the functioning of democratic principles in societies, and these developments currently threaten to have repercussions in other parts of the world as well.

Exclusionary populist movements make use of some democratic processes to subvert and destroy essential preconditions and values on which democracy depends: a sense of honesty, sincerity, responsibility, respect for the other, compromise etc. Where hate speech, fake news and methods of shallow propaganda enter the center stage of the political discourse, the space for solid and serious democratic negotiation is severely narrowed. The conference sought to identify common features of exclusionary populist discourses that seek to restrict public space and deprive people of their right to participate in democratic processes and to access just living conditions.

Exclusionary populist movements often refer to concerns about unjust distribution of power, wealth or social representation and political participation. They claim to amplify the voice of "the people" and seek "popular sovereignty" against the political power of the so-called "intellectual" or economic "elite", which gives rise to the term "populism" for this discourse in Northern American and European contexts. When these aspects are coupled with nativist ideologies, ethno-nationalist forms of populism can quickly colonize the public discourse.

Nativism circumscribes "the people" in exclusionary terms, putting "the natives" over against others. The conference discussed that these underlying dynamics of exclusionary populism are not restricted to European and Northern American contexts, but are present in other global contexts as well (e.g. the Hindutva ideology in India).

Ethno-nationalist populism seeks to redefine "the people" in binary terms through a process of "othering". Within that, those in the majority or dominant culture will identify the cultural, linguistic, religious, sexual, racial or gendered "other" as the scapegoat for social or economic anxieties and disparities. By propagating a post-truth climate of distrust of the media and other critical voices, the bases of social cohesion are eroded, and power is consolidated into patriarchal, authoritarian systems.

Ethno-nationalist populist discourse is rooted in a fundamental fear of ambiguity and the complexity of diversity. But the desire to resolve ambiguities through narratives of cultural, religious, racial or national purity results in exclusionary forms of identity politics that deny individuals' belonging to "the people" and restricts their right to fully participate in society.

Exclusion shrinks the public space and restricts access, and is the cause of the crisis as addressed above.

CHURCHES AS AGENTS FOR JUSTICE

As a way of creating public space for civil discourse, the conference opened with a public evening panel on the role of the church in times of populism. EKD Presiding Bishop Heinrich Bedford-Strohm called the church to answer the nihilistic populist narratives in Germany with an alternative narrative of hope that is rooted in the good news of God's love revealed in Christ Jesus. Church of Sweden's Archbishop Antje Jackelén underlined that the church, even if it also can be influenced by populist discourse, needs to see beyond the short-sighted and reactive politics in societies and act steadfast as a holder of visions. She highlighted the importance of being church as part of a global communion of churches, transcending boundaries of ethnicity and nation.

One of the insights of the conference was that church must always be self-critical. The church should continually ask, is the church different from society, or do we mirror patriarchal, authoritarian, discriminatory or exclusionary structures? Are churches creating spaces that encourage the full participation of every human being? During the conference we were reminded of times in history when the churches have not been able to answer in the affirmative. Churches have denied full participation of women, especially of women of color; churches have denied welcome to the stranger and succor to the needy; churches have denied love to their enemies and to their neighbors. In every generation Christians need to return to the marks of the church and the diverse epistemological sources of faith and wisdom. There we find the theological and spiritual resources that will shape and reform public theology and motivate vocation in civil society as a priesthood of all believers.

Many of our discussions revealed the difficulty of acting in unjust spaces where political persecution, the influence of media and religious fundamentalism challenge the church's ability to proclaim this inclusive narrative. Racism, sexism, xenophobia make it difficult to consistently bear faithful witness to radical inclusion that overcomes populist binaries. However, we remembered that we are called to be the salt that gives the world a taste of freedom and dignity of all, affirming meaningful participation in democratic procedures. The spiritual and theological heritage of the church provides the tools to challenge the desire to overcome creative ambiguity with simplistic binaries. The church embraces diversity as a gift and complexity as beauty. The church is a people, embodied in a diversity of genders, races, languages, ethnicities and cultures in majority and minority contexts around the world.

Belonging to the church does not depend on purity of any one society, culture, ethnicity, or political system. Rather the inclusive nature of God's love, which grants justice for every diverse and differently abled body in the world, defines this community and calls people into deep solidarity with every other creature. One implication of this call is to continually redraw the lines of belonging to include those bodies who live under marginalized conditions into new just relationships. The church is a community that witnesses to the life affirming nature of creating communities of ever widening complexity and full participation.

CONCLUSION

Conference participants encouraged churches and theological institutions:

- to promote education and spiritual formation as a means to continually transform our communities into non-violent spaces of full, just and safe participation for all,

- to acknowledge that there are different, sometimes conflicting perspectives within the church regarding populism, and to create spaces where these perspectives can be in sincere dialogue with one another to deepen discernment,

- to create spaces for neighbors to experience the transformative nature of ecumenical and interfaith encounter, and to build trust in "the other",

- to form networks with other actors in civil society, and to establish partnerships with civil society allies who share values and commitments,

- to critically remember where church and theology have been complicit in ethnonationalist populist agendas and point to the need for repentance,

- to learn about the root causes of injustices, reclaim agency for justice and give prophetic witness against oppressive, exclusionary systems and structures,

- to share narratives of hope, inclusiveness and dignity and reform the narratives that will shape public theology,

- to renegotiate the meaning of justice, liberation and freedom and to rediscover democracy in its contexts.

The conference recognized that while the church has not always acted democratically or used its agency for the liberation of all, the church strives to grow in the knowledge of how to engage in the public space. Democracy needs to be renegotiated in each generation, and churches, while not commensurate to any political system or party, must reinforce their capacity to engage in civil society, and proclaim a prophetic narrative of hope in the public sphere. In this way, we drew on the thinking of two theologians, among others, whose works were important not only for the context where the conference was held, but also for the wider ecumenical movement:

Dietrich Bonhoeffer wrote, "Christianity stands or falls with its revolutionary protest against violence, arbitrariness and pride of power, and with its apologia for the weak.—I feel that Christianity is rather doing too little in showing these points than doing too much. Christianity has adjusted itself much too easily to the worship of power. It should give much more offence, more shock to the world, than it is doing." (Dietrich Bonhoeffer, Evening Sermon on Corinthians 12:9 (London 1934), in: Dietrich Bonhoeffer Werke 13, Gütersloh 1994, 411)

Dorothee Sölle wrote, "In a theological perspective it is evident that the content of this [right wing Christianity] contradicts the message of the Jewish-Christian tradition. The God of the prophets did not preach the nation-state, but community between strangers and natives... Jesus did not make the family the central value of human life, but the solidarity of those deprived of their rights." (Dorothee Sölle, The Window of Vulnerability: A Political Spirituality, Minneapolis 1990, 138)

Conference participants came from: Argentina, Austria, Bethlehem, Brazil, Czech Republic, Denmark, Estonia, Finland, Germany, Great Britain, Haiti, Hong Kong, Hungary, India, Italy, Lesotho, Myanmar, Norway, Poland, Rwanda, South Africa, Sweden, Switzerland, USA, Zimbabwe.

List of Authors

Ádám, Zoltán, Dr, assistant professor of political economy at Corvinus University of Economics, Budapest (Hungary)

Anthony, Jeevaraj, Rev., assistant professor at the department of religion, Gurukul Lutheran Theological College, Chennai (India)

Bataringaya, Pascal, Rev. Dr, President of the Presbyterian Church in Rwanda-EPR and guest professor at PIASS, Kigali (Rwanda)

Bedford-Strohm, Heinrich, Prof. Dr, bishop of the Evangelical Lutheran Church in Bavaria, Munich (Germany) and chairperson of the Council of the Evangelical Church in Germany

Beros, Daniel Carlos, Dr, professor of systematic theology, Ecumenical Network of Theological Education (REET), Buenos Aires (Argentina)

Blasi, Marcia, Rev. Dr, professor of gender and religion, Faculdades EST, São Leopoldo (Brazil)

Bozóki, András, Dr, professor of political science, Central European University, Budapest (Hungary)

Bretschneider-Felzmann, Almut, Rev., policy advisor theology and development, Church of Sweden, Uppsala (Sweden)

Fabiny, Tamás, Dr, bishop of the Evangelical Lutheran Church in Hungary, Northern Diocese, Budapest (Hungary)

Forster, Dion, Dr, professor of public theology and ethics, director of the Beyers Naudé Center for Public Theology, Stellenbosch University, Stellenbosch (South Africa)

Gaikwad, Roger, Rev. Dr, director, Theological Education, Mission and Evangelism, Diocese of North East India of the Church of North India. (India)

Hallonsten, Gunilla, Rev. Dr, director for international affairs, Church of Sweden, Uppsala (Sweden)

Harasta, Eva, Rev. PD Dr, study secretary for theology, politics, and culture, Evangelische Akademie Sachsen-Anhalt e.V., Wittenberg (Germany)

Höhne, Florian, Dr, academic staff in systematic theology, Humboldt-Universität zu Berlin, Berlin (Germany)

Isaac, Munther, Rev. Dr, Evangelical Lutheran Church Jordan and the Holy Land, Bethlehem

Jackelén, Antje, Dr Dr h. c., archbishop of the Church of Sweden, Uppsala (Sweden)

Kaunda, Chammah J., Rev. Dr, Global Institute of Theology and United Graduate School of Theology, Yonsei University, Seoul (South Korea)

Kaunda, Mutale Mulenga, Dr, University of KwaZulu-Natal, Pietermaritzburg (South Africa)

Kim, Sung, Rev. Dr, Lutheran Theological Seminary, Hong Kong (China)

Koopmann, Nico, Dr, professor of systematic theology and ethics and vice-rector (social impact, transformation and personnel), Stellenbosch University, Stellenbosch (South Africa)

McIntosh, Esther, Dr, director, theology and religious studies, School of Humanities, Religion and Philosophy, York St. John University, York (United Kingdom)

Nausner, Michael, Rev. Dr, professor at the Church of Sweden research unit, Uppsala (Sweden)

Navrátilová, Olga, Dr, academic staff at the department of philosophy, Protestant Theological Faculty at Charles University, Prague (Czech Republic)

Pally, Marcia, Dr, professor of multilingual multicultural studies, New York University; Fordham University, New York (USA); regular guest professor, Theology Faculty, Humboldt University, Berlin (Germany)

Ribet, Elisabetta, Rev. Dr, academic staff, Faculté de Théologie Protestante, Université de Strasbourg, Strasbourg (France)

Rimmer, Chad, Rev. Dr, study secretary for Lutheran theology and practice, The Lutheran World Federation, Geneva (Switzerland)

Sekulić, Branko, doctoral student at Ludwig-Maximilians-Universität München, Munich (Germany)

Sinn, Simone, Rev. Dr, professor of ecumenical theology, Ecumenical Institute at Bossey, World Council of Churches, Geneva (Switzerland)

Sinner, Rudolf von, Rev. Dr, professor of systematic theology, ecumenics and interreligious dialogue, Faculdades EST, São Leopoldo (Brazil)

Stjerna, Kirsi I., Rev. Dr, professor of Lutheran history and theology, Pacific Lutheran Theological Seminary of California Lutheran University, Berkeley, CA (USA)

Thomas, Linda E., Rev. Dr, professor of theology and anthropology, Lutheran School of Theology, Chicago, IL (USA)

Toivanen, Joona, Rev., Estonian Evangelical Lutheran Church, Tartu (Estonia)

Werner, Dietrich, Rev. Prof. Dr Dr h.c., senior advisor theology, ecumenical education and research, Bread for the World, Berlin (Germany)

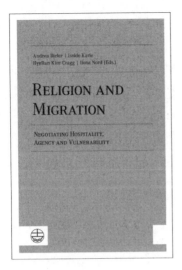

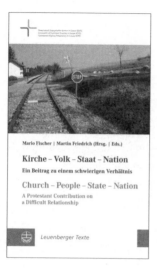